Predictiv

Write a review to receive any *FREE* eBook from our Catalogue - $99 Value!

If you recently bought this book we would love to hear from you! Benefit from receiving a free eBook from our catalogue at http://www.emereo.org/ if you write a review on Amazon (or the online store where you purchased this book) about your last purchase!

How does it work?

To post a review on Amazon, just log in to your account and click on the Create your own review button (under Customer Reviews) of the relevant product page. You can find examples of product reviews in Amazon. If you purchased from another online store, simply follow their procedures.

What happens when I submit my review?

Once you have submitted your review, send us an email at review@emereo.org with the link to your review, and the eBook you would like as our thank you from http://www.emereo.org/. Pick any book you like from the catalogue, up to $99 RRP. You will receive an email with your eBook as download link. It is that simple!

Copyright

Notice of Rights
All rights reserved. No part of this book may be reproduced or transmitted in any form by any means, electronic, mechanical, photocopying, recording, or otherwise, without the prior written permission of the publisher. No Claim to Orig. U.S. Govt. Works.

Notice of Liability
The information in this book is distributed on an As Is basis without warranty. While every precaution has been taken in the preparation of the book, neither the author nor the publisher shall have any liability to any person or entity with respect to any loss or damage caused or alleged to be caused directly or indirectly by the instructions contained in this book or by the products described in it.

Trademarks
Many of the designations used by manufacturers and sellers to distinguish their products are claimed as trademarks. Where those designations appear in this book, and the publisher was aware of a trademark claim, the designations appear as requested by the owner of the trademark. All other product names and services identified throughout this book are used in editorial fashion only and for the benefit of such companies with no intention of infringement of the trademark. No such use, or the use of any trade name, is intended to convey endorsement or other affiliation with this book.

Complete Guide to Predictive analytics.

Get the information you need--fast! This comprehensive guide offers a thorough view of key knowledge and detailed insight. It's all you need.

There is absolutely nothing that isn't thoroughly covered in the book. It is straightforward, and does an excellent job of explaining all about Predictive analytics in key topics and material.

There is no reason to invest in any other materials to learn about Predictive analytics. You'll understand it all.

Contents

Predictive analytics — 18
- Definition — 18
- Types — 18
- Predictive models — 19
- Descriptive models — 19
- Decision models — 19
- Applications — 20
- Analytical customer relationship management (CRM) — 20
- Clinical decision support systems — 20
- Collection analytics — 21
- Cross-sell — 21
- Customer retention — 21
- Direct marketing — 22
- Fraud detection — 22
- Portfolio, product or economy-level prediction — 23
- Risk management — 23
- Underwriting — 23
- Technology and Big Data influences on Predictive Analytics — 24
- Statistical techniques — 25
- Regression Models — 25
- Linear regression model — 25
- Discrete choice models — 26
- Logistic regression — 26
- Multinomial logistic regression — 26
- Probit regression — 27
- Logit versus probit — 27
- Time series models — 28
- Survival or duration analysis — 29
- Classification and regression trees — 30
- Multivariate adaptive regression splines — 30
- Machine learning techniques — 31
- Neural networks — 31
- Radial basis functions — 32
- Support vector machines — 32
- Naïve Bayes — 33
- k-nearest neighbours — 33
- Geospatial predictive modeling — 33

Tools	34
PMML	35
Autoregressive integrated moving average	**35**
Definition	36
Other special forms	36
Forecasts using ARIMA models	37
Examples	37
Implementations in statistics packages	38
Autoregressive model	**38**
Definition	39
Characteristic polynomial	39
The autocorrelation function of an AR(p) process can be expressed as	39
Graphs of AR(p) processes	40
Example: An AR(1)-process	40
Calculation of the AR parameters	41
Yule-Walker equations	42
The Yule-Walker equations are the following set of equations.	42
Estimation of AR parameters	42
The above equations (the Yule-Walker equations) provide several routes to estimating the parameters of an AR(p) model, by replacing the theoretical covariances with estimated values. Some of these variants can be described as follows:	42
Spectrum	44
AR(0)	44
For white noise (AR(0))	44
AR(1)	44
For AR(1)	44
AR(2)	44
AR(2) processes can be split into three groups depending on the characteristics of their roots:	44
Implementations in statistics packages	44
Control theory	**45**
Overview	45
An example	46
History	47
People in systems and control	48

Classical control theory ... 49
Closed-loop transfer function ... 49
PID controller ... 50
Modern control theory ... 51
Topics in control theory ... 51
Stability ... 51
Controllability and observability ... 53
Control specification ... 54
Model identification and robustness ... 55
System classifications ... 56
Linear systems control ... 56
Nonlinear systems control ... 56
Decentralized systems ... 57
Main control strategies ... 57

Credit card fraud ... **58**
Origins ... 59
Stolen cards ... 60
Compromised accounts ... 61
Card not present transaction ... 61
Identity theft ... 62
Application fraud ... 62
Account takeover ... 62
Skimming ... 63
Carding ... 64
BIN attack ... 65
Tele Phishing ... 65
Balance transfer checks ... 65
Fraudulent Charge-Back schemes ... 66
Profits, losses and punishment ... 66
United States ... 66
Cardholder liability ... 66
Merchants ... 66
United Kingdom ... 67
Credit card companies ... 67
Merchants ... 69
Famous credit fraud attacks ... 69
Countermeasures ... 69

Criminal Reduction Utilising Statistical History ... **71**
Cross-selling ... **71**

Cross-selling of professional services	72
Examples	73

Curse of dimensionality — 73

The "curse of dimensionality" as open problem	74
Curse of dimensionality in different domains	75
Combinatorics	75
Sampling	75
Optimization	75
Machine learning	76
Bayesian statistics	76
Distance functions	76
Nearest neighbor search	77
k-nearest neighbor classification	77
Anomaly detection	78

Customer attrition — 78

Industry applications	80
Research on customer attrition	80
Predicting customer attrition	81
Tools and Applications to predict attrition	82
Reducing customer attrition	82

Data mining — 82

Etymology	83
Background	84
Research and evolution	84
Process	85
Pre-processing	86
Data mining	86
Results validation	87
Standards	88
Notable uses	88
Games	88
Business	89
Science and engineering	91
Human rights	92
Spatial data mining	92
Challenges	93
Sensor data mining	94
Visual data mining	94
Music data mining	95

Surveillance 95
Pattern mining 95
Subject-based data mining 96
Knowledge grid 96
Reliability/Validity 97
Challenges 97
Privacy concerns and ethics 97
Software 99
Free open-source data mining software and applications 99
Commercial data-mining software and applications 100
Marketplace surveys 100

Decision tree learning 100
General 101
Types 102
Formulae 103
Gini impurity 103
Information gain 103
Decision tree advantages 104
Limitations 104
Extensions 105
Decision graphs 105
Search through Evolutionary Algorithms 105

Feed forward (control) 105
Overview 106
Applications 107
Physiological feed-forward system 107
Gene regulation and feed-forward 107
Feed-forward systems in computing 108
Long distance telephony 108
Automation and Machine Control 108

Forecasting 108
Categories of forecasting methods 109
Qualitative vs. quantitative methods 109
Naïve approach 110
Reference class forecasting 110
Time series methods 110
Causal / econometric forecasting methods 110
Judgmental methods 111
Artificial intelligence methods 111

Other methods	112
Forecasting accuracy	112
Fraud	**113**
By region	113
United Kingdom	113
England and Wales and Northern Ireland	113
Serious Fraud Office	114
National Fraud Authority	114
CIFAS - The UK's Fraud Prevention Service	114
Canada	114
United States	115
Cost of fraud	116
Types of fraudulent acts	116
Anti-Fraud movements	116
Fraud detection	117
Notable fraudsters	117
Related	120
Game theory	**121**
Representation of games	122
Extensive form	122
Normal form	123
Characteristic function form	123
Partition function form	124
General and applied uses	124
Description and modeling	125
Prescriptive or normative analysis	126
Economics and business	126
Political science	127
Biology	128
Computer science and logic	130
Philosophy	130
Types of games	131
Cooperative or non-cooperative	131
Symmetric and asymmetric	132
Zero-sum and non-zero-sum	133
Simultaneous and sequential	133
Perfect information and imperfect information	134
Combinatorial games	135
Infinitely long games	135
Discrete and continuous games	136

Differential games	136
Many-player and population games	136
Stochastic outcomes (and relation to other fields)	137
Metagames	138
History	138
Popular Culture	140

In-database processing — 141

History	141
Types	142
Translating Models into SQL Code	142
Loading C or C++ Libraries into the database process space	142
Out-of-Process	143
Uses	143
Vendors	143
Related Technologies	143

k-nearest neighbor algorithm — 144

Algorithm	145
Parameter selection	145
Properties	146
For estimating continuous variables	146

Learning analytics — 147

History	147
Criticism	148
Methods	148
Software	149

Linear regression — 149

Introduction to linear regression	150
Assumptions	152
Interpretation	155
Extensions	157
Simple and multiple regression	157
General linear models	157
Heteroskedastic models	157
Generalized linear models	158
Hierarchical linear models	159
Errors-in-variables	159
Others	159
Estimation methods	159

Least-squares estimation and related techniques	160
Maximum-likelihood estimation and related techniques	162
Other estimation techniques	162
Further discussion	164
Applications of linear regression	164
Trend line	165
Epidemiology	165
Finance	166
Economics	166
Environmental science	166
Machine learning	**166**
Definition	167
Generalization	167
Machine learning, knowledge discovery in databases (KDD) and data mining	167
Human interaction	168
Algorithm types	168
Theory	169
Approaches	169
Decision tree learning	170
Association rule learning	170
Artificial neural networks	170
Genetic programming	170
Inductive logic programming	171
Support vector machines	171
Clustering	171
Bayesian networks	171
Reinforcement learning	172
Representation learning	172
Sparse Dictionary Learning	173
Applications	173
Software	174
Journals and conferences	174
Marketing	**174**
Further definitions	176
Evolution of marketing	177
Earlier approaches	177
Contemporary approaches	178
Customer orientation	179
Organizational orientation	181

Herd behavior	181
Further orientations	182
Marketing research	182
Marketing environment	183
Market segmentation	183
Types of Market Research	184
Marketing planning	185
Marketing strategy	185
Marketing specializations	186
Buying behaviour	186
B2C buying behaviour	186
B2B buying behaviour	187
Use of technologies	187
Services marketing	188

Multinomial logit 188

Introduction	189
Assumptions	190
Model	191
Introduction	191
Setup	192
As a set of independent binary regressions	194
Estimating the coefficients	195
As a log-linear model	195
As a latent-variable model	197
Estimation of intercept	199
Applications	199

Multivariate adaptive regression splines 199

The basics	199
The MARS model	201
Hinge functions	202
The model building process	202
The forward pass	203
The backward pass	203
Generalized cross validation (GCV)	204
Constraints	205
Pros and cons	205

Naive Bayes classifier 207

Introduction	207
The naive Bayes probabilistic model	208

Parameter estimation	209
Sample correction	210
Constructing a classifier from the probability model	211
Discussion	211
Examples	211
Sex classification	211
Training	212
Testing	212
Document Classification	213
Neural network	**215**
Overview	216
History of the neural network analogy	217
The brain, neural networks and computers	220
Neural networks and artificial intelligence	221
Background	221
Applications of natural and of artificial neural networks	222
Neural networks and neuroscience	223
Types of models	223
Current research	224
Architecture	224
Criticism	225
Pattern recognition	**227**
Overview	227
Problem statement (supervised version)	230
Uses	231
Algorithms	232
Classification algorithms (supervised algorithms predicting categorical labels)	232
Clustering algorithms (unsupervised algorithms predicting categorical labels)	233
Regression algorithms (predicting real-valued labels)	233
Categorical sequence labeling algorithms (predicting sequences of categorical labels)	233
Real-valued sequence labeling algorithms (predicting sequences of real-valued labels)	233
Parsing algorithms (predicting tree structured labels)	234
General algorithms for predicting arbitrarily-structured labels	234
Ensemble learning algorithms (supervised meta-algorithms for combining multiple learning algorithms together)	234

Physics — 234
Prediction — 247
Informal prediction from hypothesis — 248
Opinion polls — 248
Statistics — 249
Supernatural (prophecy) — 249
Prediction in science — 249
Scientific hypothesis and prediction — 250
Finance — 251
Vision and prophecy — 251
Prediction in fiction — 252
Predictive Model Markup Language — 253
PMML Components — 253
PMML 4.0 and 4.1 — 255
Release history — 256
PMML Products — 256
Transformations Generator — 259
Pruning (decision trees) — 259
Introduction — 259
Techniques — 260
Reduced error pruning — 260
Cost complexity pruning — 260
RiskAoA — 260
Roger Jones (physicist and entrepreneur) — 264
SPSS — 265
Statistics program — 265
Versions — 267
Ownership history — 268
Add-ons — 268
Release history — 269
Tibco Software — 269
History — 270
Beginnings and Teknekron — 270
TIBCO and IPO — 270
Post-IPO — 271
Products — 272
Acquisitions — 273
Reception and awards — 274

Underwriting	**274**
Securities underwriting	275
Risk, exclusivity, and reward	275
Bank underwriting	276
Insurance underwriting	276
Other forms of underwriting	277
Real estate underwriting	278
Forensic underwriting	278
Sponsorship underwriting	278
Thomson Financial League Tables	278
Zementis Inc	**279**
The "Zementis" Name	279
The Road to ADAPA	279
Zementis Locations	280

Predictive analytics

Predictive analytics

Predictive analytics encompasses a variety of statistical techniques from modeling, machine learning, data mining and game theory that analyze current and historical facts to make predictions about future events.

In business, predictive models exploit patterns found in historical and transactional data to identify risks and opportunities. Models capture relationships among many factors to allow assessment of risk or potential associated with a particular set of conditions, guiding decision making for candidate transactions.

Predictive analytics is used in actuarial science, marketing, financial services, insurance, telecommunications, retail, travel, healthcare, pharmaceuticals and other fields.

One of the most well known applications is credit scoring, which is used throughout financial services. Scoring models process a customer's credit history, loan application, customer data, etc. , in order to rank-order individuals by their likelihood of making future credit payments on time. A well-known example would be the FICO score.

Definition

Predictive analytics is an area of statistical analysis that deals with extracting information from data and using it to predict future trends and behavior patterns. The core of predictive analytics relies on capturing relationships between explanatory variables and the predicted variables from past occurrences, and exploiting it to predict future outcomes. It is important to note, however, that the accuracy and usability of results will depend greatly on the level of data analysis and the quality of assumptions.

Types

Generally, the term predictive analytics is used to mean predictive modeling, "scoring" data with predictive models, and forecasting. However, people are increasingly using the term to describe related analytical disciplines, such as descriptive modeling and decision modeling or optimization. These disciplines also involve rigorous data analysis, and are widely used in business for segmentation and decision making, but have different purposes and the statistical techniques underlying them vary.

Predictive models

Predictive models analyze past performance to assess how likely a customer is to exhibit a specific behavior in the future in order to improve marketing effectiveness. This category also encompasses models that seek out subtle data patterns to answer questions about customer performance, such as fraud detection models. Predictive models often perform calculations during live transactions, for example, to evaluate the risk or opportunity of a given customer or transaction, in order to guide a decision. With advancement in computing speed, individual agent modeling systems can simulate human behavior or reaction to given stimuli or scenarios. The new term for animating data specifically linked to an individual in a simulated environment is avatar analytics.

Descriptive models

Descriptive models quantify relationships in data in a way that is often used to classify customers or prospects into groups. Unlike predictive models that focus on predicting a single customer behavior (such as credit risk), descriptive models identify many different relationships between customers or products. Descriptive models do not rank-order customers by their likelihood of taking a particular action the way predictive models do. Descriptive models can be used, for example, to categorize customers by their product preferences and life stage. Descriptive modeling tools can be utilized to develop further models that can simulate large number of individualized agents and make predictions.

Decision models

Decision models describe the relationship between all the elements of a decision — the known data (including results of predictive models), the decision, and the forecast results of the decision — in order to predict the results of decisions involving many variables. These models can be used in optimization, maximizing certain outcomes while minimizing others. Decision models are generally used to develop decision logic or a set of business rules that will produce the desired action for every customer or circumstance.

Applications

Although predictive analytics can be put to use in many applications, we outline a few examples where predictive analytics has shown positive impact in recent years.

Analytical customer relationship management (CRM)

Analytical Customer Relationship Management is a frequent commercial application of Predictive Analysis. Methods of predictive analysis are applied to customer data to pursue CRM objectives which is to have a holistic view of the customer no matter where their information resides in the company or the department involved. CRM uses predictive analysis in applications for marketing campaigns, sales, and customer services to name a few. These tools are required in order for a company to posture and focus their efforts effectively across the breadth of their customer base. They must analyze and understand the products in demand or have the potential for high demand, predict customer's buying habits in order to promote relevant products at multiple touch points, and proactively identify and mitigate issues that have the potential to lose customers or reduce their ability to gain new ones.

Clinical decision support systems

Experts use predictive analysis in health care primarily to determine which patients are at risk of developing certain conditions, like diabetes, asthma, heart disease and other lifetime illnesses. Additionally, sophisticated clinical decision support systems incorporate predictive analytics to support medical decision making at the point of care. A working definition has been proposed by Robert Hayward of the Centre for Health Evidence: "Clinical Decision Support Systems link health observations with health knowledge to influence health choices by clinicians for improved health care. "

Collection analytics

Every portfolio has a set of delinquent customers who do not make their payments on time. The financial institution has to undertake collection activities on these customers to recover the amounts due. A lot of collection resources are wasted on customers who are difficult or impossible to recover. Predictive analytics can help optimize the allocation of collection resources by identifying the most effective collection agencies, contact strategies, legal actions and other strategies to each customer, thus significantly increasing recovery at the same time reducing collection costs.

Cross-sell

Often corporate organizations collect and maintain abundant data (e. g. customer records, sale transactions) as exploiting hidden relationships in the data can provide a competitive advantage. For an organization that offers multiple products, predictive analytics can help analyze customers' spending, usage and other behavior, leading to efficient cross sales, or selling additional products to current customers. This directly leads to higher profitability per customer and stronger customer relationships.

Customer retention

With the number of competing services available, businesses need to focus efforts on maintaining continuous consumer satisfaction, rewarding consumer loyalty and minimizing customer attrition. Businesses tend to respond to customer attrition on a reactive basis, acting only after the customer has initiated the process to terminate service. At this stage, the chance of changing the customer's decision is almost impossible. Proper application of predictive analytics can lead to a more proactive retention strategy. By a frequent examination of a customer's past service usage, service performance, spending and other behavior patterns, predictive models can determine the likelihood of a customer terminating service sometime in the near future. An intervention with lucrative offers can increase the chance of retaining the customer. Silent attrition, the behavior of a customer to slowly but steadily reduce usage, is another problem that many companies face. Predictive analytics can also predict this behavior, so that the company can take proper actions to increase customer activity.

Direct marketing

When marketing consumer products and services, there is the challenge of keeping up with competing products and consumer behavior. Apart from identifying prospects, predictive analytics can also help to identify the most effective combination of product versions, marketing material, communication channels and timing that should be used to target a given consumer. The goal of predictive analytics is typically to lower the cost per order or cost per action.

Fraud detection

Fraud is a big problem for many businesses and can be of various types: inaccurate credit applications, fraudulent transactions (both offline and online), identity thefts and false insurance claims. These problems plague firms of all sizes in many industries. Some examples of likely victims are credit card issuers, insurance companies, retail merchants, manufacturers, business-to-business suppliers and even services providers. A predictive model can help weed out the "bads" and reduce a business's exposure to fraud.

Predictive modeling can also be used to identify high-risk fraud candidates in business or the public sector. Nigrini developed a risk-scoring method to identify audit targets. He describes the use of this approach to detect fraud in the franchisee sales reports of an international fast-food chain. Each location is scored using 10 predictors. The 10 scores are then weighted to give one final overall risk score for each location. The same scoring approach was also used to identify high-risk check kiting accounts, potentially fraudulent travel agents, and questionable vendors. A reasonably complex model was used to identify fraudulent monthly reports submitted by divisional controllers.

The Internal Revenue Service (IRS) of the United States also uses predictive analytics to mine tax returns and identify tax fraud.

Recent[when?] advancements in technology have also introduced predictive behavior analysis for web fraud detection. This type of solution utilizes heuristics in order to study normal web user behavior and detect anomalies indicating fraud attempts.

Portfolio, product or economy-level prediction

Often the focus of analysis is not the consumer but the product, portfolio, firm, industry or even the economy. For example, a retailer might be interested in predicting store-level demand for inventory management purposes. Or the Federal Reserve Board might be interested in predicting the unemployment rate for the next year. These types of problems can be addressed by predictive analytics using time series techniques (see below). They can also be addressed via machine learning approaches which transform the original time series into a feature vector space, where the learning algorithm finds patterns that have predictive power.

Risk management

When employing risk management techniques, the results are always to predict and benefit from a future scenario. The Capital asset pricing model (CAP-M) "predicts" the best portfolio to maximize return, Probabilistic Risk Assessment (PRA)--when combined with mini-Delphi Techniques and statistical approaches yields accurate forecasts and RiskAoA is a stand-alone predictive tool. These are three examples of approaches that can extend from project to market, and from near to long term. Underwriting (see below) and other business approaches identify risk management as a predictive method.

Underwriting

Many businesses have to account for risk exposure due to their different services and determine the cost needed to cover the risk. For example, auto insurance providers need to accurately determine the amount of premium to charge to cover each automobile and driver. A financial company needs to assess a borrower's potential and ability to pay before granting a loan. For a health insurance provider, predictive analytics can analyze a few years of past medical claims data, as well as lab, pharmacy and other records where available, to predict how expensive an enrollee is likely to be in the future. Predictive analytics can help underwrite these quantities by predicting the chances of illness, default, bankruptcy, etc. Predictive analytics can streamline the process of customer acquisition by predicting the future risk behavior of a customer using application level data. Predictive analytics in the form of credit scores have reduced the amount of time it takes for loan approvals, especially in the mortgage market where lending decisions are now made in a matter of hours rather than days or even weeks. Proper predictive analytics can lead to proper pricing decisions, which can help mitigate future risk of default.

Technology and Big Data influences on Predictive Analytics

Big Data is a term used to describe data sets so large and complex that they become awkward to work with using traditional database management tools. The volume, variety and velocity of Big Data have introduced challenges across the board for capture, storage, search, sharing, analysis, and visualization. Examples of big data sources include web logs, RFID and sensor data, social networks, Internet search indexing, call detail records, military surveillance, and complex data in astronomic, biogeochemical, genomics, and atmospheric sciences. Thanks to technological advances in computer hardware—faster CPUs, cheaper memory, and MPP architectures—and new technologies such as Hadoop, MapReduce, and in-database and text analytics for processing Big Data, it is now feasible to collect, analyze, and mine massive amounts of structured and unstructured data for new insights. Today, exploring Big Data and using predictive analytics is within reach of more organizations than ever before.

Statistical techniques

The approaches and techniques used to conduct predictive analytics can broadly be grouped into regression techniques and machine learning techniques.

Regression Models

Regression models are the mainstay of predictive analytics. The focus lies on establishing a mathematical equation as a model to represent the interactions between the different variables in consideration. Depending on the situation, there is a wide variety of models that can be applied while performing predictive analytics. Some of them are briefly discussed below.

Linear regression model

The linear regression model analyzes the relationship between the response or dependent variable and a set of independent or predictor variables. This relationship is expressed as an equation that predicts the response variable as a linear function of the parameters. These parameters are adjusted so that a measure of fit is optimized. Much of the effort in model fitting is focused on minimizing the size of the residual, as well as ensuring that it is randomly distributed with respect to the model predictions.

The goal of regression is to select the parameters of the model so as to minimize the sum of the squared residuals. This is referred to as ordinary least squares (OLS) estimation and results in best linear unbiased estimates (BLUE) of the parameters if and only if the Gauss-Markov assumptions are satisfied.

Once the model has been estimated we would be interested to know if the predictor variables belong in the model – i. e. is the estimate of each variable's contribution reliable? To do this we can check the statistical significance of the model's coefficients which can be measured using the t-statistic. This amounts to testing whether the coefficient is significantly different from zero. How well the model predicts the dependent variable based on the value of the independent variables can be assessed by using the R^2 statistic. It measures predictive power of the model i. e. the proportion of the total variation in the dependent variable that is "explained" (accounted for) by variation in the independent variables.

Discrete choice models

Multivariate regression (above) is generally used when the response variable is continuous and has an unbounded range. Often the response variable may not be continuous but rather discrete. While mathematically it is feasible to apply multivariate regression to discrete ordered dependent variables, some of the assumptions behind the theory of multivariate linear regression no longer hold, and there are other techniques such as discrete choice models which are better suited for this type of analysis. If the dependent variable is discrete, some of those superior methods are logistic regression, multinomial logit and probit models. Logistic regression and probit models are used when the dependent variable is binary.

Logistic regression

In a classification setting, assigning outcome probabilities to observations can be achieved through the use of a logistic model, which is basically a method which transforms information about the binary dependent variable into an unbounded continuous variable and estimates a regular multivariate model (See Allison's Logistic Regression for more information on the theory of Logistic Regression).

The Wald and likelihood-ratio test are used to test the statistical significance of each coefficient b in the model (analogous to the t tests used in OLS regression; see above). A test assessing the goodness-of-fit of a classification model is the "percentage correctly predicted."

Multinomial logistic regression

An extension of the binary logit model to cases where the dependent variable has more than 2 categories is the multinomial logit model. In such cases collapsing the data into two categories might not make good sense or may lead to loss in the richness of the data. The multinomial logit model is the appropriate technique in these cases, especially when the dependent variable categories are not ordered (for examples colors like red, blue, green). Some authors have extended multinomial regression to include feature selection/importance methods such as Random multinomial logit.

Probit regression

Probit models offer an alternative to logistic regression for modeling categorical dependent variables. Even though the outcomes tend to be similar, the underlying distributions are different. Probit models are popular in social sciences like economics.

A good way to understand the key difference between probit and logit models is to assume that there is a latent variable z.

We do not observe z but instead observe y which takes the value 0 or 1. In the logit model we assume that y follows a logistic distribution. In the probit model we assume that y follows a standard normal distribution. Note that in social sciences (e. g. economics), probit is often used to model situations where the observed variable y is continuous but takes values between 0 and 1.

Logit versus probit

The Probit model has been around longer than the logit model. They behave similarly, except that the logistic distribution tends to be slightly flatter tailed. One of the reasons the logit model was formulated was that the probit model was computationally difficult due to the requirement of numerically calculating integrals. Modern computing however has made this computation fairly simple. The coefficients obtained from the logit and probit model are fairly close. However, the odds ratio is easier to interpret in the logit model.

Practical reasons for choosing the probit model over the logistic model would be:

There is a strong belief that the underlying distribution is normal
The actual event is not a binary outcome (e. g. , bankruptcy status)

but a proportion (e. g., proportion of population at different debt levels).

Time series models

Time series models are used for predicting or forecasting the future behavior of variables. These models account for the fact that data points taken over time may have an internal structure (such as autocorrelation, trend or seasonal variation) that should be accounted for. As a result standard regression techniques cannot be applied to time series data and methodology has been developed to decompose the trend, seasonal and cyclical component of the series. Modeling the dynamic path of a variable can improve forecasts since the predictable component of the series can be projected into the future.

Time series models estimate difference equations containing stochastic components. Two commonly used forms of these models are autoregressive models (AR) and moving average (MA) models. The Box-Jenkins methodology (1976) developed by George Box and G. M. Jenkins combines the AR and MA models to produce the ARMA (autoregressive moving average) model which is the cornerstone of stationary time series analysis. ARIMA (autoregressive integrated moving average models) on the other hand are used to describe non-stationary time series. Box and Jenkins suggest differencing a non stationary time series to obtain a stationary series to which an ARMA model can be applied. Non stationary time series have a pronounced trend and do not have a constant long-run mean or variance.

Box and Jenkins proposed a three stage methodology which includes: model identification, estimation and validation. The identification stage involves identifying if the series is stationary or not and the presence of seasonality by examining plots of the series, autocorrelation and partial autocorrelation functions. In the estimation stage, models are estimated using non-linear time series or maximum likelihood estimation procedures. Finally the validation stage involves diagnostic checking such as plotting the residuals to detect outliers and evidence of model fit.

In recent years time series models have become more sophisticated and attempt to model conditional heteroskedasticity with models such as ARCH (autoregressive conditional heteroskedasticity) and GARCH (generalized autoregressive conditional heteroskedasticity) models frequently used for financial time series. In addition time series models are also used to understand inter-relationships among economic variables represented by systems of equations using VAR (vector autoregression) and structural VAR models.

Survival or duration analysis

Survival analysis is another name for time to event analysis. These techniques were primarily developed in the medical and biological sciences, but they are also widely used in the social sciences like economics, as well as in engineering (reliability and failure time analysis).

Censoring and non-normality, which are characteristic of survival data, generate difficulty when trying to analyze the data using conventional statistical models such as multiple linear regression. The normal distribution, being a symmetric distribution, takes positive as well as negative values, but duration by its very nature cannot be negative and therefore normality cannot be assumed when dealing with duration/survival data. Hence the normality assumption of regression models is violated.

The assumption is that if the data were not censored it would be representative of the population of interest. In survival analysis, censored observations arise whenever the dependent variable of interest represents the time to a terminal event, and the duration of the study is limited in time.

An important concept in survival analysis is the hazard rate, defined as the probability that the event will occur at time t conditional on surviving until time t. Another concept related to the hazard rate is the survival function which can be defined as the probability of surviving to time t.

Most models try to model the hazard rate by choosing the underlying distribution depending on the shape of the hazard function. A distribution whose hazard function slopes upward is said to have positive duration dependence, a decreasing hazard shows negative duration dependence whereas constant hazard is a process with no memory usually characterized by the exponential distribution. Some of the distributional choices in survival models are: F, gamma, Weibull, log normal, inverse normal, exponential etc. All these distributions are for a non-negative random variable.

Duration models can be parametric, non-parametric or semi-parametric. Some of the models commonly used are Kaplan-Meier and Cox proportional hazard model (non parametric).

Classification and regression trees

decision tree learning
Classification and regression trees (CART) is a non-parametric decision tree learning technique that produces either classification or regression trees, depending on whether the dependent variable is categorical or numeric, respectively.

Decision trees are formed by a collection of rules based on variables in the modeling data set:

Rules based on variables' values are selected to get the best split to differentiate observations based on the dependent variable
Once a rule is selected and splits a node into two, the same process is applied to each "child" node (i. e. it is a recursive procedure)
Splitting stops when CART detects no further gain can be made, or some pre-set stopping rules are met. (Alternatively, the data are split as much as possible and then the tree is later pruned.)
Each branch of the tree ends in a terminal node. Each observation falls into one and exactly one terminal node, and each terminal node is uniquely defined by a set of rules.

A very popular method for predictive analytics is Leo Breiman's Random forests or derived versions of this technique like Random multinomial logit.

Multivariate adaptive regression splines

Multivariate adaptive regression splines (MARS) is a non-parametric technique that builds flexible models by fitting piecewise linear regressions.

An important concept associated with regression splines is that of a knot. Knot is where one local regression model gives way to another and thus is the point of intersection between two splines.

In multivariate and adaptive regression splines, basis functions are the tool used for generalizing the search for knots. Basis functions are a set of functions used to represent the information contained in one or more variables. Multivariate and Adaptive Regression Splines model almost always creates the basis functions in pairs.

Multivariate and adaptive regression spline approach deliberately overfits the model and then prunes to get to the optimal model. The algorithm is computationally very intensive and in practice we are required to specify an upper limit on the number of basis functions.

Machine learning techniques

Machine learning, a branch of artificial intelligence, was originally employed to develop techniques to enable computers to learn. Today, since it includes a number of advanced statistical methods for regression and classification, it finds application in a wide variety of fields including medical diagnostics, credit card fraud detection, face and speech recognition and analysis of the stock market. In certain applications it is sufficient to directly predict the dependent variable without focusing on the underlying relationships between variables. In other cases, the underlying relationships can be very complex and the mathematical form of the dependencies unknown. For such cases, machine learning techniques emulate human cognition and learn from training examples to predict future events.

A brief discussion of some of these methods used commonly for predictive analytics is provided below. A detailed study of machine learning can be found in Mitchell (1997).

Neural networks

Neural networks are nonlinear sophisticated modeling techniques that are able to model complex functions. They can be applied to problems of prediction, classification or control in a wide spectrum of fields such as finance, cognitive psychology/neuroscience, medicine, engineering, and physics.

Neural networks are used when the exact nature of the relationship between inputs and output is not known. A key feature of neural networks is that they learn the relationship between inputs and output through training. There are three types of training in neural networks used by different networks, supervised and unsupervised training, reinforcement learning,with supervised being the most common one.

Some examples of neural network training techniques are backpropagation, quick propagation, conjugate gradient descent, projection operator, Delta-Bar-Delta etc. Some unsupervised network architectures are multilayer perceptrons, Kohonen networks, Hopfield networks, etc.

Radial basis functions

A radial basis function (RBF) is a function which has built into it a distance criterion with respect to a center. Such functions can be used very efficiently for interpolation and for smoothing of data. Radial basis functions have been applied in the area of neural networks where they are used as a replacement for the sigmoidal transfer function. Such networks have 3 layers, the input layer, the hidden layer with the RBF non-linearity and a linear output layer. The most popular choice for the non-linearity is the Gaussian. RBF networks have the advantage of not being locked into local minima as do the feed-forward networks such as the multilayer perceptron.

Support vector machines

Support Vector Machines (SVM) are used to detect and exploit complex patterns in data by clustering, classifying and ranking the data. They are learning machines that are used to perform binary classifications and regression estimations. They commonly use kernel based methods to apply linear classification techniques to non-linear classification problems. There are a number of types of SVM such as linear, polynomial, sigmoid etc.

Naïve Bayes

Naïve Bayes based on Bayes conditional probability rule is used for performing classification tasks. Naïve Bayes assumes the predictors are statistically independent which makes it an effective classification tool that is easy to interpret. It is best employed when faced with the problem of 'curse of dimensionality' i. e. when the number of predictors is very high.

k-nearest neighbours

The nearest neighbour algorithm (KNN) belongs to the class of pattern recognition statistical methods. The method does not impose a priori any assumptions about the distribution from which the modeling sample is drawn. It involves a training set with both positive and negative values. A new sample is classified by calculating the distance to the nearest neighbouring training case. The sign of that point will determine the classification of the sample. In the k-nearest neighbour classifier, the k nearest points are considered and the sign of the majority is used to classify the sample. The performance of the kNN algorithm is influenced by three main factors: (1) the distance measure used to locate the nearest neighbours; (2) the decision rule used to derive a classification from the k-nearest neighbours; and (3) the number of neighbours used to classify the new sample. It can be proved that, unlike other methods, this method is universally asymptotically convergent, i. e. : as the size of the training set increases, if the observations are independent and identically distributed (i. i. d.), regardless of the distribution from which the sample is drawn, the predicted class will converge to the class assignment that minimizes misclassification error. See Devroy et al.

Geospatial predictive modeling

Conceptually, geospatial predictive modeling is rooted in the principle that the occurrences of events being modeled are limited in distribution. Occurrences of events are neither uniform nor random in distribution – there are spatial environment factors (infrastructure, sociocultural, topographic, etc.) that constrain and influence where the locations of events occur. Geospatial predictive modeling attempts to describe those constraints and influences by spatially correlating occurrences of historical geospatial locations with environmental factors that represent those constraints and influences. Geospatial predictive modeling is a process for analyzing events through a geographic filter in order to make statements of likelihood for event occurrence or emergence.

Tools

Historically, using predictive analytics tools—as well as understanding the results they delivered—required advanced skills. However, modern predictive analytics tools are no longer restricted to IT specialists. As more organizations adopt predictive analytics into decision-making processes and integrate it into their operations, they're creating a shift in the market toward business users as the primary consumers of the information. Business users want tools they can use on their own. Vendors are responding by creating new software that removes the mathematical complexity, provides user-friendly graphic interfaces and/or builds in short cuts that can, for example, recognize the kind of data available and suggest an appropriate predictive model. Predictive analytics tools have become sophisticated enough to adequately present and dissect data problems, so that any data-savvy information worker can utilize them to analyze data and retrieve meaningful, useful results. For example, modern tools present findings using simple charts, graphs, and scores that indicate the likelihood of possible outcomes.

There are numerous tools available in the marketplace that help with the execution of predictive analytics. These range from those that need very little user sophistication to those that are designed for the expert practitioner. The difference between these tools is often in the level of customization and heavy data lifting allowed.

Notable predictive analytic toolset vendors include:

SAS
IBM
Information Builders, Inc.
SPSS
SAP BusinessObjects

Predictive Analysis
Revolution Analytics
StatSoft, Inc.
KXEN
FICO
Acxiom
Teradata
PROS
TIBCO Spotfire
Fuzzy Logix
Pervasive Software
Zementis
Alpine Data Labs

PMML

In an attempt to provide a standard language for expressing predictive models, the Predictive Model Markup Language (PMML) has been proposed. Such an XML-based language provides a way for the different tools to define predictive models and to share these between PMML compliant applications. PMML 4. 0 was released in June, 2009.

Autoregressive integrated moving average

Autoregressive integrated moving average

In statistics and econometrics, and in particular in time series analysis, an autoregressive integrated moving average (ARIMA) model is a generalization of an autoregressive moving average (ARMA) model. These models are fitted to time series data either to better understand the data or to predict future points in the series (forecasting). They are applied in some cases where data show evidence of non-stationarity, where an initial differencing step (corresponding to the "integrated" part of the model) can be applied to remove the non-stationarity.

The model is generally referred to as an ARIMA(p,d,q) model where p, d, and q are non-negative integers that refer to the order of the autoregressive, integrated, and moving average parts of the model respectively. ARIMA models form an important part of the Box-Jenkins approach to time-series modelling.

When one of the terms is zero, it's usual to drop AR, I or MA. For example, an I(1) model is ARIMA(0,1,0), and a MA(1) model is ARIMA(0,0,1).

Definition

Given a time series of data where is an integer index and the are real numbers, then an ARMA(p,q) model is given by:

where is the lag operator, the are the parameters of the autoregressive part of the model, the are the parameters of the moving average part and the are error terms. The error terms are generally assumed to be independent, identically distributed variables sampled from a normal distribution with zero mean.

Assume now that the polynomial has a unitary root of multiplicity d. Then it can be rewritten as:

An ARIMA(p,d,q) process expresses this polynomial factorisation property, and is given by:

and thus can be thought as a particular case of an ARMA(p+d,q) process having the auto-regressive polynomial with some roots in the unity. For this reason every ARIMA model with d>0 is not wide sense stationary.

Other special forms

The explicit identification of the factorisation of the autoregression polynomial into factors as above, can be extended to other cases, firstly to apply to the moving average polynomial and secondly to include other special factors. For example, having a factor in a model is one way of including a non-stationary seasonality of period s into the model. Another example is the factor , which includes a (non-stationary) seasonality of period 12. The effect of the first type of factor is to allow each season's value to drift separately over time, whereas with the second type values for adjacent seasons move together.

Identification and specification of appropriate factors in an ARIMA model can be an important step in modelling as it can allow a reduction in the overall number of parameters to be estimated, while allowing the imposition on the model of types of behaviour that logic and experience suggest should be there.

Forecasts using ARIMA models

ARIMA models are used for observable non-stationary processes that have some clearly identifiable trends:

a constant trend (i. e. zero average) is modeled by
a linear trend (i. e. linear growth behavior) is modeled by
a quadratic trend (i. e. quadratic growth behavior) is modeled by
In these cases the ARIMA model can be viewed as a "cascade" of two models. The first is non-stationary:

while the second is wide-sense stationary:

Now standard forecasts techniques can be formulated for the process , and then (having the sufficient number of initial conditions) can be forecast via opportune integration steps.

Examples

Some well-known special cases arise naturally. For example, an ARIMA(0,1,0) model is given by:

which is simply a random walk.

A number of variations on the ARIMA model are commonly used.

For example, if multiple time series are used then the can be thought of as vectors and a VARIMA model may be appropriate. Sometimes a seasonal effect is suspected in the model. For example, consider a model of daily road traffic volumes. Weekends clearly exhibit different behaviour from weekdays. In this case it is often considered better to use a SARIMA (seasonal ARIMA) model than to increase the order of the AR or MA parts of the model. If the time-series is suspected to exhibit long-range dependence then the parameter may be replaced by certain non-integer values in an autoregressive fractionally integrated moving average model, which is also called a Fractional ARIMA (FARIMA or ARFIMA) model.

Implementations in statistics packages

Various packages that apply methodology like Box-Jenkins parameter optimization are available to find the right parameters for the ARIMA model.

In R, the stats package includes an arima function. The function is documented in "ARIMA Modelling of Time Series". Besides the ARIMA(p,d,q) part, the function also includes seasonal factors, an intercept term, and exogenous variables (xreg, called "external regressors").
The "forecast" package in R can automatically select an ARIMA model for a given time series with the auto. arima() function. The package can also simulate seasonal and non-seasonal ARIMA models with its simulate. Arima() function. It also has a function Arima(), which is a wrapper for the arima from the "stats" package.
SAS(R) of "SAS Institute Inc. " includes extensive ARIMA processing in its Econometric and Time Series Analysis system: SAS/ETS.
Stata includes ARIMA modelling (using its arima command) as of Stata 9.
SAP(R) "SAP" allows creating models like ARIMA by using native, predictive algorithms and by employing algorithms from R.

Autoregressive model

Autoregressive model

In statistics and signal processing, an autoregressive (AR) model is a type of random process which is often used to model and predict various types of natural phenomena. The autoregressive model is one of a group of linear prediction formulas that attempt to predict an output of a system based on the previous outputs.

Contents

1 Definition
1. 1 Characteristic polynomial
2 Graphs of AR(p) processes
3 Example: An AR(1)-process
4 Calculation of the AR parameters
4. 1 Yule-Walker equations
4. 2 Estimation of AR parameters
5 Spectrum
5. 1 AR(0)
5. 2 AR(1)
5. 3 AR(2)
6 Implementations in statistics packages
7 See also
8 Notes
9 References
10 External links

Definition

The notation AR(p) indicates an autoregressive model of order p. The AR(p) model is defined as

where are the parameters of the model, is a constant (often omitted for simplicity) and is white noise.

An autoregressive model can thus be viewed as the output of an all-pole infinite impulse response filter whose input is white noise. Some constraints are necessary on the values of the parameters of this model in order that the model remains wide-sense stationary. For example, processes in the AR(1) model with |☐1| ≥ 1 are not stationary. More generally, for an AR(p) model to be wide-sense stationary, the roots of the polynomial must lie within the unit circle, i. e. , each root must satisfy .

Characteristic polynomial
The autocorrelation function of an AR(p) process can be expressed as

where are the roots of the polynomial

The autocorrelation function of an AR(p) process is a sum of decaying exponentials.
Each real root contributes a component to the autocorrelation function that decays exponentially.
Similarly, each pair of complex conjugate roots contributes an exponentially damped oscillation.

Graphs of AR(p) processes

AR(0), AR(1), and AR(2) processes with white noise
The simplest AR process is AR(0), which has no dependence between the terms. Only the error/innovation/noise term contributes to the output of the process, so in the figure, AR(0) corresponds to white noise.
For an AR(1) process with a positive , only the previous term in the process and the noise term contribute to the output. If is close to 0, then the process still looks like white noise, but as approaches 1, the output gets a larger contribution from the previous term relative to the noise. This results in a "smoothing" or integration of the output, similar to a low pass filter.
For an AR(2) process, the previous two terms and the noise term contribute to the output. If both and are positive, the output will resemble a low pass filter, with the high frequency part of the noise decreased. If is positive while is negative, then the process favors changes in sign between terms of the process. The output oscillates.

Example: An AR(1)-process

An AR(1)-process is given by:

where is a white noise process with zero mean and variance . (Note: The subscript on has been dropped.) The process is wide-sense stationary if since it is obtained as the output of a stable filter whose input is white noise. (If then has infinite variance, and is therefore not wide sense stationary.) Consequently, assuming , the mean is identical for all values of t. If the mean is denoted by , it follows from

that

and hence

In particular, if , then the mean is 0.
The variance is

where is the standard deviation of . This can be shown by noting that

and then by noticing that the quantity above is a stable fixed point of this relation.
The autocovariance is given by

It can be seen that the autocovariance function decays with a decay time (also called time constant) of [to see this, write where is independent of . Then note that and match this to the exponential decay law].
The spectral density function is the Fourier transform of the autocovariance function. In discrete terms this will be the discrete-time Fourier transform:

This expression is periodic due to the discrete nature of the , which is manifested as the cosine term in the denominator. If we assume that the sampling time () is much smaller than the decay time (), then we can use a continuum approximation to :

which yields a Lorentzian profile for the spectral density:

where is the angular frequency associated with the decay time .
An alternative expression for can be derived by first substituting for in the defining equation. Continuing this process N times yields

For N approaching infinity, will approach zero and:

It is seen that is white noise convolved with the kernel plus the constant mean. If the white noise is a Gaussian process then is also a Gaussian process. In other cases, the central limit theorem indicates that will be approximately normally distributed when is close to one.

Calculation of the AR parameters

There are many ways to estimate the coefficients, such as the ordinary least squares procedure, method of moments (through

Yule Walker equations), or Markov chain Monte Carlo methods. The AR(p) model is given by the equation

It is based on parameters where $i = 1, \ldots, p$. There is a direct correspondence between these parameters and the covariance function of the process, and this correspondence can be inverted to determine the parameters from the autocorrelation function (which is itself obtained from the covariances). This is done using the Yule-Walker equations.

Yule-Walker equations
The Yule-Walker equations are the following set of equations.

where $m = 0, \ldots, p$, yielding $p + 1$ equations. Here is the autocorrelation function of Xt, is the standard deviation of the input noise process, and is the Kronecker delta function.
Because the last part of an individual equation is non-zero only if $m = 0$, the set of equations can be solved by representing the equations for $m > 0$ in matrix form, thus getting the equation

which can be solved for all The remaining equation for $m = 0$ is

which, once are known, can be solved for
An alternative formulation is in terms of the autocorrelation function. The AR parameters are determined by the the first $p+1$ elements of the autocorrelation function. The full autocorrelation function can then be derived by recursively calculating

Examples for some Low-order AR(p) processes
p=1

Hence
p=2
The Yule-Walker equations for an AR(2) process are

Remember that
Using the first equation yields
Using the recursion formula yields

Estimation of AR parameters
The above equations (the Yule-Walker equations) provide several routes to estimating the parameters of an AR(p) model, by

replacing the theoretical covariances with estimated values. Some of these variants can be described as follows:

Estimation of autocovariances or autocorrelations. Here each of these terms is estimated separately, using conventional estimates. There are different ways of doing this and the choice between these affects the properties of the estimation scheme. For example, negative estimates of the variance can be produced by some choices.

Formulation as a least squares regression problem in which an ordinary least squares prediction problem is constructed, basing prediction of values of Xt on the p previous values of the same series. This can be thought of as a forward-prediction scheme. The normal equations for this problem can be seen to correspond to an approximation of the matrix form of the Yule-Walker equations in which each appearance of an autocovariance of the same lag is replaced by a slightly different estimate.

Formulation as an extended form of ordinary least squares prediction problem. Here two sets of prediction equations are combined into a single estimation scheme and a single set of norma equations. One set is the set of forward-prediction equations and the other is a corresponding set of backward prediction equations, relating to the backward representation of the AR model:

Here predicted of values of Xt would be based on the p future values of the same series. This way of estimating the AR parameters is due to Burg, and call the Burg method: Burg and later authors called these particular estimates "maximum entropy estimates", but the reasoning behind this applies to the use of any set of estimated AR parameters. Compared to the estimation scheme using only the forward prediction equations, different estimates of the autocovariances are produced, and the estimates have different stability properties. Burg estimates are particularly associated with maximum entropy spectral estimation.

Other possible approaches to estimation include maximum likelihood estimation. Two distinct variants of maximum likelihood are available: in one (broadly equivalent to the forward prediction least squares scheme) the likelihood function considered is that corrresponding to the conditional distribution of later values in the series given the initial p values in the series; in the second, the likelihood function considered is that corrresponding to the unconditional joint distribution of all the values in the observed series. Substantial differences in the results of these approaches can occur if the observed series is short, or if the process is close to non-stationarity.

Spectrum

The power spectral density of an AR(p) process with noise variance is

AR(0)
For white noise (AR(0))

AR(1)
For AR(1)

If there is a single spectral peak at f=0, often referred to as red noise. As becomes nearer 1, there is stronger power at low frequencies, i. e. larger time lags.
If there is a minimum at f=0, often referred to as blue noise

AR(2)
AR(2) processes can be split into three groups depending on the characteristics of their roots:

When , the process has a pair of complex-conjugate roots, creating a mid-frequency peak at:

Otherwise the process has real roots, and:
When it acts as a low-pass filter on the white noise with a spectral peak at
When it acts as a high-pass filter on the white noise with a spectral peak at .
The process is stable when the roots are within the unit circle, or equivalently when the coefficients are in the triangle .
The full PSD function can be expressed in real form as:

Implementations in statistics packages

R, the stats package includes an ar function.
Matlab and Octave: the TSA toolbox contains several estimation

functions for uni-variate, multivariate and adaptive autoregressive models.

Control theory

Control theory

Control theory is an interdisciplinary branch of engineering and mathematics that deals with the behavior of dynamical systems with inputs. The external input of a system is called the reference. When one or more output variables of a system need to follow a certain reference over time, a controller manipulates the inputs to a system to obtain the desired effect on the output of the system.

The usual objective of a control theory is to calculate solutions for the proper corrective action from the controller that result in system stability, that is, the system will hold the set point and not oscillate around it.

The inputs and outputs of a continuous control system are generally related by differential equations. If these are linear with constant coefficients, a transfer function relating the input and output can be obtained by taking their Laplace transform. If the differential equations are nonlinear and have a known solution, it may be possible to linearize the nonlinear differential equations at that solution. If the resulting linear differential equations have constant coefficients one can take their Laplace transform to obtain a transfer function.

The transfer function is also known as the system function or network function. The transfer function is a mathematical representation, in terms of spatial or temporal frequency, of the relation between the input and output of a linear time-invariant solution of the nonlinear differential equations describing the system.

Extensive use is usually made of a diagrammatic style known as the block diagram.

Overview

Control theory is

a theory that deals with influencing the behavior of dynamical systems
an interdisciplinary subfield of science, which originated in engineering and mathematics, and evolved into use by the social sciences, like psychology, sociology, criminology and in the financial system.
Control systems can be thought of as having four functions; Measure, Compare, Compute, and Correct. These four functions are completed by five elements; Detector, Transducer, Transmitter, Controller, and Final Control Element. The measuring function is completed by the detector, transducer and transmitter. In practical applications these three elements are typically contained in one unit. A standard example is a Resistance thermometer.
The compare and compute functions are completed within the controller which may be completed electronically through a Proportional Control, PI Controller, PID Controller, Bistable, Hysteretic control or Programmable logic controller. The correct function is completed with a final control element. The final control element changes an input or output in the control system which affect the manipulated or controlled variable.

An example

Consider a car's cruise control, which is a device designed to maintain vehicle speed at a constant desired or reference speed provided by the driver. The controller is the cruise control, the plant is the car, and the system is the car and the cruise control. The system output is the car's speed, and the control itself is the engine's throttle position which determines how much power the engine generates.

A primitive way to implement cruise control is simply to lock the throttle position when the driver engages cruise control. However, if the cruise control is engaged on a stretch of flat road, then the car will travel slower going uphill and faster when going downhill. This type of controller is called an open-loop controller because no measurement of the system output (the car's speed) is used to alter the control (the throttle position.) As a result, the controller cannot compensate for changes acting on the car, like a change in the slope of the road.

In a closed-loop control system, a sensor monitors the system output (the car's speed) and feeds the data to a controller which adjusts the control (the throttle position) as necessary to maintain the desired system output (match the car's speed to the reference speed.) Now when the car goes uphill the decrease in speed is measured, and the throttle position changed to increase engine power, speeding the vehicle. Feedback from measuring the car's speed has allowed the controller to dynamically compensate for changes to the car's speed. It is from this feedback that the paradigm of the control loop arises: the control affects the system output, which in turn is measured and looped back to alter the control.

History

Although control systems of various types date back to antiquity, a more formal analysis of the field began with a dynamics analysis of the centrifugal governor, conducted by the physicist James Clerk Maxwell in 1868 entitled On Governors. This described and analyzed the phenomenon of "hunting", in which lags in the system can lead to overcompensation and unstable behavior. This generated a flurry of interest in the topic, during which Maxwell's classmate Edward John Routh generalized Maxwell's results for the general class of linear systems. Independently, Adolf Hurwitz analyzed system stability using differential equations in 1877, resulting in what is now known as the Routh–Hurwitz theorem.

A notable application of dynamic control was in the area of manned flight. The Wright brothers made their first successful test flights on December 17, 1903 and were distinguished by their ability to control their flights for substantial periods (more so than the ability to produce lift from an airfoil, which was known). Continuous, reliable control of the airplane was necessary for flights lasting longer than a few seconds.

By World War II, control theory was an important part of fire-control systems, guidance systems and electronics.

Sometimes mechanical methods are used to improve the stability of systems. For example, ship stabilizers are fins mounted beneath the waterline and emerging laterally. In contemporary vessels, they may be gyroscopically controlled active fins, which have the capacity to change their angle of attack to counteract roll caused by wind or waves acting on the ship.

The Sidewinder missile uses small control surfaces placed at the rear of the missile with spinning disks on their outer surface; these are known as rollerons. Airflow over the disk spins them to a high speed. If the missile starts to roll, the gyroscopic force of the disk drives the control surface into the airflow, cancelling the motion. Thus the Sidewinder team replaced a potentially complex control system with a simple mechanical solution.

The Space Race also depended on accurate spacecraft control. However, control theory also saw an increasing use in fields such as economics.

People in systems and control

People in systems and control
Many active and historical figures made significant contribution to control theory, including, for example:

Pierre-Simon Laplace (1749-1827) invented the z-transform used to solve discrete-time control theory problems.
Alexander Lyapunov (1857–1918) in the 1890s marks the beginning of stability theory.
Harold S. Black (1898–1983), invented the concept of negative feedback amplifiers in 1927. He managed to develop stable negative feedback amplifiers in the 1930s.
Harry Nyquist (1889–1976), developed the Nyquist stability criterion for feedback systems in the 1930s.
Richard Bellman (1920–1984), developed dynamic programming since the 1940s.
Andrey Kolmogorov (1903–1987) co-developed the Wiener–Kolmogorov filter (1941).
Norbert Wiener (1894–1964) co-developed the Wiener–Kolmogorov filter and coined the term cybernetics in the 1940s.
John R. Ragazzini (1912–1988) introduced digital control and the z-transform in the 1950s.
Lev Pontryagin (1908–1988) introduced the maximum principle and the bang-bang principle.

Classical control theory

To overcome the limitations of the open-loop controller, control theory introduces feedback. A closed-loop controller uses feedback to control states or outputs of a dynamical system. Its name comes from the information path in the system: process inputs (e. g. , voltage applied to an electric motor) have an effect on the process outputs (e. g. , speed or torque of the motor), which is measured with sensors and processed by the controller; the result (the control signal) is used as input to the process, closing the loop.

Closed-loop controllers have the following advantages over open-loop controllers:

disturbance rejection (such as hills in the cruise control example above)
guaranteed performance even with model uncertainties, when the model structure does not match perfectly the real process and the model parameters are not exact
unstable processes can be stabilized
reduced sensitivity to parameter variations
improved reference tracking performance
In some systems, closed-loop and open-loop control are used simultaneously. In such systems, the open-loop control is termed feedforward and serves to further improve reference tracking performance.

A common closed-loop controller architecture is the PID controller.

Closed-loop transfer function

The output of the system y(t) is fed back through a sensor measurement F to the reference value r(t). The controller C then takes the error e (difference) between the reference and the output to change the inputs u to the system under control P. This is shown in the figure. This kind of controller is a closed-loop controller or feedback controller.

This is called a single-input-single-output (SISO) control system; MIMO (i. e. , Multi-Input-Multi-Output) systems, with more than one input/output, are common. In such cases variables are represented through vectors instead of simple scalar values. For some distributed parameter systems the vectors may be infinite-dimensional (typically functions).

If we assume the controller C, the plant P, and the sensor F are linear and time-invariant (i. e. , elements of their transfer function C(s), P(s), and F(s) do not depend on time), the systems above can be analysed using the Laplace transform on the variables. This gives the following relations:

Solving for Y(s) in terms of R(s) gives:

The expression is referred to as the closed-loop transfer function of the system. The numerator is the forward (open-loop) gain from r to y, and the denominator is one plus the gain in going around the feedback loop, the so-called loop gain. If , i. e. , it has a large norm with each value of s, and if , then Y(s) is approximately equal to R(s) and the output closely tracks the reference input.

PID controller

The PID controller is probably the most-used feedback control design. PID is an acronym for Proportional-Integral-Derivative, referring to the three terms operating on the error signal to produce a control signal. If u(t) is the control signal sent to the system, y(t) is the measured output and r(t) is the desired output, and tracking error , a PID controller has the general form

The desired closed loop dynamics is obtained by adjusting the three parameters , and , often iteratively by "tuning" and without specific knowledge of a plant model. Stability can often be ensured using only the proportional term. The integral term permits the rejection of a step disturbance (often a striking specification in process control). The derivative term is used to provide damping or shaping of the response. PID controllers are the most well established class of control systems: however, they cannot be used in several more complicated cases, especially if MIMO systems are considered.

Applying Laplace transformation results in the transformed PID controller equation

with the PID controller transfer function

Modern control theory

In contrast to the frequency domain analysis of the classical control theory, modern control theory utilizes the time-domain state space representation, a mathematical model of a physical system as a set of input, output and state variables related by first-order differential equations. To abstract from the number of inputs, outputs and states, the variables are expressed as vectors and the differential and algebraic equations are written in matrix form (the latter only being possible when the dynamical system is linear). The state space representation (also known as the "time-domain approach") provides a convenient and compact way to model and analyze systems with multiple inputs and outputs. With inputs and outputs, we would otherwise have to write down Laplace transforms to encode all the information about a system. Unlike the frequency domain approach, the use of the state space representation is not limited to systems with linear components and zero initial conditions. "State space" refers to the space whose axes are the state variables. The state of the system can be represented as a vector within that space.

Topics in control theory

Stability

The stability of a general dynamical system with no input can be described with Lyapunov stability criteria. A linear system that takes an input is called bounded-input bounded-output (BIBO) stable if its output will stay bounded for any bounded input. Stability for nonlinear systems that take an input is input-to-state stability

(ISS), which combines Lyapunov stability and a notion similar to BIBO stability. For simplicity, the following descriptions focus on continuous-time and discrete-time linear systems.

Mathematically, this means that for a causal linear system to be stable all of the poles of its transfer function must have negative-real values, i. e. the real part of all the poles are less than zero. Practically speaking, stability requires that the transfer function complex poles reside

in the open left half of the complex plane for continuous time, when the Laplace transform is used to obtain the transfer function. inside the unit circle for discrete time, when the Z-transform is used. The difference between the two cases is simply due to the traditional method of plotting continuous time versus discrete time transfer functions. The continuous Laplace transform is in Cartesian coordinates where the axis is the real axis and the discrete Z-transform is in circular coordinates where the axis is the real axis.

When the appropriate conditions above are satisfied a system is said to be asymptotically stable: the variables of an asymptotically stable control system always decrease from their initial value and do not show permanent oscillations. Permanent oscillations occur when a pole has a real part exactly equal to zero (in the continuous time case) or a modulus equal to one (in the discrete time case). If a simply stable system response neither decays nor grows over time, and has no oscillations, it is marginally stable: in this case the system transfer function has non-repeated poles at complex plane origin (i. e. their real and complex component is zero in the continuous time case). Oscillations are present when poles with real part equal to zero have an imaginary part not equal to zero.

If a system in question has an impulse response of

then the Z-transform (see this example), is given by

which has a pole in (zero imaginary part). This system is BIBO (asymptotically) stable since the pole is inside the unit circle.

However, if the impulse response was

then the Z-transform is

which has a pole at and is not BIBO stable since the pole has a modulus strictly greater than one.

Numerous tools exist for the analysis of the poles of a system. These include graphical systems like the root locus, Bode plots or the Nyquist plots.

Mechanical changes can make equipment (and control systems) more stable. Sailors add ballast to improve the stability of ships. Cruise ships use antiroll fins that extend transversely from the side of the ship for perhaps 30 feet (10 m) and are continuously rotated about their axes to develop forces that oppose the roll.

Controllability and observability

Controllability and observability are main issues in the analysis of a system before deciding the best control strategy to be applied, or whether it is even possible to control or stabilize the system. Controllability is related to the possibility of forcing the system into a particular state by using an appropriate control signal. If a state is not controllable, then no signal will ever be able to control the state. If a state is not controllable, but its dynamics are stable, then the state is termed Stabilizable. Observability instead is related to the possibility of "observing", through output measurements, the state of a system. If a state is not observable, the controller will never be able to determine the behaviour of an unobservable state and hence cannot use it to stabilize the system. However, similar to the stabilizability condition above, if a state cannot be observed it might still be detectable.

From a geometrical point of view, looking at the states of each variable of the system to be controlled, every "bad" state of these variables must be controllable and observable to ensure a good behaviour in the closed-loop system. That is, if one of the eigenvalues of the system is not both controllable and observable, this part of the dynamics will remain untouched in the closed-loop system. If such an eigenvalue is not stable, the dynamics of this eigenvalue will be present in the closed-loop system which therefore will be unstable. Unobservable poles are not present in the transfer function realization of a state-space representation, which is why sometimes the latter is preferred in dynamical systems analysis.

Solutions to problems of uncontrollable or unobservable system include adding actuators and sensors.

Control specification

Several different control strategies have been devised in the past years. These vary from extremely general ones (PID controller), to others devoted to very particular classes of systems (especially robotics or aircraft cruise control).

A control problem can have several specifications. Stability, of course, is always present: the controller must ensure that the closed-loop system is stable, regardless of the open-loop stability. A poor choice of controller can even worsen the stability of the open-loop system, which must normally be avoided. Sometimes it would be desired to obtain particular dynamics in the closed loop: i. e. that the poles have , where is a fixed value strictly greater than zero, instead of simply asking that .

Another typical specification is the rejection of a step disturbance; including an integrator in the open-loop chain (i. e. directly before the system under control) easily achieves this. Other classes of disturbances need different types of sub-systems to be included.

Other "classical" control theory specifications regard the time-response of the closed-loop system: these include the rise time (the time needed by the control system to reach the desired value after a perturbation), peak overshoot (the highest value reached by the response before reaching the desired value) and others (settling time, quarter-decay). Frequency domain specifications are usually related to robustness (see after).

Modern performance assessments use some variation of integrated tracking error (IAE,ISA,CQI).

Model identification and robustness

A control system must always have some robustness property. A robust controller is such that its properties do not change much if applied to a system slightly different from the mathematical one used for its synthesis. This specification is important: no real physical system truly behaves like the series of differential equations used to represent it mathematically. Typically a simpler mathematical model is chosen in order to simplify calculations, otherwise the true system dynamics can be so complicated that a complete model is impossible.

System identification
The process of determining the equations that govern the model's dynamics is called system identification. This can be done off-line: for example, executing a series of measures from which to calculate an approximated mathematical model, typically its transfer function or matrix. Such identification from the output, however, cannot take account of unobservable dynamics. Sometimes the model is built directly starting from known physical equations: for example, in the case of a mass-spring-damper system we know that . Even assuming that a "complete" model is used in designing the controller, all the parameters included in these equations (called "nominal parameters") are never known with absolute precision; the control system will have to behave correctly even when connected to physical system with true parameter values away from nominal.

Some advanced control techniques include an "on-line" identification process (see later). The parameters of the model are calculated ("identified") while the controller itself is running: in this way, if a drastic variation of the parameters ensues (for example, if the robot's arm releases a weight), the controller will adjust itself consequently in order to ensure the correct performance.

Analysis
Analysis of the robustness of a SISO (single input single output) control system can be performed in the frequency domain, considering the system's transfer function and using Nyquist and Bode diagrams. Topics include gain and phase margin and amplitude margin. For MIMO (multi input multi output) and, in general, more complicated control systems one must consider the

theoretical results devised for each control technique (see next section): i. e. , if particular robustness qualities are needed, the engineer must shift his attention to a control technique by including them in its properties.

Constraints
A particular robustness issue is the requirement for a control system to perform properly in the presence of input and state constraints. In the physical world every signal is limited. It could happen that a controller will send control signals that cannot be followed by the physical system: for example, trying to rotate a valve at excessive speed. This can produce undesired behavior of the closed-loop system, or even damage or break actuators or other subsystems. Specific control techniques are available to solve the problem: model predictive control (see later), and anti-wind up systems. The latter consists of an additional control block that ensures that the control signal never exceeds a given threshold.

System classifications

Linear systems control

State space (controls)
For MIMO systems, pole placement can be performed mathematically using a state space representation of the open-loop system and calculating a feedback matrix assigning poles in the desired positions. In complicated systems this can require computer-assisted calculation capabilities, and cannot always ensure robustness. Furthermore, all system states are not in general measured and so observers must be included and incorporated in pole placement design.

Nonlinear systems control

Nonlinear control
Processes in industries like robotics and the aerospace industry typically have strong nonlinear dynamics. In control theory it is sometimes possible to linearize such classes of systems and apply linear techniques, but in many cases it can be necessary to devise from scratch theories permitting control of nonlinear systems. These,

e. g. , feedback linearization, backstepping, sliding mode control, trajectory linearization control normally take advantage of results based on Lyapunov's theory. Differential geometry has been widely used as a tool for generalizing well-known linear control concepts to the non-linear case, as well as showing the subtleties that make it a more challenging problem.

Decentralized systems

Decentralized/distributed control
When the system is controlled by multiple controllers, the problem is one of decentralized control. Decentralization is helpful in many ways, for instance, it helps control systems operate over a larger geographical area. The agents in decentralized control systems can interact using communication channels and coordinate their actions.

Main control strategies

Every control system must guarantee first the stability of the closed-loop behavior. For linear systems, this can be obtained by directly placing the poles. Non-linear control systems use specific theories (normally based on Aleksandr Lyapunov's Theory) to ensure stability without regard to the inner dynamics of the system. The possibility to fulfill different specifications varies from the model considered and the control strategy chosen. Here a summary list of the main control techniques is shown:

Adaptive control
Adaptive control uses on-line identification of the process parameters, or modification of controller gains, thereby obtaining strong robustness properties. Adaptive controls were applied for the first time in the aerospace industry in the 1950s, and have found particular success in that field.
Hierarchical control
A Hierarchical control system is a type of Control System in which a set of devices and governing software is arranged in a hierarchical tree. When the links in the tree are implemented by a computer network, then that hierarchical control system is also a form of Networked control system.
Intelligent control

Intelligent control uses various AI computing approaches like neural networks, Bayesian probability, fuzzy logic, machine learning, evolutionary computation and genetic algorithms to control a dynamic system.

Optimal control

Optimal control is a particular control technique in which the control signal optimizes a certain "cost index": for example, in the case of a satellite, the jet thrusts needed to bring it to desired trajectory that consume the least amount of fuel. Two optimal control design methods have been widely used in industrial applications, as it has been shown they can guarantee closed-loop stability. These are Model Predictive Control (MPC) and linear-quadratic-Gaussian control (LQG). The first can more explicitly take into account constraints on the signals in the system, which is an important feature in many industrial processes. However, the "optimal control" structure in MPC is only a means to achieve such a result, as it does not optimize a true performance index of the closed-loop control system. Together with PID controllers, MPC systems are the most widely used control technique in process control.

Robust control

Robust control deals explicitly with uncertainty in its approach to controller design. Controllers designed using robust control methods tend to be able to cope with small differences between the true system and the nominal model used for design. The early methods of Bode and others were fairly robust; the state-space methods invented in the 1960s and 1970s were sometimes found to lack robustness. A modern example of a robust control technique is H-infinity loop-shaping developed by Duncan McFarlane and Keith Glover of Cambridge University, United Kingdom. Robust methods aim to achieve robust performance and/or stability in the presence of small modeling errors.

Stochastic control

Stochastic control deals with control design with uncertainty in the model. In typical stochastic control problems, it is assumed that there exist random noise and disturbances in the model and the controller, and the control design must take into account these random deviations.

Credit card fraud

Credit card fraud

Credit card fraud is a wide-ranging term for theft and fraud committed using a credit card or any similar payment mechanism as a fraudulent source of funds in a transaction. The purpose may be to obtain goods without paying, or to obtain unauthorized funds from an account. Credit card fraud is also an adjunct to identity theft. According to the Federal Trade Commission, while identity theft had been holding steady for the last few years, it saw a 21 percent increase in 2008. However, credit card fraud, that crime which most people associate with ID theft, decreased as a percentage of all ID theft complaints for the sixth year in a row.

The cost of card fraud in 2006 were 7 cents per 100 dollars worth of transactions (7 basis points). Due to the high volume of transactions this translates to billions of dollars. In 2006, fraud in the United Kingdom alone was estimated at £535 million, or US$750–830 million at prevailing 2006 exchange rates.

Origins

The fraud begins with either the theft of the physical card or the compromise of data associated with the account, including the card account number or other information that would routinely and necessarily be available to a merchant during a legitimate transaction. The compromise can occur by many common routes and can usually be conducted without tipping off the card holder, the merchant or the issuer, at least until the account is ultimately used for fraud. A simple example is that of a store clerk copying sales receipts for later use. The rapid growth of credit card use on the Internet has made database security lapses particularly costly; in some cases, millions of accounts have been compromised.

Stolen cards can be reported quickly by cardholders, but a compromised account can be hoarded by a thief for weeks or months before any fraudulent use, making it difficult to identify the source of the compromise. The cardholder may not discover fraudulent use until receiving a billing statement, which may be delivered infrequently. Cardholders can mitigate against this fraud risk by checking their account frequently to ensure constant awareness in case there are any suspicious, unknown transactions or activities.

Stolen cards

When a credit card is lost or stolen, it remains usable until the holder notifies the issuer that the card is lost. Most issuers have free 24-hour telephone numbers to encourage prompt reporting. Still, it is possible for a thief to make unauthorized purchases on a card until it is canceled. Without other security measures, a thief could potentially purchase thousands of dollars in merchandise or services before the cardholder or the card issuer realize that the card is in the wrong hands.

The only common security measure on all cards is a signature panel, but signatures are relatively easy to forge. Some merchants will demand to see a picture ID, such as a driver's license, to verify the identity of the purchaser, and some credit cards include the holder's picture on the card itself. In some jurisdictions, it is illegal for merchants to demand card holder identification. Self-serve payment systems (gas stations, kiosks, etc.) are common targets for stolen cards, as there is no way to verify the card holder's identity.

A common countermeasure is to require the user to key in some identifying information, such as the user's ZIP or postal code. This method may deter casual theft of a card found alone, but if the card holder's wallet is stolen, it may be trivial for the thief to deduce the information by looking at other items in the wallet. For instance, a U. S. driver license commonly has the holder's home address and ZIP code printed on it. Visa Inc. offers merchants lower rates on transactions if the customer provides a zip code.

In Europe, most cards are equipped with an EMV chip which requires a 4 digit PIN to be entered in to the merchants terminal before payment will be authorised. However, a PIN isn't required for online transactions, and is often not required for transactions using the magnetic strip.

Requiring a customer's ZIP code is illegal in California, where the state's 1971 law prohibits merchants from requesting or requiring a card-holder's "personal identification information" as a condition of accepting the card for payment. The California Supreme Court has ruled that the ZIP code qualifies as personal identification information because it is part of the cardholder's address. Companies face fines of $250–1000 for each violation. Requiring a "personal identification number" (PIN) may also be a violation.

Card issuers have several countermeasures, including sophisticated software that can, prior to an authorized transaction, estimate the probability of fraud. For example, a large transaction occurring a great distance from the cardholder's home might seem suspicious. The merchant may be instructed to call the card issuer for verification, or to decline the transaction, or even to hold the card and refuse to return it to the customer. The customer must contact the issuer and prove who they are to get their card back (if it is not fraud and they are actually buying a product).

Compromised accounts

Card account information is stored in a number of formats. Account numbers – formally the Primary Account Number (PAN) – are often embossed or imprinted on the card, and a magnetic stripe on the back contains the data in machine readable format. Fields can vary, but the most common include:

Name of card holder
Account number
Expiration date
Verification/CVV code

Card not present transaction

Card not present transaction
The mail and the Internet are major routes for fraud against merchants who sell and ship products, and affects legitimate mail-order and Internet merchants. If the card is not physically present (called CNP, card not present) the merchant must rely on the holder (or someone purporting to be so) presenting the information indirectly, whether by mail, telephone or over the Internet. While there are safeguards to this, it is still more risky than presenting in person, and indeed card issuers tend to charge a greater transaction rate for CNP, because of the greater risk.

It is difficult for a merchant to verify that the actual cardholder is indeed authorising the purchase. Shipping companies can guarantee delivery to a location, but they are not required to check identification and they are usually not involved in processing payments for the merchandise. A common recent preventive measure for merchants is to allow shipment only to an address approved by the cardholder, and merchant banking systems offer simple methods of verifying this information. Before this and similar countermeasures were introduced, mail order carding was rampant as early as 1992. A carder would obtain the credit card information for a local resident and then intercept delivery of the illegitimately purchased merchandise at the shipping address, often by staking out the porch of the residence.

Small transactions generally undergo less scrutiny, and are less likely to be investigated by either the card issuer or the merchant. CNP merchants must take extra precaution against fraud exposure and associated losses, and they pay higher rates for the privilege of accepting cards. Fraudsters bet on the fact that many fraud prevention features are not used for small transactions.

Merchant associations have developed some prevention measures, such as single use card numbers, but these have not met with much success. Customers expect to be able to use their credit card without any hassles, and have little incentive to pursue additional security due to laws limiting customer liability in the event of fraud. Merchants can implement these prevention measures but risk losing business if the customer chooses not to use the measures.

Identity theft

Identity theft can be divided into two broad categories: Application fraud and account takeover.

Application fraud

Application fraud happens when a criminal uses stolen or fake documents to open an account in someone else's name. Criminals may try to steal documents such as utility bills and bank statements to build up useful personal information. Or they may create counterfeit documents.

Account takeover

Account takeover happens when a criminal tries to take over another person's account, first by gathering information about the intended victim, and then contacting their card issuer while impersonating the genuine cardholder, and asking for mail to be redirected to a new address. The criminal then reports the card lost and asks for a replacement to be sent.

Some merchants added a new practice to protect their consumers and their own reputation, where they ask the buyer to send a photocopy of the physical card and statement to ensure the legitimate usage of a card.

Skimming

Skimming is the theft of credit card information used in an otherwise legitimate transaction. The thief can procure a victim's credit card number using basic methods such as photocopying receipts or more advanced methods such as using a small electronic device (skimmer) to swipe and store hundreds of victims' credit card numbers. Common scenarios for skimming are restaurants or bars where the skimmer has possession of the victim's credit card out of their immediate view. The thief may also use a small keypad to unobtrusively transcribe the 3 or 4 digit Card Security Code which is not present on the magnetic strip. Call centers are another area where skimming can easily occur. Skimming can also occur at merchants such as gas stations when a third-party card-reading device is installed either outside or inside a fuel dispenser or other card-swiping terminal. This device allows a thief to capture a customer's credit and debit card information, including their PIN, with each card swipe.

Instances of skimming have been reported where the perpetrator has put a device over the card slot of an ATM (automated teller machine), which reads the magnetic strip as the user unknowingly passes their card through it. These devices are often used in conjunction with a miniature camera (inconspicuously attached to the ATM) to read the user's PIN at the same time. This method is being used very frequently in many parts of the world, including South America, Argentina, and Europe. Another technique used is a keypad overlay that matches up with the buttons of the legitimate keypad below it and presses them when operated, but records or transmits the keylog of the PIN entered by wireless.

The device or group of devices illicitly installed on an ATM are also colloquially known as a "skimmer". Recently-made ATMs now often run a picture of what the slot and keypad are supposed to look like as a background, so that consumers can identify foreign devices attached.

Skimming is difficult for the typical cardholder to detect, but given a large enough sample, it is fairly easy for the card issuer to detect. The issuer collects a list of all the cardholders who have complained about fraudulent transactions, and then uses data mining to discover relationships among them and the merchants they use. For example, if many of the cardholders use a particular merchant, that merchant can be directly investigated. Sophisticated algorithms can also search for patterns of fraud. Merchants must ensure the physical security of their terminals, and penalties for merchants can be severe if they are compromised, ranging from large fines by the issuer to complete exclusion from the system, which can be a death blow to businesses such as restaurants where credit card transactions are the norm.

Carding

Carding is a term used for a process to verify the validity of stolen card data. The thief presents the card information on a website that has real-time transaction processing. If the card is processed successfully, the thief knows that the card is still good. The specific item purchased is immaterial, and the thief does not need to purchase an actual product; a web site subscription or charitable donation would be sufficient. The purchase is usually for a small monetary amount, both to avoid using the card's credit limit, and also to avoid attracting the card issuer's attention. A website known to be susceptible to carding is known as a cardable website.

In the past, carders used computer programs called "generators" to produce a sequence of credit card numbers, and then test them to see which were valid accounts. Another variation would be to take false card numbers to a location that does not immediately process card numbers, such as a trade show or special event. However, this process is no longer viable due to widespread requirement by internet credit card processing systems for additional data such as the billing address, the 3 to 4 digit Card

Security Code and/or the card's expiration date, as well as the more prevalent use of wireless card scanners that can process transactions right away. Nowadays, carding is more typically used to verify credit card data obtained directly from the victims by skimming or phishing.

A set of credit card details that has been verified in this way is known in fraud circles as a phish. A carder will typically sell data files of the phish to other individuals who will carry out the actual fraud. Market price for a phish ranges from US$1. 00 to US$50. 00 depending on the type of card, freshness of the data and credit status of the victim.

BIN attack

Credit cards are produced in BIN ranges. Where an issuer does not use random generation of the card number, it is possible for an attacker to obtain one good card number and generate valid card numbers by changing the last four numbers using a generator. The expiry date of these cards would most likely be the same as the good card.

Tele Phishing

Scammers may obtain a list of individuals with their name and phone number luring the victim into thinking that they are speaking with a trusted organization handing over sensitive information such as credit card details.

Balance transfer checks

Some promotional offers include active balance transfer checks which may be tied directly to a credit card account. These are often sent unsolicited, and may occur as often as once per month by some financial institutions. In cases where checks are stolen from a victims mailbox they can be used at point of sales locations thereby leaving the victim responsible for the losses. They are one path at times used by fraudsters.

Fraudulent Charge-Back schemes

There is a class of email spam (usually sent to commercial / corporate email addresses) where the spammer makes an offer to purchase goods (usually not specifically identified) from a vendor. In the email, the spammer makes it clear that they intend to pay for the goods using a credit card. The spammer provides the shipping address for the goods, and requests a product and price-list from the vendor in the initial email. It has been speculated[by whom?] that this is some form of charge-back scheme, whereby the spammer is using a valid credit card but intends to request a charge-back to reverse the charge while at the same time retaining the goods that were shipped to them.

Profits, losses and punishment

United States

Cardholder liability

In the US, federal law limits the liability of card holders to $50 in the event of theft of the actual credit card, regardless of the amount charged on the card, if reported within 60 days of receiving the statement. In practice many issuers will waive this small payment and simply remove the fraudulent charges from the customer's account if the customer signs an affidavit confirming that the charges are indeed fraudulent. If the physical card is not lost or stolen, but rather just the credit card account number itself is stolen, then Federal Law guarantees card holders have zero liability to the credit card issuer.

Merchants

The merchants and the financial institutions bear the loss. The merchant loses the value of any goods or services sold, and any associated fees. If the financial institution does not have a chargeback right then the financial institution bears the loss and the merchant does not suffer at all. These losses incline merchants to be cautious and often they ban legitimate transactions and lose potential revenues. Online merchants can choose to apply for additional services that credit card companies offer, such as Verified by Visa and MasterCard SecureCode. However, these are fiddly for consumers so there is a trade-off of making a sale easy and making it secure.

The liability for the fraud is determined by the details of the transaction. If the merchant retrieved all the necessary pieces of information and followed all of the rules and regulations the financial institution would bear the liability for the fraud. If the merchant did not get all of the necessary information they would be required to return the funds to the financial institution. This is all determined through the credit card processory.

High-risk industries such as online shops anticipate losses and spread them over the prices that are paid by honest buyers. The FBI's Financial Report to the Public in 2007 estimated such losses to be $52. 6 billion that are borne by 9. 91 million US consumers. Recently[when?] several attempts have been made to amend the legislation to protect cardholders and merchants from fraud, but credit card companies are heavily resistant to such initiatives.

United Kingdom

In the UK, credit cards are regulated by the Consumer Credit Act 1974 (amended 2006). This provides a number of protections and requirements.

Any misuse of the card, unless deliberately criminal on the part of the cardholder, must be refunded by the merchant or card issuer.

Distance Selling Regulations require goods ordered by telephone, Internet or mail order to be delivered to the cardholder's address. There is also a 7-day "cooling off period" where they can be returned without charge. The aim is more to protect people from mis-selling, but it also helps protect against fraud.

Credit card companies

To prevent being "charged back" for fraud transactions merchants can sign up for services offered by Visa and MasterCard called Verified by Visa and MasterCard SecureCode, under the umbrella term 3-D Secure. This requires consumers to add additional information to confirm a transaction.

Often enough online merchants do not take adequate measures to protect their websites from fraud attacks, for example by being blind to sequencing. In contrast to more automated product transactions, a clerk overseeing "card present" authorization requests must approve the customer's removal of the goods from the premise in real time.

Credit card merchant associations, like Visa and MasterCard, receive profits from transaction fees, charging between 0% and 3.25% of the purchase price plus a per transaction fee of between 0.00 USD and 40.00 USD. Cash costs more to bank up, so it is worthwhile for merchants to take cards. Issuers are thus motivated to pursue policies which increase the money transferred by their systems. Many merchants believe this pursuit of revenue reduces the incentive for credit card issuers to adopt procedures to reduce crime, particularly because the cost of investigating a fraud is usually higher than the cost of just writing it off. But in the US and Australia credit card issuers do not take these costs; they are passed on to the merchants as "chargebacks". This can result in substantial additional costs: not only has the merchant been defrauded for the amount of the transaction, he is also obliged to pay the chargeback fee, and to add insult to injury the transaction fees still stand.

Merchants have started to request changes in state and federal laws to protect themselves and their consumers from fraud, but the credit card industry has opposed many of the requests. In many cases, merchants have little ability to fight fraud, and must simply accept a proportion of fraud as a cost of doing business.

Because all card-accepting merchants and card-carrying customers are bound by civil contract law there are few criminal laws covering the fraud. Payment transfer associations enact changes to regulations, and the three parties— the issuer, the consumer, and the merchant— are all generally bound to the conditions, by a self-acceptance term in the contract that it can be changed.

Merchants

The merchant loses the goods or services sold, the payment, the fees for processing the payment, any currency conversion commissions, and the amount of the chargeback penalty. For obvious reasons, many merchants take steps to avoid chargebacks—such as not accepting suspicious transactions. This may spawn collateral damage, where the merchant additionally loses legitimate sales by incorrectly blocking legitimate transactions. Mail Order/Telephone Order (MOTO) merchants are implementing Agent-assisted automation which allows the call center agent to collect the credit card number and other personally identifiable information without ever seeing or hearing it. This greatly reduces the probability of chargebacks and increases the likelihood that fraudulent chargebacks will be successfully overturned.

Famous credit fraud attacks

Between July 2005 and mid-January 2007, a breach of systems at TJX Companies exposed data from more than 45. 6 million credit cards. Albert Gonzalez is accused of being the ringleader of the group responsible for the thefts.

In August 2009 Gonzalez was also indicted for the biggest known credit card theft to date — information from more than 130 million credit and debit cards was stolen at Heartland Payment Systems, retailers 7-Eleven and Hannaford Brothers, and two unidentified companies.

Countermeasures

Countermeasures to combat credit card fraud include the following.

By merchants:

PAN truncation – not displaying the full number on receipts

Tokenization (data security) – not storing the full number in computer systems
Requesting additional information, such as a PIN, ZIP code, or Card Security Code

By card issuers:

Fraud detection and prevention software that analyzes patterns of normal and unusual behavior as well as individual transactions in order to flag likely fraud. Profiles include such information as IP address
Fraud detection and response business processes such as:
Contacting the cardholder to request verification
Placing preventative controls/holds on accounts which may have been victimized
Blocking card until transactions are verified by cardholder
Investigating fraudulent activity
Strong Authentication measures such as:
Multi-factor Authentication, verifying that the account is being accessed by the cardholder through requirement of additional information such as account number, PIN, ZIP, challenge questions
Out-of-band Authentication, verifying that the transaction is being done by the cardholder through a "known" or "trusted" communication channel such as text message, phone call, or security token device
Industry collaboration and information sharing about known fraudsters and emerging threat vectors

By Governmental and Regulatory Bodies:

Enacting consumer protection laws related to card fraud
Performing regular examinations and risk assessments of credit card issuers
Publishing standards, guidance, and guidelines for protecting cardholder information and monitoring for fraudulent activity

By cardholders:

Reporting lost or stolen cards
Reviewing charges regularly and reporting unauthorized transactions immediately
Installing virus protection software on personal computers
Using caution when using credit cards for online purchases, especially on non-trusted websites
Keeping a record of account numbers, their expiration dates, and the phone number and address of each company in a secure place.

Additional technological features:

EMV
3-D Secure

Criminal Reduction Utilising Statistical History

Criminal Reduction Utilising Statistical History

Criminal Reduction Utilizing Statistical History is an IBM predictive analytics system that attempts to predict the location of future crimes. It was developed as part of the Blue CRUSH program in conjunction with Memphis Police Department and the University of Memphis Criminology and Research department.
As of July 2010, it is being trialled by two British police forces.

Cross-selling

Cross-selling

Cross-selling is the action or practice of selling among or between established clients, markets, traders, etc. or the action or practice of selling an additional product or service to an existing customer. This article deals exclusively with the latter meaning. In practice, businesses define cross-selling in many different ways. Elements that might influence the definition might include the size of the business, the industry sector it operates within and the financial motivations of those required to define the term.

The objectives of cross-selling can be either to increase the income derived from the client or clients or to protect the relationship with the client or clients. The approach to the process of cross-selling can be varied.

Unlike the acquiring of new business, cross-selling involves an element of risk that existing relationships with the client could be disrupted. For that reason, it is important to ensure that the additional product or service being sold to the client or clients enhances the value the client or clients get from the organization.

In practice, large businesses usually combine cross-selling and up-selling techniques to enhance the value that the client or clients gets from the organization (and vice versa).

Cross-selling of professional services

Benefits that can accrue to the customer include the efficiency and leverage that result from using a single supplier for multiple products. When buying complex professional services, like consulting needed to make and integrate an acquisition, the use of one firm reduces the fingerpointing that is common when a problem occurs in an area that straddles two or more services; if only one firm is responsible, fingerpointing is eliminated.

For the vendor, the benefits are also substantial. The most obvious example is an increase in revenue. There are also efficiency benefits in servicing one account rather than several. Most importantly, vendors that sell more services to a client are less likely to be displaced by a competitor. The more a client buys from a vendor, the higher the switching cost.

Though there are some ethical issues with most cross-selling, in some cases they can be huge. Arthur Andersen's dealings with Enron provide a highly visible example. It is commonly felt that the firm's objectivity, being an auditor, was compromised by selling internal audit services and massive amounts of consulting work to the account.

Though most companies want more cross-selling, there can be substantial barriers:

A customer policy requiring the use of multiple vendors.
Different purchasing points within an account, which reduce the ability to treat the customer like a single account.
The fear of the incumbent business unit that its colleagues would botch their work at the client, resulting with the loss of the account for all units of the firm.
Broadly speaking, cross-selling takes three forms. First, while servicing an account, the product or service provider may hear of an additional need, unrelated to the first, that the client has and offer to meet it. Thus, for example, in conducting an audit,

an accountant is likely to learn about a range of needs for tax services, for valuation services and others. To the degree that regulations allow, the accounts may be able to sell services that meet these needs. This kind of cross-selling helped major accounting firms to expand their businesses considerably. Because of the potential for abuse, this kind of selling by auditors has been greatly curtailed under the Sarbanes-Oxley Act.

Selling add-on services is another form of cross-selling. That happens when a supplier shows a customer that it can enhance the value of its service by buying another from a different part of the supplier's company. When one buys an appliance, the salesperson will offer to sell insurance beyond the terms of the warranty. Though common, that kind of cross-selling can leave a customer feeling poorly used. The customer might ask the appliance salesperson why he needs insurance on a brand new refrigerator, "Is it really likely to break in just nine months?"[original research?]

The third kind of cross-selling can be called selling a solution. In this case, the customer buying air conditioners is sold a package of both the air conditioners and installation services. The customer can be considered buying relief from the heat, unlike just air conditioners.

Examples

A Life Insurance company suggesting its customer sign up for car or health insurance.
A wholesale mobile retailer suggesting a customer choose a network or carrier after one purchases a mobile.
A television brand suggesting its customers go for a home theater of its or another's brand.
A laptop seller offering a customer a mouse, pen-drive, and or accessories.

Curse of dimensionality

Curse of dimensionality

The curse of dimensionality refers to various phenomena that arise when analyzing and organizing data in high-dimensional spaces (often with hundreds or thousands of dimensions) that do not occur in low-dimensional settings such as the physical space commonly modeled with just three dimensions.

There are multiple phenomena referred to by this name in domains such as numerical analysis, sampling, combinatorics, machine learning, data mining and databases. The common theme of these problems is that when the dimensionality increases, the volume of the space increases so fast that the available data becomes sparse. This sparsity is problematic for any method that requires statistical significance. In order to obtain a statistically sound and reliable result, the amount of data needed to support the result often grows exponentially with the dimensionality. Also organizing and searching data often relies on detecting areas where objects form groups with similar properties; in high dimensional data however all objects appear to be sparse and dissimilar in many ways which prevents common data organization strategies from being efficient.

The term curse of dimensionality was coined by Richard E. Bellman when considering problems in dynamic optimization.

The "curse of dimensionality" as open problem

The "curse of dimensionality" is often used as a blanket excuse for not dealing with high-dimensional data. However, the effects are not yet completely understood by the scientific community, and there is ongoing research. On one hand, the notion of intrinsic dimension refers to the fact that any low-dimensional data space can trivially be turned into a higher dimensional space by adding redundant (e. g. duplicate) or randomized dimensions, and in turn many high-dimensional data sets can be reduced to lower dimensional data without significant information loss. This is also reflected by the effectiveness of dimension reduction methods such as principal component analysis in many situations. For distance functions and nearest neighbor search, recent research also showed that data sets that exhibit the curse of dimensionality properties can still be processed unless there are too many irrelevant dimensions, while relevant dimensions can make some problems such as cluster analysis actually easier. Secondly, methods such as Markov chain Monte Carlo or shared nearest neighbor methods often work very well on data that were considered intractable by other methods due to high dimensionality.

Curse of dimensionality in different domains

Combinatorics

In some problems, each variable can take one of several discrete values, or the range of possible values is divided to give a finite number of possibilities. Taking the variables together, a huge number of combinations of values must be considered. This effect is also known as the combinatorial explosion. Even in the simplest case of binary variables, the number of possible combinations already is , exponential in the dimensionality. Naively, each additional dimension doubles the effort needed to try all combinations.

Sampling

There is an exponential increase in volume associated with adding extra dimensions to a mathematical space. For example, $10^2=100$ evenly-spaced sample points suffice to sample a unit interval (a "1-dimensional cube") with no more than $10^{-2}=0.01$ distance between points; an equivalent sampling of a 10-dimensional unit hypercube with a lattice that has a spacing of $10^{-2}=0.01$ between adjacent points would require 10^{20} sample points. In general, with a spacing distance of 10^{-n} the 10-dimensional hypercube appears to be a factor of $10^{n(10-1)}$ "larger" than the 1-dimensional hypercube, which is the unit interval. In the above example n=2: when using a sampling distance of 0.01 the 10-dimensional hypercube appears to be 10^{18} "larger" than the unit interval. This effect is a combination of the combinatorics problems above and the distance function problems explained below.

Optimization

When solving dynamic optimization problems by numerical

backward induction, the objective function must be computed for each combination of values. This is a significant obstacle when the dimension of the "state variable" is large.

Machine learning

In machine learning problems that involve learning a "state-of-nature" (maybe an infinite distribution) from a finite number of data samples in a high-dimensional feature space with each feature having a number of possible values, an enormous amount of training data are required to ensure that there are several samples with each combination of values. With a fixed number of training samples, the predictive power reduces as the dimensionality increases, and this is known as the Hughes effect or Hughes phenomenon (named after Gordon F. Hughes).

Bayesian statistics

The curse of dimensionality has often been a difficulty with Bayesian statistics, for which the posterior distributions often have many parameters.

However, this problem has been largely overcome by the advent of simulation-based Bayesian inference, especially using Markov chain Monte Carlo methods, which suffices for many practical problems. Of course, simulation-based methods converge slowly and therefore simulation-based methods are not a panacea for high-dimensional problems.

Distance functions

When a measure such as a Euclidean distance is defined using many coordinates, there is little difference in the distances between different pairs of samples.

One way to illustrate the "vastness" of high-dimensional Euclidean space is to compare the proportion of a hypersphere with radius and dimension , to that of a hypercube with sides of length , and equivalent dimension. The volume of such a sphere is: The volume of the cube would be: As the dimension of the space increases, the hypersphere becomes an insignificant volume relative to that of the hypercube. This can clearly be seen by comparing the proportions as the dimension goes to infinity: . as .

Thus, in some sense, nearly all of the high-dimensional space is "far away" from the centre, or, to put it another way, the high-dimensional unit space can be said to consist almost entirely of the "corners" of the hypercube, with almost no "middle". This is an important intuition for understanding the chi-squared distribution. [why?]

Given a single distribution, the minimum and the maximum occurring distances become indiscernible as the difference between the minimum and maximum value compared to the minimum value converges to 0: .

This is often cited as distance functions losing their usefulness in high dimensionality.

Nearest neighbor search

The effect complicates nearest neighbor search in high dimensional space. It is not possible to quickly reject candidates by using the difference in one coordinate as a lower bound for a distance based on all the dimensions.

However, recent research indicates that the mere number of dimensions does not necessarily result in problems, since relevant additional dimensions can also increase the contrast. In addition, the resulting ranking remains useful to discern close and far neighbors. Irrelevant ("noise") dimensions however reduce the contrast as expected. In time series analysis, where the data are inherently high-dimensional, distance functions also work reliably as long as the signal-to-noise ratio is high enough.

k-nearest neighbor classification

Another effect of high dimensionality on distance functions concerns k-nearest neighbor (k-NN) graphs constructed from a data set using some distance functions. As dimensionality increases, the indegree distribution of the k-NN digraph becomes skewed to the right, resulting in the emergence of hubs, as data instances that appear in many more k-NN lists of other instances from the data set than expected. This phenomenon can have a considerable impact on various techniques for classification (including the k-NN classifier), semi-supervised learning, and clustering, and it also affects information retrieval.

Anomaly detection

In a recent survey, Zimek et al. identified the following problems when searching for anomalies in high-dimensional data:

Concentration of scores and distances: derived values such as distances become numerically similar
Irrelevant attributes: in high dimensional data, a signficiant amount of attributes may be irrelevant
Definition of reference sets: for local methods, reference sets are often nearest-neighbor based
Incomparable scores for different dimensionalities: different subspaces produce incomparable scores
Interpretability of scores: the scores often no longer convey a semantic meaning
Exponential search space: the search space can no longer be systematically scanned
Data snooping bias: given the large search space, for every desired significance an hypothesis can be found
Hubness: certain objects occur more frequent in neighbor lists than others.
Many of the analyzed specialized methods tackle one or another of these problems, but there remain many open research questions.

Customer attrition

Customer attrition

Customer attrition, also known as customer churn, customer turnover, or customer defection, is a business term used to describe loss of clients or customers.

Banks, telephone service companies, Internet service providers, pay TV companies, insurance firms, and alarm monitoring services, often use customer attrition analysis and customer attrition rates as one of their key business metrics (along with cash flow, EBITDA, etc.) because the ". . . cost of retaining an existing customer is far less than acquiring a new one. " Companies from these sectors often have customer service branches which attempt to win back defecting clients, because recovered long-term customers can be worth much more to a company than newly recruited clients.

Companies usually make a distinction between voluntary churn and involuntary churn. Voluntary churn occurs due to a decision by the customer to switch to another company or service provider, involuntary churn occurs due to circumstances such as a customer's relocation to a long-term care facility, death, or the relocation to a distant location. In most applications, involuntary reasons for churn are excluded from the analytical models. Analysts tend to concentrate on voluntary churn, because it typically occurs due to factors of the company-customer relationship which companies control, such as how billing interactions are handled or how after-sales help is provided.

When companies are measuring their customer turnover, they typically make the distinction between gross attrition and net attrition. Gross attrition is the loss of existing customers and their associated recurring revenue for contracted goods or services during a particular period. Net attrition is gross attrition plus the addition or recruitment of similar customers at the original location. Financial institutions often track and measure attrition using a weighted calculation called Recurring Monthly Revenue (or RMR). In the 2000s, there are also a number of business intelligence software programs which can mine databases of customer information and analyze the factors that are associated with customer attrition, such as dissatisfaction with service or technical support, billing disputes, or a disagreement over company policies. More sophisticated predictive analytics software use churn prediction models that predict customer churn by assessing their propensity of risk to churn. Since these models generate a small prioritized list of potential defectors, they are effective at focusing customer retention marketing programs on the subset of the customer base who are most vulnerable to churn.

Industry applications

Financial services such as banking and insurance use applications of predictive analytics for churn modeling, because customer retention is an essential part of most financial services' business models. Other sectors have also discovered the power of predictive analytics, including retailing, telecommunications and pay-TV operators. One of the main objectives of modeling customer churn is to determine the causal factors, so that the company can try to prevent the attrition from happening in the future. Some companies want to prevent their good customers from deteriorating (e. g. , by falling behind in their payments) and becoming less profitable customers, so they introduced the notion of partial customer churn.

Customer attrition merits special attention by mobile telecom service providers worldwide. This is due to the low barriers to switching to a competing service provider especially with the advent of Mobile Number Portability (MNP) in several countries. This allows customers to switch to another provider while preserving their phone numbers. While mature markets with high teledensity (phone market penetration) have churn rates ranging from 1% to 2% per month, high growth developing markets such as India and China are experiencing churn rates between 3% to 4% per month. By deploying new technologies such churn prediction models coupled with effective retention programs, customer attrition could be better managed to stem the significant revenue loss from defecting customers.

Customer attrition is a major concern for US and Canadian banks, because they have much higher churn rates than banks in Western Europe. US and Canadian banks with the lowest churn rates have achieved customer turnover rates as low as 12% per year, by using tactics such as free checking accounts, online banking and bill payment, and improved customer service. However, once banks can improve their churn rates by improving customer service, they can reach a point beyond which further customer service will not improve retention; other tactics or approaches need to be explored.

Research on customer attrition

Scholars have studied customer attrition at European financial services companies, and investigated the predictors of churn and how the use of customer relationship management (CRM) approaches can impact churn rates. Several studies combine several different types of predictors to develop a churn model. This model can take demographic characteristics, environmental changes, and other factors into account.

Research on customer attrition data modeling may provide businesses with several tools for enhancing customer retention. Using data mining and software, one may apply statistical methods to develop nonlinear attrition causation models. One researcher notes that ". . . retaining existing customers is more profitable than acquiring new customers due primarily to savings on acquisition costs, the higher volume of service consumption, and customer referrals. " The argument is that to build an ". . . effective customer retention program," managers have to come to an understanding of ". . . why customers leave" and ". . . identify the customers with high risk of leaving" by accurately predicting customer attrition.

Predicting customer attrition

In the business context, "churn" refers both to customers' migration and to their loss of value. So, "churn rate" refers, on the one hand, to the percentage of customers who end their relation with the organization or, on the other hand, to the customers who still perceive their services, but not as much or not as often as they used to. Current organizations face therefore a huge challenge: to be able to anticipate to customers' abandon in order to retain them on time, reducing this way costs and risks and gaining efficiency and competitivity. There are in the market advanced analytics tools and applications, especially designed to analyze in depth the enormous amount of data inside the organizations, and to make predictions based on the information obtained from analyzing and exploring those data. Their aim, to put at the service of marketing departments and agencies –and of all business users- the necessary weapons to:

Detect soon which customers are about to abandon and to know them in depth, answering to questions such as: Who are they? or How do they behave?
Know the real value of the potential loss of those customers, with

the aim of establishing priorities and distributing business efforts and resources efficiently, optimizing resources and maximizing the value of the current customers' portfolio.
Put into practice personalized retention plans in order to reduce or avoid their migration, increasing the capability to react and anticipating to possible non-predicted fugues.

Tools and Applications to predict attrition

Mineful, Data Analysis and Automated Actions to promote customer retention.
Dynamic Data Web, 2. 0 BI platform based on Data Mining and Predictive Analysis techniques.

Reducing customer attrition

There are organizations that have developed international standards regarding recognition and sharing of global best practice in customer service in order to reduce customer attrition. The International Customer Service Institute has developed The International Customer Service Standard to strategically align organizations so they focus on delivering excellence in customer service, whilst at the same time providing recognition of success through a 3rd Party registration scheme.

Data mining

Data mining

Data mining (the analysis step of the "Knowledge Discovery in Databases" process, or KDD), is a field at the intersection of computer science and statistics, is the process that attempts to discover patterns in large data sets. It utilizes methods at the intersection of artificial intelligence, machine learning, statistics, and database systems. The overall goal of the data mining process is to extract information from a data set and transform it into an understandable structure for further use. Aside from the raw analysis step, it involves database and data management aspects, data preprocessing, model and inference considerations, interestingness metrics, complexity considerations, post-processing of discovered structures, visualization, and online updating.

The term is a buzzword, and is frequently misused to mean any form of large-scale data or information processing (collection, extraction, warehousing, analysis, and statistics) but is also generalized to any kind of computer decision support system, including artificial intelligence, machine learning, and business intelligence. In the proper use of the word, the key term is discovery, commonly defined as "detecting something new". Even the popular book "Data mining: Practical machine learning tools and techniques with Java" (which covers mostly machine learning material) was originally to be named just "Practical machine learning", and the term "data mining" was only added for marketing reasons. Often the more general terms "(large scale) data analysis", or "analytics" – or when referring to actual methods, artificial intelligence and machine learning – are more appropriate.

The actual data mining task is the automatic or semi-automatic analysis of large quantities of data to extract previously unknown interesting patterns such as groups of data records (cluster analysis), unusual records (anomaly detection) and dependencies (association rule mining). This usually involves using database techniques such as spatial indexes. These patterns can then be seen as a kind of summary of the input data, and may be used in further analysis or, for example, in machine learning and predictive analytics. For example, the data mining step might identify multiple groups in the data, which can then be used to obtain more accurate prediction results by a decision support system. Neither the data collection, data preparation, nor result interpretation and reporting are part of the data mining step, but do belong to the overall KDD process as additional steps.

The related terms data dredging, data fishing, and data snooping refer to the use of data mining methods to sample parts of a larger population data set that are (or may be) too small for reliable statistical inferences to be made about the validity of any patterns discovered. These methods can, however, be used in creating new hypotheses to test against the larger data populations.

Etymology

In the 1960s, statisticians used terms like "Data Fishing" or "Data

Dredging" to refer to what they considered the bad practice of analyzing data without an a-priori hypothesis. The term "Data Mining" appeared around 1990 in the database community. At the beginning of the century, there was a phrase "database mining"™, trademarked by HNC, a San Diego-based company (now merged into FICO), to pitch their Data Mining Workstation; researchers consequently turned to "data mining". Other terms used include Data Archaeology, Information Harvesting, Information Discovery, Knowledge Extraction, etc. Gregory Piatetsky-Shapiro coined the term "Knowledge Discovery in Databases" for the first workshop on the same topic (1989) and this term became more popular in AI and Machine Learning Community. However, the term data mining became more popular in the business and press communities. Currently, Data Mining and Knowledge Discovery are used interchangeably.

Background

The manual extraction of patterns from data has occurred for centuries. Early methods of identifying patterns in data include Bayes' theorem (1700s) and regression analysis (1800s). The proliferation, ubiquity and increasing power of computer technology has dramatically increased data collection, storage, and manipulation ability. As data sets have grown in size and complexity, direct "hands-on" data analysis has increasingly been augmented with indirect, automated data processing, aided by other discoveries in computer science, such as neural networks, cluster analysis, genetic algorithms (1950s), decision trees (1960s), and support vector machines (1990s). Data mining is the process of applying these methods with the intention of uncovering hidden patterns in large data sets. It bridges the gap from applied statistics and artificial intelligence (which usually provide the mathematical background) to database management by exploiting the way data is stored and indexed in databases to execute the actual learning and discovery algorithms more efficiently, allowing such methods to be applied to ever larger data sets.

Research and evolution

The premier professional body in the field is the Association for Computing Machinery's Special Interest Group on Knowledge

Discovery and Data Mining (SIGKDD). Since 1989 they have hosted an annual international conference and published its proceedings, and since 1999 have published a biannual academic journal titled "SIGKDD Explorations".

Computer science conferences on data mining include:

CIKM Conference – ACM Conference on Information and Knowledge Management
DMIN Conference – International Conference on Data Mining
DMKD Conference – Research Issues on Data Mining and Knowledge Discovery
ECDM Conference – European Conference on Data Mining
ECML-PKDD Conference – European Conference on Machine Learning and Principles and Practice of Knowledge Discovery in Databases
EDM Conference – International Conference on Educational Data Mining
ICDM Conference – IEEE International Conference on Data Mining
KDD Conference – ACM SIGKDD Conference on Knowledge Discovery and Data Mining
MLDM Conference – Machine Learning and Data Mining in Pattern Recognition
PAKDD Conference – The annual Pacific-Asia Conference on Knowledge Discovery and Data Mining
PAW Event – Predictialytics World
SDM Conference – SIAM International Conference on Data Mining (SIAM)
SSTD Symposium – Symposium on Spatial and Temporal Databases
WSDM Conference – ACM Conference on Web Search and Data Mining
Data mining topics are also present on many data management/database conferences such as the ICDE Conference, SIGMOD Conference and International Conference on Very Large Data Bases

Process

The Knowledge Discovery in Databases (KDD) process is commonly defined with the stages:

(1) Selection

(2) Pre-processing
(3) Transformation
(4) Data Mining
(5) Interpretation/Evaluation.
It exists, however, in many variations on this theme, such as the Cross Industry Standard Process for Data Mining (CRISP-DM) which defines six phases:

(1) Business Understanding
(2) Data Understanding
(3) Data Preparation
(4) Modeling
(5) Evaluation
(6) Deployment
or a simplified process such as (1) pre-processing, (2) data mining, and (3) results validation.

Pre-processing

Before data mining algorithms can be used, a target data set must be assembled. As data mining can only uncover patterns actually present in the data, the target dataset must be large enough to contain these patterns while remaining concise enough to be mined within an acceptable time limit. A common source for data is a data mart or data warehouse. Pre-processing is essential to analyze the multivariate datasets before data mining. The target set is then cleaned. Data cleaning removes the observations containing noise and those with missing data.

Data mining

Data mining involves six common classes of tasks:

Anomaly detection (Outlier/change/deviation detection) – The identification of unusual data records, that might be interesting or data errors and require further investigation.
Association rule learning (Dependency modeling) – Searches for relationships between variables. For example a supermarket might gather data on customer purchasing habits. Using association rule learning, the supermarket can determine which products are frequently bought together and use this information for marketing

purposes. This is sometimes referred to as market basket analysis.
Clustering – is the task of discovering groups and structures in the data that are in some way or another "similar", without using known structures in the data.
Classification – is the task of generalizing known structure to apply to new data. For example, an e-mail program might attempt to classify an e-mail as "legitimate" or as "spam".
Regression – Attempts to find a function which models the data with the least error.
Summarization – providing a more compact representation of the data set, including visualization and report generation.

Results validation

This section is missing information about non-classification tasks in data mining, it only covers machine learning. This concern has been noted on the talk page where whether or not to include such information may be discussed. (September 2011)
The final step of knowledge discovery from data is to verify that the patterns produced by the data mining algorithms occur in the wider data set. Not all patterns found by the data mining algorithms are necessarily valid. It is common for the data mining algorithms to find patterns in the training set which are not present in the general data set. This is called overfitting. To overcome this, the evaluation uses a test set of data on which the data mining algorithm was not trained. The learned patterns are applied to this test set and the resulting output is compared to the desired output. For example, a data mining algorithm trying to distinguish "spam" from "legitimate" emails would be trained on a training set of sample e-mails. Once trained, the learned patterns would be applied to the test set of e-mails on which it had not been trained. The accuracy of the patterns can then be measured from how many e-mails they correctly classify. A number of statistical methods may be used to evaluate the algorithm, such as ROC curves.

If the learned patterns do not meet the desired standards, then it is necessary to re-evaluate and change the pre-processing and data mining steps. If the learned patterns do meet the desired standards, then the final step is to interpret the learned patterns and turn them into knowledge.

Standards

There have been some efforts to define standards for the data mining process, for example the 1999 European Cross Industry Standard Process for Data Mining (CRISP-DM 1. 0) and the 2004 Java Data Mining standard (JDM 1. 0). Development on successors to these processes (CRISP-DM 2. 0 and JDM 2. 0) was active in 2006, but has stalled since. JDM 2. 0 was withdrawn without reaching a final draft.

For exchanging the extracted models – in particular for use in predictive analytics – the key standard is the Predictive Model Markup Language (PMML), which is an XML-based language developed by the Data Mining Group (DMG) and supported as exchange format by many data mining applications. As the name suggests, it only covers prediction models, a particular data mining task of high importance to business applications. However, extensions to cover (for example) subspace clustering have been proposed independently of the DMG.

Notable uses

Games

Since the early 1960s, with the availability of oracles for certain combinatorial games, also called tablebases (e. g. for 3x3-chess) with any beginning configuration, small-board dots-and-boxes, small-board-hex, and certain endgames in chess, dots-and-boxes, and hex; a new area for data mining has been opened. This is the extraction of human-usable strategies from these oracles. Current pattern recognition approaches do not seem to fully acquire the high level of abstraction required to be applied successfully. Instead, extensive experimentation with the tablebases – combined with an intensive study of tablebase-answers to well designed problems, and with knowledge of prior art (i. e. pre-tablebase knowledge) – is used to yield insightful patterns. Berlekamp (in dots-and-boxes, etc.) and John Nunn (in chess endgames) are notable examples of researchers doing this work, though they were not – and are not – involved in tablebase generation.

Business

Data mining in customer relationship management applications can contribute significantly to the bottom line. Rather than randomly contacting a prospect or customer through a call center or sending mail, a company can concentrate its efforts on prospects that are predicted to have a high likelihood of responding to an offer. More sophisticated methods may be used to optimize resources across campaigns so that one may predict to which channel and to which offer an individual is most likely to respond (across all potential offers). Additionally, sophisticated applications could be used to automate mailing. Once the results from data mining (potential prospect/customer and channel/offer) are determined, this "sophisticated application" can either automatically send an e-mail or a regular mail. Finally, in cases where many people will take an action without an offer, "uplift modeling" can be used to determine which people have the greatest increase in response if given an offer. Data clustering can also be used to automatically discover the segments or groups within a customer data set.

Businesses employing data mining may see a return on investment, but also they recognize that the number of predictive models can quickly become very large. Rather than using one model to predict how many customers will churn, a business could build a separate model for each region and customer type. Then, instead of sending an offer to all people that are likely to churn, it may only want to send offers to loyal customers. Finally, the business may want to determine which customers are going to be profitable over a certain window in time, and only send the offers to those that are likely to be profitable. In order to maintain this quantity of models, they need to manage model versions and move on to automated data mining.

Data mining can also be helpful to human resources (HR) departments in identifying the characteristics of their most successful employees. Information obtained – such as universities attended by highly successful employees – can help HR focus recruiting efforts accordingly. Additionally, Strategic Enterprise Management applications help a company translate corporate-level goals, such as profit and margin share targets, into operational decisions, such as production plans and workforce levels.

Another example of data mining, often called the market basket analysis, relates to its use in retail sales. If a clothing store records the purchases of customers, a data mining system could identify those customers who favor silk shirts over cotton ones. Although some explanations of relationships may be difficult, taking advantage of it is easier. The example deals with association rules within transaction-based data. Not all data are transaction based and logical, or inexact rules may also be present within a database.

Market basket analysis has also been used to identify the purchase patterns of the Alpha Consumer. Alpha Consumers are people that play a key role in connecting with the concept behind a product, then adopting that product, and finally validating it for the rest of society. Analyzing the data collected on this type of user has allowed companies to predict future buying trends and forecast supply demands.

Data mining is a highly effective tool in the catalog marketing industry. Catalogers have a rich database of history of their customer transactions for millions of customers dating back a number of years. Data mining tools can identify patterns among customers and help identify the most likely customers to respond to upcoming mailing campaigns.

Data mining for business applications is a component which needs to be integrated into a complex modeling and decision making process. Reactive business intelligence (RBI) advocates a "holistic" approach that integrates data mining, modeling, and interactive visualization into an end-to-end discovery and continuous innovation process powered by human and automated learning.

In the area of decision making, the RBI approach has been used to mine knowledge that is progressively acquired from the decision maker, and then self-tune the decision method accordingly.

An example of data mining related to an integrated-circuit production line is described in the paper "Mining IC Test Data to Optimize VLSI Testing. " In this paper, the application of data mining and decision analysis to the problem of die-level functional testing is described. Experiments mentioned demonstrate the ability to apply a system of mining historical die-test data to create a probabilistic model of patterns of die failure. These patterns are then utilized to decide, in real time, which die to test next and when to stop testing. This system has been shown, based on experiments with historical test data, to have the potential to improve profits on mature IC products.

Science and engineering

In recent years, data mining has been used widely in the areas of science and engineering, such as bioinformatics, genetics, medicine, education and electrical power engineering.

In the study of human genetics, sequence mining helps address the important goal of understanding the mapping relationship between the inter-individual variations in human DNA sequence and the variability in disease susceptibility. In simple terms, it aims to find out how the changes in an individual's DNA sequence affects the risks of developing common diseases such as cancer, which is of great importance to improving methods of diagnosing, preventing, and treating these diseases. The data mining method that is used to perform this task is known as multifactor dimensionality reduction.

In the area of electrical power engineering, data mining methods have been widely used for condition monitoring of high voltage electrical equipment. The purpose of condition monitoring is to obtain valuable information on, for example, the status of the insulation (or other important safety-related parameters). Data clustering techniques – such as the self-organizing map (SOM), have been applied to vibration monitoring and analysis of transformer on-load tap-changers (OLTCS). Using vibration monitoring, it can be observed that each tap change operation generates a signal that contains information about the condition of the tap changer contacts and the drive mechanisms. Obviously, different tap positions will generate different signals. However, there was considerable variability amongst normal condition signals for exactly the same tap position. SOM has been applied to detect abnormal conditions and to hypothesize about the nature of the abnormalities.

Data mining methods have also been applied to dissolved gas analysis (DGA) in power transformers. DGA, as a diagnostics for power transformers, has been available for many years. Methods such as SOM has been applied to analyze generated data and to determine trends which are not obvious to the standard DGA ratio methods (such as Duval Triangle).

Another example of data mining in science and engineering is found in educational research, where data mining has been used to study the factors leading students to choose to engage in behaviors which reduce their learning, and to understand factors influencing university student retention. A similar example of social application of data mining is its use in expertise finding systems, whereby descriptors of human expertise are extracted, normalized, and classified so as to facilitate the finding of experts, particularly in scientific and technical fields. In this way, data mining can facilitate institutional memory.

Other examples of application of data mining methods are biomedical data facilitated by domain ontologies, mining clinical trial data, and traffic analysis using SOM.

In adverse drug reaction surveillance, the Uppsala Monitoring Centre has, since 1998, used data mining methods to routinely screen for reporting patterns indicative of emerging drug safety issues in the WHO global database of 4.6 million suspected adverse drug reaction incidents. Recently, similar methodology has been developed to mine large collections of electronic health records for temporal patterns associating drug prescriptions to medical diagnoses.

Data mining has been applied software artifacts within the realm of software engineering: Mining Software Repositories.

Human rights

Data mining of government records – particularly records of the justice system (i.e. courts, prisons) – enables the discovery of systemic human rights violations in connection to generation and publication of invalid or fraudulent legal records by various government agencies.

Spatial data mining

Spatial data mining is the application of data mining methods to spatial data. The end objective of spatial data mining is to find patterns in data with respect to geography. So far, data mining and Geographic Information Systems (GIS) have existed as two separate technologies, each with its own methods, traditions, and approaches to visualization and data analysis. Particularly, most contemporary GIS have only very basic spatial analysis functionality. The immense explosion in geographically referenced data occasioned by developments in IT, digital mapping, remote sensing, and the global diffusion of GIS emphasizes the importance of developing data-driven inductive approaches to geographical analysis and modeling.

Data mining offers great potential benefits for GIS-based applied decision-making. Recently, the task of integrating these two technologies has become of critical importance, especially as various public and private sector organizations possessing huge databases with thematic and geographically referenced data begin to realize the huge potential of the information contained therein. Among those organizations are:

offices requiring analysis or dissemination of geo-referenced statistical data
public health services searching for explanations of disease clustering
environmental agencies assessing the impact of changing land-use patterns on climate change
geo-marketing companies doing customer segmentation based on spatial location.

Challenges

Geospatial data repositories tend to be very large. Moreover, existing GIS datasets are often splintered into feature and attribute components that are conventionally archived in hybrid data management systems. Algorithmic requirements differ substantially for relational (attribute) data management and for topological (feature) data management. Related to this is the range and diversity of geographic data formats, which present unique challenges. The digital geographic data revolution is creating new types of data formats beyond the traditional "vector" and "raster" formats. Geographic data repositories increasingly include ill-structured data, such as imagery and geo-referenced multi-media.

There are several critical research challenges in geographic knowledge discovery and data mining. Miller and Han offer the following list of emerging research topics in the field:

Developing and supporting geographic data warehouses (GDW's): Spatial properties are often reduced to simple aspatial attributes in mainstream data warehouses. Creating an integrated GDW requires solving issues of spatial and temporal data interoperability – including differences in semantics, referencing systems, geometry, accuracy, and position.
Better spatio-temporal representations in geographic knowledge discovery: Current geographic knowledge discovery (GKD) methods generally use very simple representations of geographic objects and spatial relationships. Geographic data mining methods should recognize more complex geographic objects (i. e. lines and polygons) and relationships (i. e. non-Euclidean distances, direction, connectivity, and interaction through attributed geographic space such as terrain). Furthermore, the time dimension needs to be more fully integrated into these geographic representations and relationships.
Geographic knowledge discovery using diverse data types: GKD methods should be developed that can handle diverse data types beyond the traditional raster and vector models, including imagery and geo-referenced multimedia, as well as dynamic data types (video streams, animation).

Sensor data mining

Wireless sensor networks can be used for facilitating the collection of data for spatial data mining for a variety of applications such as air pollution monitoring. A characteristic of such networks is that nearby sensor nodes monitoring an environmental feature typically register similar values. This kind of data redundancy due to the spatial correlation between sensor observations inspires the techniques for in-network data aggregation and mining. By measuring the spatial correlation between data sampled by different sensors, a wide class of specialized algorithms can be developed to develop more efficient spatial data mining algorithms.

Visual data mining

In the process of turning from analogical into digital, large data sets have been generated, collected, and stored discovering statistical patterns, trends and information which is hidden in data, in order to build predictive patterns. Studies suggest visual data mining is faster and much more intuitive than is traditional data mining.

Music data mining

Data mining techniques, and in particular co-occurrence analysis, has been used to discover relevant similarities among music corpora (radio lists, CD databases) for the purpose of classifying music into genres in a more objective manner.

Surveillance

Data mining has been used to stop terrorist programs under the U. S. government, including the Total Information Awareness (TIA) program, Secure Flight (formerly known as Computer-Assisted Passenger Prescreening System (CAPPS II)), Analysis, Dissemination, Visualization, Insight, Semantic Enhancement (ADVISE), and the Multi-state Anti-Terrorism Information Exchange (MATRIX). These programs have been discontinued due to controversy over whether they violate the 4th Amendment to the United States Constitution, although many programs that were formed under them continue to be funded by different organizations or under different names.

In the context of combating terrorism, two particularly plausible methods of data mining are "pattern mining" and "subject-based data mining".

Pattern mining

"Pattern mining" is a data mining method that involves finding existing patterns in data. In this context patterns often means association rules. The original motivation for searching association rules came from the desire to analyze supermarket transaction data, that is, to examine customer behavior in terms of the purchased products. For example, an association rule "beer potato chips (80%)" states that four out of five customers that bought beer also bought potato chips.

In the context of pattern mining as a tool to identify terrorist activity, the National Research Council provides the following definition: "Pattern-based data mining looks for patterns (including anomalous data patterns) that might be associated with terrorist activity — these patterns might be regarded as small signals in a large ocean of noise. " Pattern Mining includes new areas such a Music Information Retrieval (MIR) where patterns seen both in the temporal and non temporal domains are imported to classical knowledge discovery search methods.

Subject-based data mining

"Subject-based data mining" is a data mining method involving the search for associations between individuals in data. In the context of combating terrorism, the National Research Council provides the following definition: "Subject-based data mining uses an initiating individual or other datum that is considered, based on other information, to be of high interest, and the goal is to determine what other persons or financial transactions or movements, etc. , are related to that initiating datum. "

Knowledge grid

Knowledge discovery "On the Grid" generally refers to conducting knowledge discovery in an open environment using grid computing concepts, allowing users to integrate data from various online data sources, as well make use of remote resources, for executing their data mining tasks. The earliest example was the Discovery Net, developed at Imperial College London, which won the "Most Innovative Data-Intensive Application Award" at the ACM SC02 (Supercomputing 2002) conference and exhibition, based on a demonstration of a fully interactive distributed knowledge discovery application for a bioinformatics application. Other examples include work conducted by researchers at the University of Calabria, who developed a Knowledge Grid architecture for distributed knowledge discovery, based on grid computing.

Reliability/Validity

Data mining can be misused, and can also unintentionally produce results which appear significant but which do not actually predict future behavior and cannot be reproduced on a new sample of data. See Data snooping, Data dredging.

Challenges

In four annual surveys of data miners, data mining practitioners consistently identify three key challenges that they face more than any others, specifically (a) dirty data, (b) explaining data mining to others, and (c) unavailability of data/difficult access to data. In the 2010 survey data miners also shared their experiences in overcoming these particular challenges.

Privacy concerns and ethics

Some people believe that data mining itself is ethically neutral. It is important to note that the term "data mining" has no ethical implications, but is often associated with the mining of information in relation to peoples' behavior (ethical and otherwise). To be precise, data mining is a statistical method that is applied to a set of information (i. e. a data set). Associating these data sets with people is an extreme narrowing of the types of data that are available in today's technological society. Examples could range from a set of crash test data for passenger vehicles, to the performance of a group of stocks. These types of data sets make up a great proportion of the information available to be acted on by data mining methods, and rarely have ethical concerns associated with them. However, the ways in which data mining can be used can in some cases and contexts raise questions regarding privacy, legality, and ethics. In particular, data mining government or commercial data sets for national security or law enforcement purposes, such as in the Total Information Awareness Program or in ADVISE, has raised privacy concerns.

Data mining requires data preparation which can uncover information or patterns which may compromise confidentiality and privacy obligations. A common way for this to occur is through data aggregation. Data aggregation involves combining data together (possibly from various sources) in a way that facilitates analysis (but that also might make identification of private, individual-level data deducible or otherwise apparent). This is not data mining per se, but a result of the preparation of data before – and for the purposes of – the analysis. The threat to an individual's privacy comes into play when the data, once compiled, cause the data miner, or anyone who has access to the newly compiled data set, to be able to identify specific individuals, especially when the data were originally anonymous.

It is recommended that an individual is made aware of the following before data are collected:

the purpose of the data collection and any (known) data mining projects
how the data will be used
who will be able to mine the data and use the data and their derivatives
the status of security surrounding access to the data
how collected data can be updated.
In America, privacy concerns have been addressed to some extent by the US Congress via the passage of regulatory controls such as the Health Insurance Portability and Accountability Act (HIPAA). The HIPAA requires individuals to give their "informed consent" regarding information they provide and its intended present and future uses. According to an article in Biotech Business Week', "'[i]n practice, HIPAA may not offer any greater protection than the longstanding regulations in the research arena,' says the AAHC. More importantly, the rule's goal of protection through informed consent is undermined by the complexity of consent forms that are required of patients and participants, which approach a level of incomprehensibility to average individuals. " This underscores the necessity for data anonymity in data aggregation and mining practices.

Data may also be modified so as to become anonymous, so that individuals may not readily be identified. However, even "de-identified"/"anonymized" data sets can potentially contain enough information to allow identification of individuals, as occurred when journalists were able to find several individuals based on a set of search histories that were inadvertently released by AOL.

Software

Free open-source data mining software and applications

Carrot2: Text and search results clustering framework.
Chemicalize. org: A chemical structure miner and web search engine.
ELKI: A university research project with advanced cluster analysis and outlier detection methods written in the Java language.
GATE: a natural language processing and language engineering tool.
JHepWork: Java cross-platform data analysis framework developed at Argonne National Laboratory.
KNIME: The Konstanz Information Miner, a user friendly and comprehensive data analytics framework.
NLTK (Natural Language Toolkit): A suite of libraries and programs for symbolic and statistical natural language processing (NLP) for the Python language.
Orange: A component-based data mining and machine learning software suite written in the Python language.
R: A programming language and software environment for statistical computing, data mining, and graphics. It is part of the GNU project.
RapidMiner: An environment for machine learning and data mining experiments.
UIMA: The UIMA (Unstructured Information Management Architecture) is a component framework for analyzing unstructured content such as text, audio and video – originally developed by IBM.
Weka: A suite of machine learning software applications written in the Java programming language.
ML-Flex: A software package that enables users to integrate with third-party machine-learning packages written in any programming language, execute classification analyses in parallel across multiple computing nodes, and produce HTML reports of classification results.
In 2010, the open source R language overtook other tools to become the application used by more data miners (43%) than any other, according to a well-known annual survey.

Commercial data-mining software and applications

Microsoft Analysis Services: data mining software provided by Microsoft
SAS: Enterprise Miner – data mining software provided by the SAS Institute.
STATISTICA: Data Miner – data mining software provided by StatSoft.
Oracle Data Mining: data mining software by Oracle.
LIONsolver: an integrated software application for data mining, business intelligence, and modeling that implements the Learning and Intelligent OptimizatioN (LION) approach
According to Rexer's Annual Data Miner Survey in 2010, IBM SPSS Modeler, STATISTICA Data Miner, and the R received the strongest satisfaction ratings.

Marketplace surveys

Several researchers and organizations have conducted reviews of data mining tools and surveys of data miners. These identify some of the strengths and weaknesses of the software packages. They also provide an overview of the behaviors, preferences and views of data miners. Some of these reports include:

Annual Rexer Analytics Data Miner Surveys
Forrester Research 2010 Predictive Analytics and Data Mining Solutions report
Gartner 2008 "Magic Quadrant" report
Haughton et al.'s 2003 Review of Data Mining Software Packages in The American Statistician
Robert A. Nisbet's 2006 Three Part Series of articles "Data Mining Tools: Which One is Best For CRM?"
2011 Wiley Interdisciplinary Reviews: Data Mining and Knowledge Discovery

Decision tree learning

Decision tree learning

Decision tree learning, used in statistics, data mining and machine learning, uses a decision tree as a predictive model which maps observations about an item to conclusions about the item's target value. More descriptive names for such tree models are classification trees or regression trees. In these tree structures, leaves represent class labels and branches represent conjunctions of features that lead to those class labels.

In decision analysis, a decision tree can be used to visually and explicitly represent decisions and decision making. In data mining, a decision tree describes data but not decisions; rather the resulting classification tree can be an input for decision making. This page deals with decision trees in data mining.

General

A tree showing survival of passengers on the Titanic ("sibsp" is the number of spouses or siblings aboard). The figures under the leaves show the probability of survival and the percentage of observations in the leaf.
Decision tree learning is a method commonly used in data mining. The goal is to create a model that predicts the value of a target variable based on several input variables. An example is shown on the right. Each interior node corresponds to one of the input variables; there are edges to children for each of the possible values of that input variable. Each leaf represents a value of the target variable given the values of the input variables represented by the path from the root to the leaf.

A tree can be "learned" by splitting the source set into subsets based on an attribute value test. This process is repeated on each derived subset in a recursive manner called recursive partitioning. The recursion is completed when the subset at a node has all the same value of the target variable, or when splitting no longer adds value to the predictions. This process of top-down induction of decision trees (TDIDT) is an example of a greedy algorithm, and it is by far the most common strategy for learning decision trees from data, but it is not the only strategy.

In data mining, decision trees can be described also as the combination of mathematical and computational techniques to aid the description, categorisation and generalisation of a given set of data.

Data comes in records of the form:

The dependent variable, Y, is the target variable that we are trying to understand, classify or generalise. The vector x is composed of the input variables, x1, x2, x3 etc., that are used for that task.

Types

Decision trees used in data mining are of two main types:

Classification tree analysis is when the predicted outcome is the class to which the data belongs.
Regression tree analysis is when the predicted outcome can be considered a real number (e. g. the price of a house, or a patient's length of stay in a hospital).
The term Classification And Regression Tree (CART) analysis is an umbrella term used to refer to both of the above procedures, first introduced by Breiman et al. Trees used for regression and trees used for classification have some similarities - but also some differences, such as the procedure used to determine where to split.

Some techniques, often called ensemble methods, construct more than one decision tree:

Bagging decision trees, an early ensemble method, builds multiple decision trees by repeatedly resampling training data with replacement, and voting the trees for a consensus prediction.
A Random Forest classifier uses a number of decision trees, in order to improve the classification rate.
Boosted Trees can be used for regression-type and classification-type problems.
Rotation forest - in which every decision tree is trained by first applying principal component analysis (PCA) on a random subset of the input features.
There are many specific decision-tree algorithms. Notable ones include:

ID3 algorithm
C4. 5 algorithm

CHi-squared Automatic Interaction Detector (CHAID). Performs multi-level splits when computing classification trees.
MARS: extends decision trees to better handle numerical data

Formulae

The algorithms that are used for constructing decision trees usually work top-down by choosing a variable at each step that is the next best variable to use in splitting the set of items. "Best" is defined by how well the variable splits the set into homogeneous subsets that have the same value of the target variable. Different algorithms use different formulae for measuring "best". This section presents a few of the most common formulae. These formulae are applied to each candidate subset, and the resulting values are combined (e.g., averaged) to provide a measure of the quality of the split.

Gini impurity

Gini coefficient
Used by the CART algorithm, Gini impurity is a measure of how often a randomly chosen element from the set would be incorrectly labeled if it were randomly labeled according to the distribution of labels in the subset. Gini impurity can be computed by summing the probability of each item being chosen times the probability of a mistake in categorizing that item. It reaches its minimum (zero) when all cases in the node fall into a single target category.

To compute Gini impurity for a set of items, suppose y takes on values in $\{1, 2, \ldots, m\}$, and let f_i = the fraction of items labeled with value i in the set.

Information gain

Information gain in decision trees
Used by the ID3, C4.5 and C5.0 tree generation algorithms. Information gain is based on the concept of entropy used in information theory.

Decision tree advantages

Amongst other data mining methods, decision trees have various advantages:

Simple to understand and interpret. People are able to understand decision tree models after a brief explanation.
Requires little data preparation. Other techniques often require data normalisation, dummy variables need to be created and blank values to be removed.
Able to handle both numerical and categorical data. Other techniques are usually specialised in analysing datasets that have only one type of variable. Ex: relation rules can be used only with nominal variables while neural networks can be used only with numerical variables.
Uses a white box model. If a given situation is observable in a model the explanation for the condition is easily explained by boolean logic. An example of a black box model is an artificial neural network since the explanation for the results is difficult to understand.
Possible to validate a model using statistical tests. That makes it possible to account for the reliability of the model.
Robust. Performs well even if its assumptions are somewhat violated by the true model from which the data were generated.
Performs well with large data in a short time. Large amounts of data can be analysed using standard computing resources.

Limitations

The problem of learning an optimal decision tree is known to be NP-complete under several aspects of optimality and even for simple concepts. Consequently, practical decision-tree learning algorithms are based on heuristic algorithms such as the greedy algorithm where locally optimal decisions are made at each node. Such algorithms cannot guarantee to return the globally optimal decision tree.
Decision-tree learners can create over-complex trees that do not generalise the data well. This is called overfitting. Mechanisms such as pruning are necessary to avoid this problem.
There are concepts that are hard to learn because decision trees do not express them easily, such as XOR, parity or

multiplexer problems. In such cases, the decision tree becomes prohibitively large. Approaches to solve the problem involve either changing the representation of the problem domain (known as propositionalisation) or using learning algorithms based on more expressive representations (such as statistical relational learning or inductive logic programming).

For data including categorical variables with different numbers of levels, information gain in decision trees are biased in favor of those attributes with more levels.

Extensions

Decision graphs

In a decision tree, all paths from the root node to the leaf node proceed by way of conjunction, or AND. In a decision graph, it is possible to use disjunctions (ORs) to join two more paths together using Minimum Message Length (MML). Decision graphs have been further extended to allow for previously unstated new attributes to be learnt dynamically and used at different places within the graph. The more general coding scheme results in better predictive accuracy and log-loss probabilistic scoring. In general, decision graphs infer models with fewer leaves than decision trees.

Search through Evolutionary Algorithms

Evolutionary algorithms have been used to avoid local optimal decisions and search the decision tree space with little a priori bias.

Feed forward (control)

Feed forward (control)

Feed-forward is a term describing an element or pathway within a control system which passes a controlling signal from a source in the control system's external environment, often a command signal from an external operator, to a load elsewhere in its external environment. A control system which has only feed-forward behavior responds to its control signal in a pre-defined way without responding to how the load reacts; it is in contrast with a system that also has feedback, which adjusts the output to take account of how it affects the load, and how the load itself may vary unpredictably; the load is considered to belong to the external environment of the system.

Some prerequisites are needed for control scheme to be reliable by pure feed-forward without feedback: the external command or controlling signal must be available, and the effect of the output of the system on the load should be known (that usually means that the load must be predictably unchanging with time). Sometimes pure feed-forward control without feedback is called 'ballistic', because once a control signal has been sent, it cannot be further adjusted; any corrective adjustment must be by way of a new control signal. In contrast 'cruise control' adjusts the output in response to the load that it encounters, by a feedback mechanism.

These systems could be in control theory, physiology or computing.

Overview

With feed-forward control, the disturbances are measured and accounted for before they have time to affect the system. In the house example, a feed-forward system may measure the fact that the door is opened and automatically turn on the heater before the house can get too cold. The difficulty with feed-forward control is that the effect of the disturbances on the system must be accurately predicted, and there must not be any unmeasured disturbances. For instance, if a window was opened that was not being measured, the feed-forward-controlled thermostat might still let the house cool down.

There are three types of control systems: open loop, feed-forward, and feedback. An example of a pure open loop control system is manual non-power-assisted steering of a motor car; the steering system does not have access to an auxiliary power source and does not respond to varying resistance to turning of the direction wheels; the driver must make that response without help from the steering system. In comparison, power steering has access to a controlled auxiliary power source, which depends on the engine speed. When the steering wheel is turned, a valve is opened which allows fluid under pressure to turn the driving wheels. A sensor monitors that pressure so that the valve only opens enough to cause the correct pressure to reach the wheel turning mechanism. This is feed-forward control where the output of the system, the change in direction of travel of the vehicle, plays no part in the system. See Model predictive control.

If you include the driver in the system, then he does provide a feedback path by observing the direction of travel and compensating for errors by turning the steering wheel. In that case you have a feedback system, and the block labeled "System" in Figure(c) is a feed-forward system.

In other words, systems of different types can be nested, and the overall system regarded as a black-box.

Applications

Physiological feed-forward system

In physiology, feed-forward control is exemplified by the normal anticipatory regulation of heartbeat in advance of actual physical exertion. Feed-forward control can be likened to learned anticipatory responses to known cues. Feedback regulation of the heartbeat provides further adaptiveness to the running eventualities of physical exertion.

A pure feed-forward system is distinct from a homeostatic control system, which has the function of keeping the internal environment of the body steady or constant or in a prolonged steady state of readiness, and relies mainly on feedback, indeed on negative feedback, in addition to the feedforward elements of the system.

Gene regulation and feed-forward

The cross regulation of genes can be represented by a graph, where genes are the nodes and one node is linked to another if the former is a transcription factor for the latter. A motif which predominantly appears in all known networks (E. coli, Yeast,...) is A activates B, A and B activate C. This motif has been shown to be a feed forward system, detecting non-temporary change of environment. This feed forward control theme is commonly observed in hematopoietic cell lineage development, where irreversible commitments are made.

Feed-forward systems in computing

Perceptron
In computing, feed-forward normally refers to a perceptron network in which the outputs from all neurons go to following but not preceding layers, so there are no feedback loops. The connections are set up during a training phase, which in effect is when the system is a feedback system.

Long distance telephony

In the early 1970s, intercity coaxial transmission systems, including L-carrier, used feed-forward amplifiers to diminish linear distortion. This more complex method allowed wider bandwidth than earlier feedback systems. Optical fiber, however, made such systems obsolete before many were built.

Automation and Machine Control

Feedforward control is a discipline within the field of automatic controls used in automation.

Forecasting

Forecasting

Forecasting is the process of making statements about events whose actual outcomes (typically) have not yet been observed.

A commonplace example might be estimation of some variable of interest at some specified future date. Prediction is a similar, but more general term. Both might refer to formal statistical methods employing time series, cross-sectional or longitudinal data, or alternatively to less formal judgemental methods. Usage can differ between areas of application: for example, in hydrology, the terms "forecast" and "forecasting" are sometimes reserved for estimates of values at certain specific future times, while the term "prediction" is used for more general estimates, such as the number of times floods will occur over a long period.

Risk and uncertainty are central to forecasting and prediction; it is generally considered good practice to indicate the degree of uncertainty attaching to forecasts. In any case, the data must be up to date in order for the forecast to be as accurate as possible.

Although quantitative analysis can be very precise, it is not always appropriate. Some experts in the field of forecasting have advised against the use of mean square error to compare forecasting methods.

Categories of forecasting methods

Qualitative vs. quantitative methods

Qualitative forecasting techniques are subjective, based on the opinion and judgment of consumers, experts; appropriate when past data is not available. It is usually applied to intermediate-long range decisions. Examples of qualitative forecasting methods are: informed opinion and judgment, the Delphi method, market research, historical life-cycle analogy.

Quantitative forecasting models are used to estimate future demands as a function of past data; appropriate when past data are available. The method is usually applied to short-intermediate range decisions. Examples of quantitative forecasting methods are: last period demand, simple and weighted moving averages (N-Period), simple exponential smoothing, multiplicative seasonal indexes.

Naïve approach

Naïve forecasts are the most cost-effective and efficient objective forecasting model, and provide a benchmark against which more sophisticated models can be compared. For stable time series data, this approach says that the forecast for any period equals the previous period's actual value.

Reference class forecasting

Reference class forecasting was developed by Oxford professor Bent Flyvbjerg to eliminate or reduce bias in forecasting by focusing on distributional information about past, similar outcomes to that being forecasted. Daniel Kahneman, Nobel Prize winner in economics, calls Flyvbjerg's counsel to use reference class forecasting to de-bias forecasts, "the single most important piece of advice regarding how to increase accuracy in forecasting."

Time series methods

Time series methods use historical data as the basis of estimating future outcomes some notable methods are.

Moving average
Weighted moving average
Kalman filtering
Exponential smoothing
Autoregressive moving average (ARMA)
Autoregressive integrated moving average (ARIMA)
e. g. Box-Jenkins
Extrapolation
Linear prediction
Trend estimation
Growth curve

Causal / econometric forecasting methods

Some forecasting methods use the assumption that it is possible to identify the underlying factors that might influence the variable that is being forecast. For example, including information about weather conditions might improve the ability of a model to predict umbrella sales. This is a model of seasonality which shows a regular pattern of up and down fluctuations. In addition to weather, seasonality can also be due to holidays and customs such as predicting that sales in college football apparel will be higher during football season as opposed to the off season.

Casual forecasting methods are also subject to the discretion of the forecaster. There are several informal methods which do not have strict algorithms, but rather modest and unstructured guidance. One can forecast based on, for example, linear relationships. If one variable is linearly related to the other for a long enough period of time, it may be beneficial to predict such a relationship in the future. This is quite different from the aforementioned model of seasonality whose graph would more closely resemble a sine or cosine wave. The most important factor when performing this operation is using concrete and substantiated data. Forecasting off of another forecast produces inconclusive and possibly erroneous results.

Such methods include:

Regression analysis includes a large group of methods that can be used to predict future values of a variable using information about other variables. These methods include both parametric (linear or non-linear) and non-parametric techniques.
Autoregressive moving average with exogenous inputs (ARMAX)

Judgmental methods

Judgmental forecasting methods incorporate intuitive judgements, opinions and subjective probability estimates.

Composite forecasts
Delphi method
Forecast by analogy
Scenario building
Statistical surveys
Technology forecasting

Artificial intelligence methods

Artificial neural networks
Group method of data handling
Support vector machines
Often these are done today by specialized programs loosely labeled

Data mining

Other methods

Simulation
Prediction market
Probabilistic forecasting and Ensemble forecasting

Forecasting accuracy

The forecast error is the difference between the actual value and the forecast value for the corresponding period.

where E is the forecast error at period t, Y is the actual value at period t, and F is the forecast for period t.

Measures of aggregate error:

Business forecasters and practitioners sometimes use different terminology in the industry. They refer to the PMAD as the MAPE, although they compute this as a volume weighted MAPE. For more information see Calculating demand forecast accuracy.

Reference class forecasting was developed to increase forecasting accuracy by framing the forecasting problem so as to take into account available distributional information. Daniel Kahneman, winner of the Nobel Prize in economics, calls the use of reference class forecasting "the single most important piece of advice regarding how to increase accuracy in forecasting. " Forecasting accuracy, in contrary to belief, cannot be increased by the addition of experts in the subject area relevant to the phenomenon to be forecast.

Fraud

Fraud - ,

In criminal law, a fraud is an intentional deception made for personal gain or to damage another individual; the related adjective is fraudulent. The specific legal definition varies by legal jurisdiction. Fraud is a crime, and also a civil law violation. Defrauding people or entities of money or valuables is a common purpose of fraud.

A hoax also involves deception, but without the intention of gain or of damaging or depriving the victim.

By region

United Kingdom

England and Wales and Northern Ireland

Fraud Act 2006
The government's 2006 Fraud Review concluded that fraud is a significantly under-reported crime, and while various agencies and organisations were attempting to tackle the issue, greater co-operation was needed to achieve a real impact in the public sector. The scale of the problem pointed to the need for a small but high-powered body to bring together the numerous counter-fraud initiatives that existed. Baker (Dennis J. Baker, Glanville Williams Textbook of Criminal Law, (London: Sweet & Maxwell, 2012) at p. 1161 writes that the new offences are inchoate and therefore: "The new fraud offences are almost unlimited as to the dishonest conduct they criminalize. A particular problem with the new offences is that everyone is labelled the same. Those who attempt fraud are labelled as though they consummated their act of fraud. " The National Fraud Authority was established as a result of this recommendation. Baker also writes (ibid at pp. 1162 and following) that fraud by false representation is the offence that will do most of the work in the 2006 Act.

Serious Fraud Office

See Serious Fraud Office (United Kingdom) is an arm of the Government of the United Kingdom, accountable to the Attorney-General.

National Fraud Authority

The National Fraud Authority (NFA) is the government agency co-ordinating the counter-fraud response in the UK.

CIFAS - The UK's Fraud Prevention Service

CIFAS - The UK's Fraud Prevention Service, is a not-for-profit membership association representing the private and public sectors. CIFAS is dedicated to the prevention of fraud, including staff fraud, and the identification of financial and related crime.

Canada

Section 380(1) of the Criminal Code of Canada provides the general definition for fraud in Canada:

380. (1) Every one who, by deceit, falsehood or other fraudulent means, whether or not it is a false pretence within the meaning of this Act, defrauds the public or any person, whether ascertained or not, of any property, money or valuable security or any service,

(a) is guilty of an indictable offence and liable to a term of imprisonment not exceeding fourteen years, where the subject-matter of the offence is a testamentary instrument or the value of the subject-matter of the offence exceeds five thousand dollars; or
(b) is guilty
(i) of an indictable offence and is liable to imprisonment for a term not exceeding two years, or
(ii) of an offence punishable on summary conviction,
where the value of the subject-matter of the offence does not exceed five thousand dollars.

In addition to the penalties outlined above, the court can also issue a prohibition order under s. 380. 2 (preventing a person from "seeking, obtaining or continuing any employment, or becoming or being a volunteer in any capacity, that involves having authority over the real property, money or valuable security of another person"). It can also make a restitution order under s. 380. 3.

The Canadian courts have held that the offence consists of two distinct elements:

A prohibited act of deceit, falsehood or other fraudulent means. In the absence of deceit or falsehood, the courts will look objectively for a "dishonest act"; and
The deprivation must be caused by the prohibited act, and deprivation must relate to property, money, valuable security, or any service.
The Supreme Court of Canada has held that deprivation is satisfied on proof of detriment, prejudice or risk of prejudice; it is not essential that there be actual loss. Deprivation of confidential information, in the nature of a trade secret or copyrighted material that has commercial value, has also been held to fall within the scope of the offence.

United States

Common law fraud has nine elements:

a representation of an existing fact;
its materiality;
its falsity;
the speaker's knowledge of its falsity;
the speaker's intent that it shall be acted upon by the plaintiff;
plaintiff's ignorance of its falsity;
plaintiff's reliance on the truth of the representation;
plaintiff's right to rely upon it; and
consequent damages suffered by plaintiff.
Most jurisdictions in the United States require that each element be pled with particularity and be proved with clear, cogent, and convincing evidence (very probable evidence) to establish a claim of fraud. The measure of damages in fraud cases is to be computed by the "benefit of bargain" rule, which is the difference

between the value of the property had it been as represented, and its actual value. Special damages may be allowed if shown proximately caused by defendant's fraud and the damage amounts are proved with specificity.

Cost of fraud

The typical organization loses five percent of its annual revenue to fraud, with a median loss of $160,000. Frauds committed by owners and executives were more than nine times as costly as employee fraud. The industries most commonly affected are banking, manufacturing, and government.

Types of fraudulent acts

Fraud can be committed through many media, including mail, wire, phone, and the Internet (computer crime and Internet fraud). The international dimensions of the web and ease with which users can hide their location, the difficulty of checking identity and legitimacy online, and the simplicity with which hackers can divert browsers to dishonest sites and steal credit card details have all contributed to the very rapid growth of Internet fraud. In some countries, tax fraud is also prosecuted under false billing or tax forgery. There have also been fraudulent "discoveries", e. g. , in science, to gain prestige rather than immediate monetary gain.

Anti-Fraud movements

Beyond laws that aim at prevention of fraud, there are also governmental and non-governmental organizations that aim to fight fraud. Between 1911 and 1933, 47 states adopted the so-called Blue Sky Laws status. These laws were enacted and enforced at the state level and regulated the offering and sale of securities to protect the public from fraud. Though the specific provisions of these laws varied among states, they all required the registration of all securities offerings and sales, as well as of every US stockbroker and brokerage firm. However, these Blue Sky laws were generally found to be ineffective. To increase public trust in the capital markets the United States President, Franklin D. Roosevelt, established the U. S. Securities and Exchange Commission (SEC).

The main reason for the creation of the SEC was to regulate the stock market and prevent corporate abuses relating to the offering and sale of securities and corporate reporting. The SEC was given the power to license and regulate stock exchanges, the companies whose securities traded on them, and the brokers and dealers who conducted the trading.

Fraud detection

For detection of fraudulent activities on the large scale, massive use of (online) data analysis is required, in particular predictive analytics or forensic analytics. Forensic analytics is the use of electronic data to reconstruct or detect financial fraud. The steps in the process are data collection, data preparation, data analysis, and the preparation of a report and possibly a presentation of the results. Using computer-based analytic methods Nigrini's wider goal is the detection of fraud, errors, anomalies, inefficiencies, and biases which refer to people gravitating to certain dollar amounts to get past internal control thresholds. The analytic tests usually start with high-level data overview tests to spot highly significant irregularities. In a recent purchasing card application these tests identified a purchasing card transaction for 3,000,000 Costa Rica Colons. This was neither a fraud nor an error, but it was a highly unusual amount for a purchasing card transaction. These high-level tests include tests related to Benford's Law and possibly also those statistics known as descriptive statistics. These high-tests are always followed by more focused tests to look for small samples of highly irregular transactions. The famillar methods of correlation and time-series analysis can also be used to detect fraud and other irregularities. Forensic analytics also includes the use of a fraud risk-scoring model to identify high risk forensic units (customers, employees, locations, insurance claims and so on). Forensic analytics also includes suggested tests to identify financial statement irregularities, but the general rule is that analytic methods alone are not too successful at detecting financial statement fraud.

Notable fraudsters

Frank Abagnale Jr. , US impostor who wrote bad checks and falsely represented himself as a qualified member of professions such as airline pilot, doctor, attorney, and teacher. The film Catch Me If You Can is based on his life.

John Bodkin Adams, British doctor and suspected serial killer, but only found guilty of forging wills and prescriptions

Eddie Antar, founder of Crazy Eddie, who has about $1 billion worth of judgments against him stemming from fraudulent accounting practices at that company.

Cassie Chadwick, who pretended to be Andrew Carnegie's illegitimate daughter to get loans.

Columbia/HCA Medicare fraud. Columbia/HCA pleaded guilty to 14 felony counts and paid out more than $2 billion to settle lawsuits arising from the fraud. The company's board of directors forced then–Chairman and CEO Rick Scott to resign at the beginning of the federal investigation; Scott was subsequently elected Governor of Florida in 2010.

Salim Damji is a convicted fraud artist who defrauded millions of dollars in an affinity fraud. The money came mostly from relatives and members of the close-knit Ismaili community. His $78 million scam was among the largest in Canadian history.

Charles Dawson, an amateur British archeologist who claimed to have found the Piltdown man.

Marc Dreier, Managing founder of Attorney firm Dreir LLP. Prosecutors allege that from 2004 through December 2008, He sold approximately $700 million worth of fictitious promissory notes.

Bernard Ebbers, founder of WorldCom, which inflated its asset statements by about $11 billion.

Ramón Báez Figueroa, banker from the Dominican Republic and former President of Banco Intercontinental. Sentenced on October 21, 2007 to ten years in prison for a US $2.2 billion fraud case that drove the Caribbean nation into an economic crisis in 2003.

Martin Frankel is a former U.S. financier, convicted in 2002 of insurance fraud worth $208 million, racketeering and money laundering.

Pearlasia Gamboa, president of the micronation of Melchizedek, hundreds of aliases; in 2002, one of Gamboa's banking and investor fraud schemes was described by the Italian newspaper La Republica as "one of the most diabolical international scams ever devised in recent years", and in 2000, the Asia Times described Gamboa's operations as "an astonishing series of worldwide swindles".

Samuel Israel III, former hedge fund manager that ran the former fraudulent Bayou Hedge Fund Group. He faked suicide.

Ashok Jadeja has been accused of cheating people from across India of scores of rupees on the pretext of having divine blessings.

Konrad Kujau, German fraudster and forger responsible for the "Hitler Diaries".

Kenneth Lay, the American businessman who built energy company Enron. He was one of the highest paid CEOs in America until he was ousted as Chairman and was convicted of fraud and conspiracy, although as a result of his death, his conviction was vacated.

Nick Leeson, English trader whose unsupervised speculative trading caused the collapse of Barings Bank.

James Paul Lewis, Jr. , ran one of the biggest ($311 million) and longest running Ponzi Schemes (20 years) in US history.

Gregor MacGregor, Scottish conman who tried to attract investment and settlers for the non-existent country of Poyais.

Bernard Madoff, creator of a $65 billion Ponzi scheme – the largest investor fraud ever attributed to a single individual.

Colleen McCabe, British headmistress who stole £½ million from her school.

Gaston Means, a professional conman during U. S. President Warren G. Harding's administration.

Matt the Knife, American born con artist, card cheat and pickpocket who, from the ages of approximately 14 through 21, bilked dozens of casinos, corporations and at least one Mafia crime family out of untold sums.

Barry Minkow and the ZZZZ Best scam.

Michael Monus, founder of Phar-Mor, which ultimately cost its investors more than $1 billion.

F. Bam Morrison, who conned the town of Wetumka, Oklahoma by promoting a circus that never came.

Lou Pearlman, former boy-band manager indicted by a federal grand jury in Orlando on charges that he schemed to bilk banks out of more than $100 million.

Frederick Emerson Peters, US impersonator who wrote bad checks.

Thomas Petters is an American masquerading as a business man who turned out to be a con man and was the former CEO and chairman of Petters Group Worldwide. Petters resigned his position as CEO on September 29, 2008, amid mounting criminal investigations. He later was convicted for turning Petters Group Worldwide into a $3. 65 billion Ponzi scheme and was sentenced to 50 years in federal prison.

Charles Ponzi and the Ponzi scheme.

Alves Reis, who forged documents to print 100,000,000 PTE in official escudo banknotes (adjusted for inflation, it would be worth about US$150 million today).

John Rigas, cable television entrepreneur, cofounder of Adelphia

Communications Corporation and owner of the Buffalo Sabres hockey team. Defrauded investors of over $2 billion and was sentenced to a 12 year term in federal prison.
Christopher Rocancourt, a Rockefeller impersonator who defrauded Hollywood celebrities.
Joseph Rothe, of Fonthill, Ontario, ordered to pay $500,000 in restitution, received a four-year prison sentence, along with Ewaryst Prokofiew, of Mississauga, Ontario, in the biggest GST fraud in Canadian history. Code named Project Phantom for the lengthy police investigation, the organizers lined up a steady supply of vehicles that were to be sold at the auctions. The cars never materialized and were never purchased. But the operators of the fraud claimed that they had been sold, and because of the natives' tax-exempt status were able to claim the GST exemption. Authorities could only guess at the full loss sustained by the Canada Revenue Agency. Madam Justice Lynda Templeton of Superior Court said the scheme siphoned at least $11-million from Ottawa, possibly a great deal more.
Scott W. Rothstein, a disbarred lawyer from Ft. Lauderdale, Florida, who perpetrated a Ponzi scheme which defrauded investors of over $1 billion.
Michael Sabo, best known as a check, stocks and bonds forger. He became notorious in the 1960s throughout the 1990s as a "Great Impostor" over 100 aliases, and earned millions from such.
John Spano, a struggling businessman who faked massive success in an attempt to buy out the New York Islanders of the NHL.
John Stonehouse, the last Postmaster-General of the UK and MP who faked his death to marry his mistress.
Kevin Trudeau, US writer and billiards promoter, convicted of fraud and larceny in 1991, known for a series of late-night infomercials and his series of books about "Natural Cures "They" Don't Want You to Know About".
Andrew Wakefield, UK physician who claimed links between the MMR vaccine, autism and inflammatory bowel disease. He was found guilty of dishonesty in his research and banned from medicine by the UK General Medical Council following an investigation by Brian Deer of the London Sunday Times.
Richard Whitney, who stole from the New York Stock Exchange Gratuity Fund in the 1930s.

Related

Apart from fraud, there are several related categories of intentional deceptions that may or may not include the elements of personal gain or damage to another individual:

Obstruction of justice
18 U. S. C. § 704 which criminalizes false representation of having been awarded any decoration or medal authorized by Congress for the Armed Forces of the United States

Game theory

Game theory

Game theory is the study of strategic decision making. More formally, it is "the study of mathematical models of conflict and cooperation between intelligent rational decision-makers. " An alternative term suggested "as a more descriptive name for the discipline" is interactive decision theory. Game theory is mainly used in economics, political science, and psychology, as well as logic and biology. The subject first addressed zero-sum games, such that one person's gains exactly equal net losses of the other participant(s). Today, however, game theory applies to a wide range of class relations, and has developed into an umbrella term for the logical side of science, to include both human and non-humans, like computers. Classic uses include a sense of balance in numerous games, where each person has found or developed a tactic that cannot successfully better his results, given the other approach.

Modern game theory began with the idea regarding the existence of mixed-strategy equilibria in two-person zero-sum games and its proof by John von Neumann. Von Neumann's original proof used Brouwer's fixed-point theorem on continuous mappings into compact convex sets, which became a standard method in game theory and mathematical economics. His paper was followed by his 1944 book Theory of Games and Economic Behavior, with Oskar Morgenstern, which considered cooperative games of several players. The second edition of this book provided an axiomatic theory of expected utility, which allowed mathematical statisticians and economists to treat decision-making under uncertainty.

This theory was developed extensively in the 1950s by many scholars. Game theory was later explicitly applied to biology in the

1970s, although similar developments go back at least as far as the 1930s. Game theory has been widely recognized as an important tool in many fields. Eight game-theorists have won the Nobel Memorial Prize in Economic Sciences, and John Maynard Smith was awarded the Crafoord Prize for his application of game theory to biology.

Representation of games

The games studied in game theory are well-defined mathematical objects. A game consists of a set of players, a set of moves (or strategies) available to those players, and a specification of payoffs for each combination of strategies. Most cooperative games are presented in the characteristic function form, while the extensive and the normal forms are used to define noncooperative games.

Extensive form

Extensive form game
The extensive form can be used to formalize games with a time sequencing of moves. Games here are played on trees (as pictured to the left). Here each vertex (or node) represents a point of choice for a player. The player is specified by a number listed by the vertex. The lines out of the vertex represent a possible action for that player. The payoffs are specified at the bottom of the tree. The extensive form can be viewed as a multi-player generalization of a decision tree. (Fudenberg & Tirole 1991, p. 67)

In the game pictured to the left, there are two players. Player 1 moves first and chooses either F or U. Player 2 sees Player 1's move and then chooses A or R. Suppose that Player 1 chooses U and then Player 2 chooses A, then Player 1 gets 8 and Player 2 gets 2.

The extensive form can also capture simultaneous-move games and games with imperfect information. To represent it, either a dotted line connects different vertices to represent them as being part of the same information set (i. e. , the players do not know at which point they are), or a closed line is drawn around them. (See example in the imperfect information section.)

Normal form

	Player 2 chooses Left	Player 2 chooses Right
Player 1 chooses Up	4, 3	−1, −1
Player 1 chooses Down	0, 0	3, 4

Normal form or payoff matrix of a 2-player, 2-strategy game

Normal-form game
The normal (or strategic form) game is usually represented by a matrix which shows the players, strategies, and pay-offs (see the example to the right). More generally it can be represented by any function that associates a payoff for each player with every possible combination of actions. In the accompanying example there are two players; one chooses the row and the other chooses the column. Each player has two strategies, which are specified by the number of rows and the number of columns. The payoffs are provided in the interior. The first number is the payoff received by the row player (Player 1 in our example); the second is the payoff for the column player (Player 2 in our example). Suppose that Player 1 plays Up and that Player 2 plays Left. Then Player 1 gets a payoff of 4, and Player 2 gets 3.

When a game is presented in normal form, it is presumed that each player acts simultaneously or, at least, without knowing the actions of the other. If players have some information about the choices of other players, the game is usually presented in extensive form.

Every extensive-form game has an equivalent normal-form game, however the transformation to normal form may result in an exponential blowup in the size of the representation, making it computationally impractical. (Leyton-Brown & Shoham 2008, p. 35)

Characteristic function form

Cooperative game
In games that possess removable utility separate rewards are not given; rather, the characteristic function decides the payoff of each unity. The idea is that the unity that is 'empty', so to speak, does not receive a reward at all.

The origin of this form is to be found in John von Neumann and Oskar Morgenstern's book; when looking at these instances, they guessed that when a union C appears, it works against the fraction (N/C) as if two individuals were playing a normal game. The balanced payoff of C is a basic function. Although there are differing examples that help determine coalitional amounts from normal games, not all appear that in their function form can be derived from such.

Formally, a characteristic function is seen as: (N,v), where N represents the group of people and $v:2^N \to R$ is a normal utility.

Such characteristic functions have expanded to describe games where there is no removable utility.

Partition function form

The characteristic function form ignores the possible externalities of coalition formation. In the partition function form the payoff of a coalition depends not only on its members, but also on the way the rest of the players are partitioned (Thrall & Lucas 1963).

General and applied uses

As a method of applied mathematics, game theory has been used to study a wide variety of human and animal behaviors. It was initially developed in economics to understand a large collection of economic behaviors, including behaviors of firms, markets, and consumers. The use of game theory in the social sciences has expanded, and game theory has been applied to political, sociological, and psychological behaviors as well.

Game-theoretic analysis was initially used to study animal behavior by Ronald Fisher in the 1930s (although even Charles Darwin makes a few informal game-theoretic statements). This work predates the name "game theory", but it shares many important features with this field. The developments in economics were later applied to biology largely by John Maynard Smith in his book Evolution and the Theory of Games.

In addition to being used to describe, predict, and explain behavior, game theory has also been used to develop theories of ethical or normative behavior and to prescribe such behavior. In economics and philosophy, scholars have applied game theory to help in the understanding of good or proper behavior. Game-theoretic arguments of this type can be found as far back as Plato.

Description and modeling

The first known use is to describe and model how human populations behave. Some[who?] scholars believe that by finding the equilibria of games they can predict how actual human populations will behave when confronted with situations analogous to the game being studied. This particular view of game theory has come under recent criticism. First, it is criticized because the assumptions made by game theorists are often violated. Game theorists may assume players always act in a way to directly maximize their wins (the Homo economicus model), but in practice, human behavior often deviates from this model. Explanations of this phenomenon are many; irrationality, new models of deliberation, or even different motives (like that of altruism). Game theorists respond by comparing their assumptions to those used in physics. Thus while their assumptions do not always hold, they can treat game theory as a reasonable scientific ideal akin to the models used by physicists. However, in the centipede game, guess 2/3 of the average game, and the dictator game, people regularly do not play Nash equilibria. These experiments have demonstrated that individuals do not play equilibrium strategies. There is an ongoing debate regarding the importance of these experiments.

Alternatively, some[who?] authors claim that Nash equilibria do not provide predictions for human populations, but rather provide an explanation for why populations that play Nash equilibria remain in that state. However, the question of how populations reach those points remains open.

Some[who?] game theorists have turned to evolutionary game theory in order to resolve these issues. These models presume either no rationality or bounded rationality on the part of players. Despite the name, evolutionary game theory does not necessarily presume natural selection in the biological sense. Evolutionary game theory includes both biological as well as cultural evolution and also models of individual learning (for example, fictitious play dynamics).

Prescriptive or normative analysis

	Cooperate	Defect
Cooperate	-1, -1	-10, 0
Defect	0, -10	-5, -5

The Prisoner's Dilemma

On the other hand, some[who?] scholars see game theory not as a predictive tool for the behavior of human beings, but as a suggestion for how people ought to behave. Since a Nash equilibrium of a game constitutes one's best response to the actions of the other players, playing a strategy that is part of a Nash equilibrium seems appropriate. However, this use for game theory has also come under criticism. First, in some cases it is appropriate to play a non-equilibrium strategy if one expects others to play non-equilibrium strategies as well. For an example, see Guess 2/3 of the average.

Second, the Prisoner's dilemma presents another potential counterexample. In the Prisoner's Dilemma, each player pursuing his own self-interest leads both players to be worse off than had they not pursued their own self-interests.

Economics and business

This article is incomplete. Please help to improve the article, or discuss the issue on the talk page. (November 2010)
Game theory is a major method used in mathematical economics and business for modeling competing behaviors of interacting agents. Applications include a wide array of economic phenomena and approaches, such as auctions, bargaining, mergers & acquisitions pricing, fair division, duopolies, oligopolies, social network formation, agent-based computational economics, general equilibrium, mechanism design, and voting systems, and across such broad areas as experimental economics, behavioral economics, information economics, industrial organization, and political economy.

This research usually focuses on particular sets of strategies known as equilibria in games. These "solution concepts" are usually based on what is required by norms of rationality. In non-cooperative games, the most famous of these is the Nash equilibrium. A set of strategies is a Nash equilibrium if each represents a best response to the other strategies. So, if all the players are playing the strategies in a Nash equilibrium, they have no unilateral incentive to deviate, since their strategy is the best they can do given what others are doing.

The payoffs of the game are generally taken to represent the utility of individual players. Often in modeling situations the payoffs represent money, which presumably corresponds to an individual's utility. This assumption, however, can be faulty.

A prototypical paper on game theory in economics begins by presenting a game that is an abstraction of a particular economic situation. One or more solution concepts are chosen, and the author demonstrates which strategy sets in the presented game are equilibria of the appropriate type. Naturally one might wonder to what use should this information be put. Economists and business professors suggest two primary uses (noted above): descriptive and prescriptive.

Political science

The application of game theory to political science is focused in the overlapping areas of fair division, political economy, public choice, war bargaining, positive political theory, and social choice theory. In each of these areas, researchers have developed game-theoretic models in which the players are often voters, states, special interest groups, and politicians.

For early examples of game theory applied to political science, see the work of Anthony Downs. In his book An Economic Theory of Democracy (Downs 1957), he applies the Hotelling firm location model to the political process. In the Downsian model, political candidates commit to ideologies on a one-dimensional policy space. Downs first shows how the political candidates will converge to the ideology preferred by the median voter if voters are fully informed, but then argues that voters choose to remain rationally ignorant which allows for candidate divergence.

A game-theoretic explanation for democratic peace is that public and open debate in democracies send clear and reliable information regarding their intentions to other states. In contrast, it is difficult to know the intentions of nondemocratic leaders, what effect concessions will have, and if promises will be kept. Thus there will be mistrust and unwillingness to make concessions if at least one of the parties in a dispute is a non-democracy (Levy & Razin 2003).

Biology

	Hawk	Dove
Hawk	20, 20	80, 40
Dove	40, 80	60, 60

The hawk-dove game

Unlike economics, the payoffs for games in biology are often interpreted as corresponding to fitness. In addition, the focus has been less on equilibria that correspond to a notion of rationality, but rather on ones that would be maintained by evolutionary forces. The best known equilibrium in biology is known as the evolutionarily stable strategy (or ESS), and was first introduced in (Smith & Price 1973). Although its initial motivation did not involve any of the mental requirements of the Nash equilibrium, every ESS is a Nash equilibrium.

In biology, game theory has been used to understand many different phenomena. It was first used to explain the evolution (and stability) of the approximate 1:1 sex ratios. (Fisher 1930) suggested that the 1:1 sex ratios are a result of evolutionary forces acting on individuals who could be seen as trying to maximize their number of grandchildren.

Additionally, biologists have used evolutionary game theory and the ESS to explain the emergence of animal communication (Harper & Maynard Smith 2003). The analysis of signaling games and other communication games has provided insight into the evolution of communication among animals. For example, the mobbing behavior of many species, in which a large number of prey animals attack a larger predator, seems to be an example of spontaneous emergent organization. Ants have also been shown to exhibit feed-forward behavior akin to fashion, see Butterfly Economics.

Biologists have used the game of chicken to analyze fighting behavior and territoriality.

Maynard Smith, in the preface to Evolution and the Theory of Games, writes, "paradoxically, it has turned out that game theory is more readily applied to biology than to the field of economic behaviour for which it was originally designed". Evolutionary game theory has been used to explain many seemingly incongruous phenomena in nature.

One such phenomenon is known as biological altruism. This is a situation in which an organism appears to act in a way that benefits other organisms and is detrimental to itself. This is distinct from traditional notions of altruism because such actions are not conscious, but appear to be evolutionary adaptations to increase overall fitness. Examples can be found in species ranging from vampire bats that regurgitate blood they have obtained from a night's hunting and give it to group members who have failed to feed, to worker bees that care for the queen bee for their entire lives and never mate, to Vervet monkeys that warn group members of a predator's approach, even when it endangers that individual's chance of survival. All of these actions increase the overall fitness of a group, but occur at a cost to the individual.

Evolutionary game theory explains this altruism with the idea of kin selection. Altruists discriminate between the individuals they help and favor relatives. Hamilton's rule explains the evolutionary reasoning behind this selection with the equation $c < b*r$ where the cost (c) to the altruist must be less than the benefit (b) to the recipient multiplied by the coefficient of relatedness (r). The more closely related two organisms are causes the incidences of altruism to increase because they share many of the same alleles. This means that the altruistic individual, by ensuring that the alleles of its close relative are passed on, (through survival of its offspring) can forgo the option of having offspring itself because the same number of alleles are passed on. Helping a sibling for example (in diploid animals), has a coefficient of ½, because (on average) an individual shares ½ of the alleles in its sibling's offspring. Ensuring that enough of a sibling's offspring survive to adulthood precludes the necessity of the altruistic individual producing offspring. The coefficient values depend heavily on the scope of the playing field; for example if the choice of whom to favor includes all genetic living things, not just all relatives, we assume the discrepancy between all humans only accounts for approximately 1% of the diversity in the playing field, a co-efficient that was ½ in the smaller field becomes 0. 995. Similarly if it is considered that information other than that of a genetic nature (e. g. epigenetics, religion, science, etc.) persisted through time the playing field becomes larger still, and the discrepancies smaller.

Computer science and logic

Game theory has come to play an increasingly important role in logic and in computer science. Several logical theories have a basis in game semantics. In addition, computer scientists have used games to model interactive computations. Also, game theory provides a theoretical basis to the field of multi-agent systems.

Separately, game theory has played a role in online algorithms. In particular, the k-server problem, which has in the past been referred to as games with moving costs and request-answer games (Ben David, Borodin & Karp et al. 1994). Yao's principle is a game-theoretic technique for proving lower bounds on the computational complexity of randomized algorithms, and especially of online algorithms.

The emergence of the internet has motivated the development of algorithms for finding equilibria in games, markets, computational auctions, peer-to-peer systems, and security and information markets. Algorithmic game theory and within it algorithmic mechanism design combine computational algorithm design and analysis of complex systems with economic theory.

Philosophy

	Stag	Hare
Stag	3, 3	0, 2
Hare	2, 0	2, 2

Stag hunt

Game theory has been put to several uses in philosophy. Responding to two papers by W. V. O. Quine (1960, 1967), Lewis (1969) used game theory to develop a philosophical account of convention. In so doing, he provided the first analysis of common knowledge and employed it in analyzing play in coordination games. In addition, he first suggested that one can understand meaning in terms of signaling games. This later suggestion has been pursued by several philosophers since Lewis (Skyrms (1996), Grim, Kokalis, and Alai-Tafti et al. (2004)). Following Lewis (1969) game-theoretic account of conventions, Edna Ullmann-Margalit (1977) and Bicchieri (2006) have developed theories of social norms that define them as Nash equilibria that result from transforming a mixed-motive game into a coordination game.

Game theory has also challenged philosophers to think in terms of interactive epistemology: what it means for a collective to have common beliefs or knowledge, and what are the consequences of this knowledge for the social outcomes resulting from agents' interactions. Philosophers who have worked in this area include Bicchieri (1989, 1993), Skyrms (1990), and Stalnaker (1999).

In ethics, some[who?] authors have attempted to pursue the project, begun by Thomas Hobbes, of deriving morality from self-interest. Since games like the Prisoner's dilemma present an apparent conflict between morality and self-interest, explaining why cooperation is required by self-interest is an important component of this project. This general strategy is a component of the general social contract view in political philosophy (for examples, see Gauthier (1986) and Kavka (1986).

Other authors have attempted to use evolutionary game theory in order to explain the emergence of human attitudes about morality and corresponding animal behaviors. These authors look at several games including the Prisoner's dilemma, Stag hunt, and the Nash bargaining game as providing an explanation for the emergence of attitudes about morality (see, e. g. , Skyrms (1996, 2004) and Sober and Wilson (1999)).

Some[which?] assumptions used in some[which?] parts of game theory have been challenged in philosophy; psychological egoism states that rationality reduces to self-interest—a claim debated among philosophers. (see Psychological egoism#Criticisms)

Types of games

Cooperative or non-cooperative

A game is cooperative if the players are able to form binding commitments. For instance the legal system requires them to adhere to their promises. In noncooperative games this is not possible.

Often it is assumed that communication among players is allowed in cooperative games, but not in noncooperative ones. However, this classification on two binary criteria has been questioned, and sometimes rejected (Harsanyi 1974).

Of the two types of games, noncooperative games are able to model situations to the finest details, producing accurate results. Cooperative games focus on the game at large. Considerable efforts have been made to link the two approaches. The so-called Nash-programme[clarification needed] has already established many of the cooperative solutions as noncooperative equilibria.

Hybrid games contain cooperative and non-cooperative elements. For instance, coalitions of players are formed in a cooperative game, but these play in a non-cooperative fashion.

Symmetric and asymmetric

	E	F
E	1, 2	0, 0
F	0, 0	1, 2

An asymmetric game
Symmetric game
A symmetric game is a game where the payoffs for playing a particular strategy depend only on the other strategies employed, not on who is playing them. If the identities of the players can be changed without changing the payoff to the strategies, then a game is symmetric. Many of the commonly studied 2×2 games are symmetric. The standard representations of chicken, the prisoner's dilemma, and the stag hunt are all symmetric games. Some[who?] scholars would consider certain asymmetric games as examples of these games as well. However, the most common payoffs for each of these games are symmetric.

Most commonly studied asymmetric games are games where there are not identical strategy sets for both players. For instance, the ultimatum game and similarly the dictator game have different strategies for each player. It is possible, however, for a game to have identical strategies for both players, yet be asymmetric. For example, the game pictured to the right is asymmetric despite having identical strategy sets for both players.

Zero-sum and non-zero-sum

	A	B
A	−1, 1	3, −3
B	0, 0	−2, 2

A zero-sum game

Zero–sum game

Zero-sum games are a special case of constant-sum games, in which choices by players can neither increase nor decrease the available resources. In zero-sum games the total benefit to all players in the game, for every combination of strategies, always adds to zero (more informally, a player benefits only at the equal expense of others). Poker exemplifies a zero-sum game (ignoring the possibility of the house's cut), because one wins exactly the amount one's opponents lose. Other zero-sum games include matching pennies and most classical board games including Go and chess.

Many games studied by game theorists (including the infamous prisoner's dilemma) are non-zero-sum games, because the outcome has net results greater or less than zero. Informally, in non-zero-sum games, a gain by one player does not necessarily correspond with a loss by another.

Constant-sum games correspond to activities like theft and gambling, but not to the fundamental economic situation in which there are potential gains from trade. It is possible to transform any game into a (possibly asymmetric) zero-sum game by adding an additional dummy player (often called "the board"), whose losses compensate the players' net winnings.

Simultaneous and sequential

Sequential game
Simultaneous games are games where both players move

simultaneously, or if they do not move simultaneously, the later players are unaware of the earlier players' actions (making them effectively simultaneous). Sequential games (or dynamic games) are games where later players have some knowledge about earlier actions. This need not be perfect information about every action of earlier players; it might be very little knowledge. For instance, a player may know that an earlier player did not perform one particular action, while he does not know which of the other available actions the first player actually performed.

The difference between simultaneous and sequential games is captured in the different representations discussed above. Often, normal form is used to represent simultaneous games, and extensive form is used to represent sequential ones. The transformation of extensive to normal form is one way, meaning that multiple extensive form games correspond to the same normal form. Consequently, notions of equilibrium for simultaneous games are insufficient for reasoning about sequential games; see subgame perfection.

Perfect information and imperfect information

An important subset of sequential games consists of games of perfect information. A game is one of perfect information if all players know the moves previously made by all other players. Thus, only sequential games can be games of perfect information because players in simultaneous games do not know the actions of the other players. Most games studied in game theory are imperfect-information games. Interesting examples of perfect-information games include the ultimatum game and centipede game. Recreational games of perfect information games include chess, go, and mancala. Many card games are games of imperfect information, for instance poker or contract bridge.

Perfect information is often confused with complete information, which is a similar concept. Complete information requires that every player know the strategies and payoffs available to the other players but not necessarily the actions taken. Games of incomplete information can be reduced, however, to games of imperfect information by introducing "moves by nature" (Leyton-Brown & Shoham 2008, p. 60).

Combinatorial games

Games in which the difficulty of finding an optimal strategy stems from the multiplicity of possible moves are called combinatorial games. Examples include chess and go. Games that involve imperfect or incomplete information may also have a strong combinatorial character, for instance backgammon. There is no unified theory addressing combinatorial elements in games. There are, however, mathematical tools that can solve particular problems and answer some[which?] general questions.

Games of perfect information have been studied in combinatorial game theory, which has developed novel representations, e. g. surreal numbers, as well as combinatorial and algebraic (and sometimes non-constructive) proof methods to solve games of certain types, including some[which?] "loopy" games that may result in infinitely long sequences of moves. These methods address games with higher combinatorial complexity than those usually considered in traditional (or "economic") game theory. A typical game that has been solved this way is hex. A related field of study, drawing from computational complexity theory, is game complexity, which is concerned with estimating the computational difficulty of finding optimal strategies.

Research in artificial intelligence has addressed both perfect and imperfect (or incomplete) information games that have very complex combinatorial structures (like chess, go, or backgammon) for which no provable optimal strategies have been found. The practical solutions involve computational heuristics, like alpha-beta pruning or use of artificial neural networks trained by reinforcement learning, which make games more tractable in computing practice.

Infinitely long games

Determinacy
Games, as studied by economists and real-world game players, are generally finished in finitely many moves. Pure mathematicians are not so constrained, and set theorists in particular study games that last for infinitely many moves, with the winner (or other payoff) not known until after all those moves are completed.

The focus of attention is usually not so much on what is the best way to play such a game, but simply on whether one or the other player has a winning strategy. (It can be proven, using the axiom of choice, that there are games—even with perfect information, and where the only outcomes are "win" or "lose"—for which neither player has a winning strategy.) The existence of such strategies, for cleverly designed games, has important consequences in descriptive set theory.

Discrete and continuous games

Much of game theory is concerned with finite, discrete games, that have a finite number of players, moves, events, outcomes, etc. Many concepts can be extended, however. Continuous games allow players to choose a strategy from a continuous strategy set. For instance, Cournot competition is typically modeled with players' strategies being any non-negative quantities, including fractional quantities.

Differential games

Differential games such as the continuous pursuit and evasion game are continuous games where the evolution of the players' state variables is governed by differential equations. The problem of finding an optimal strategy in a differential game is closely related to the optimal control theory. In particular, there are two types of strategies: the open-loop strategies are found using the Pontryagin Maximum Principle while the closed-loop strategies are found using Bellman's Dynamic Programming method.

A particular case of differential games are the games with random time horizon. In such games, the terminal time is a random variable with a given probability distribution function. Therefore, the players maximize the mathematical expectancy of the cost function. It was shown that the modified optimization problem can be reformulated as a discounted differential game over an infinite time interval.

Many-player and population games

Games with an arbitrary, but finite, number of players are often called n-person games (Luce & Raiffa 1957). Evolutionary game theory considers games involving a population of decision makers, where the frequency with which a particular decision is made can change over time in response to the decisions made by all individuals in the population. In biology, this is intended to model (biological) evolution, where genetically programmed organisms pass along some of their strategy programming to their offspring. In economics, the same theory is intended to capture population changes because people play the game many times within their lifetime, and consciously (and perhaps rationally) switch strategies (Webb 2007).

Stochastic outcomes (and relation to other fields)

Individual decision problems with stochastic outcomes are sometimes considered "one-player games". These situations are not considered game theoretical by some authors. [by whom?] They may be modeled using similar tools within the related disciplines of decision theory, operations research, and areas of artificial intelligence, particularly AI planning (with uncertainty) and multi-agent system. Although these fields may have different motivators, the mathematics involved are substantially the same, e. g. using Markov decision processes (MDP).

Stochastic outcomes can also be modeled in terms of game theory by adding a randomly acting player who makes "chance moves", also known as "moves by nature" (Osborne & Rubinstein 1994). This player is not typically considered a third player in what is otherwise a two-player game, but merely serves to provide a roll of the dice where required by the game.

For some[which?] problems, different approaches to modeling stochastic outcomes may lead to different solutions. For example, the difference in approach between MDPs and the minimax solution is that the latter considers the worst-case over a set of adversarial moves, rather than reasoning in expectation about these moves given a fixed probability distribution. The minimax approach may be advantageous where stochastic models of uncertainty are not available, but may also be overestimating extremely unlikely (but costly) events, dramatically swaying the strategy in such scenarios if it is assumed that an adversary can force such an event to happen. (See black swan theory for more discussion on this kind of modeling issue, particularly as it relates to predicting and limiting losses in investment banking.)

General models that include all elements of stochastic outcomes, adversaries, and partial or noisy observability (of moves by other players) have also been studied. The "gold standard" is considered to be partially observable stochastic game (POSG), but few realistic problems are computationally feasible in POSG representation.

Metagames

These are games the play of which is the development of the rules for another game, the target or subject game. Metagames seek to maximize the utility value of the rule set developed. The theory of metagames is related to mechanism design theory.

The term metagame analysis is also used to refer to a practical approach developed by Nigel Howard (Howard 1971) whereby a situation is framed as a strategic game in which stakeholders try to realise their objectives by means of the options available to them. Subsequent developments have led to the formulation of Confrontation analysis.

History

Early discussions of examples of two-person games occurred long before the rise of modern, mathematical game theory. The first known discussion of game theory occurred in a letter written by James Waldegrave in 1713. In this letter, Waldegrave provides a minimax mixed strategy solution to a two-person version of the card game le Her. James Madison made what we now recognize as a game-theoretic analysis of the ways states can be expected to behave under different systems of taxation. In his 1838 Recherches sur les principes mathématiques de la théorie des richesses (Researches into the Mathematical Principles of the Theory of Wealth), Antoine Augustin Cournot considered a duopoly and presents a solution that is a restricted version of the Nash equilibrium.

The Danish mathematician Zeuthen proved that a mathematical model has a winning strategy by using Brouwer's fixed point theorem. In his 1938 book Applications aux Jeux de Hasard and earlier notes, Émile Borel proved a minimax theorem for two-person zero-sum matrix games only when the pay-off matrix was symmetric. Borel conjectured that non-existence of mixed-strategy equilibria in two-person zero-sum games would occur, a conjecture that was proved false.

Game theory did not really exist as a unique field until John von Neumann published a paper in 1928. Von Neumann's original proof used Brouwer's fixed-point theorem on continuous mappings into compact convex sets, which became a standard method in game theory and mathematical economics. His paper was followed by his 1944 book Theory of Games and Economic Behavior, with Oskar Morgenstern, which considered cooperative games of several players. The second edition of this book provided an axiomatic theory of expected utility, which allowed mathematical statisticians and economists to treat decision-making under uncertainty. Von Neumann's work in game theory culminated in the 1944 book Theory of Games and Economic Behavior by von Neumann and Oskar Morgenstern. This foundational work contains the method for finding mutually consistent solutions for two-person zero-sum games. During this time period, work on game theory was primarily focused on cooperative game theory, which analyzes optimal strategies for groups of individuals, presuming that they can enforce agreements between them about proper strategies.

In 1950, the first discussion of the prisoner's dilemma appeared, and an experiment was undertaken by notable mathematicians Merrill M. Flood and Melvin Dresher, as part of the RAND corporation's investigations into game theory. Rand pursued the studies because of possible applications to global nuclear strategy. Around this same time, John Nash developed a criterion for mutual consistency of players' strategies, known as Nash equilibrium, applicable to a wider variety of games than the criterion proposed by von Neumann and Morgenstern. This equilibrium is sufficiently general to allow for the analysis of non-cooperative games in addition to cooperative ones.

Game theory experienced a flurry of activity in the 1950s, during which time the concepts of the core, the extensive form game, fictitious play, repeated games, and the Shapley value were developed. In addition, the first applications of Game theory to philosophy and political science occurred during this time.

In 1965, Reinhard Selten introduced his solution concept of subgame perfect equilibria, which further refined the Nash equilibrium (later he would introduce trembling hand perfection as well). In 1967, John Harsanyi developed the concepts of complete information and Bayesian games. Nash, Selten and Harsanyi became Economics Nobel Laureates in 1994 for their contributions to economic game theory.

In the 1970s, game theory was extensively applied in biology, largely as a result of the work of John Maynard Smith and his evolutionarily stable strategy. In addition, the concepts of correlated equilibrium, trembling hand perfection, and common knowledge were introduced and analyzed.

In 2005, game theorists Thomas Schelling and Robert Aumann followed Nash, Selten and Harsanyi as Nobel Laureates. Schelling worked on dynamic models, early examples of evolutionary game theory. Aumann contributed more to the equilibrium school, introducing an equilibrium coarsening, correlated equilibrium, and developing an extensive formal analysis of the assumption of common knowledge and of its consequences.

In 2007, Leonid Hurwicz, together with Eric Maskin and Roger Myerson, was awarded the Nobel Prize in Economics "for having laid the foundations of mechanism design theory. " Myerson's contributions include the notion of proper equilibrium, and an important graduate text: Game Theory, Analysis of Conflict (Myerson 1997). Hurwicz introduced and formalized the concept of incentive compatibility.

Popular Culture

The life story of Mathematician John Nash, was turned into a biopic Beautiful Mind starring Russel Crowe, based on the namesake book by Sylvia Nasar,

In-database processing

In-database processing

In-database processing, sometimes referred to as in-database analytics, refers to the integration of data analytics into data warehousing functionality. Today, many large databases, such as those used for credit card fraud detection and investment bank risk management, use this technology because it provides significant performance improvements over traditional methods.

History

Traditional approaches to data analysis require data to be moved out of the database into a separate analytics environment for processing, and then back to the database. (SAS and SPSS from IBM are examples of tools that still do this today.) Doing the analysis in the database, where the data resides, eliminates the costs, time and security issues associated with the old approach by doing the processing in the data warehouse itself.

Though in-database capabilities were first commercially offered in the mid-1990s, as object-related database systems from vendors including IBM, Illustra/Informix (now IBM) and Oracle, the technology did not begin to catch on until the mid-2000s.

At that point, the need for in-database processing had become more pressing as the amount of data available to collect and analyze continues to grow exponentially (due largely to the rise of the Internet), from megabytes to gigabytes, terabytes and petabytes. This "big data" is one of the primary reasons it has become important to collect, process and analyze data efficiently and accurately.

Also, the speed of business has accelerated to the point where a performance gain of nanoseconds can make a difference in some industries. Additionally, as more people and industries use data to answer important questions, the questions they ask become more complex, demanding more sophisticated tools and more precise results.

All of these factors in combination have created the need for in-database processing. The introduction of the column-oriented database, specifically designed for analytics, data warehousing and reporting, has helped make the technology possible.

Types

There are three main types of in-database processing: translating a model into SQL code, loading C or C++ libraries into the database process space as a built-in user-defined function (UDF), and out-of-process libraries typically written in C, C++ or JAVA and registering them in the database as a built-in UDFs in a SQL statement.

Translating Models into SQL Code

In this type of in-database processing, a predictive model is converted from its source language into SQL that can run in the database usually in a stored procedure. Many analytic model-building tools have the ability to export their models in either in SQL or PMML (Predictive Modeling Markup Language). Once the SQL is loaded into a stored procedure, values can be passed in through parameters and the model is executed natively in the database. Tools that can use this approach include SAS, R and KXEN.

Loading C or C++ Libraries into the database process space

With C or C++ UDF libraries that run in process, the functions are typically registered as built-in functions within the database server and called like any other built-in function in a SQL statement. Running in process allows the function to have full access to the database server's memory, parallelism and processing management capabilities. Because of this, the functions must be well-behaved so as not to negatively impact the database or the engine. This type of UDF gives the highest performance out of any method for OLAP, mathematical, statistical, univariate distributions and data mining algorithms. Vendors such as Fuzzy Logix (DBLytix) and RogueWave (IMSL) have pre-built libraries available. IBM Netezza, EMC Greenplum, Sybase and Teradata (AsterData) have the capability to do this type of in-database analytics. Some of these vendors allow customers to write their own custom in-process UDFs.

Out-of-Process

Out-of-Process UDFs are typically written in C, C++ or JAVA. By running out of process, they do not run the same risk to the database or the engine as they run in their own process space with their own resources. Here, they wouldn't be expected to have the same performance as an in-process UDF. They are still typically registered in the database engine and called through standard SQL, usually in a stored procedure. A vendor, Zementis, has plug-ins for different database vendors that can be used to take a PMML model and convert it to a JAVA UDF that can be called through the native SQL. Out-of-process UDFs are a safe way to extend the capabilities of a database server and are an ideal way to add custom data mining libraries.

Uses

In-database processing makes data analysis more accessible and relevant for high-throughput, real-time applications including fraud detection, credit scoring, risk management, transaction processing, pricing and margin analysis, usage-based micro-segmenting, behavioral ad targeting and recommendation engines, such as those used by customer service organizations to determine next-best actions.

Vendors

In-database processing is performed and promoted as a feature by many of the major data warehousing vendors, including Teradata (and acquired Aster Data Systems), IBM Netezza, EMC Greenplum and Sybase.

Related Technologies

In-database processing is one of several technologies focused on improving data warehousing performance. Others include parallel computing, shared everything architectures, shared nothing architectures and massive parallel processing. It is an important step towards improving predictive analytics capabilities.

k-nearest neighbor algorithm

k-nearest neighbor algorithm

In pattern recognition, the k-nearest neighbor algorithm (k-NN) is a method for classifying objects based on closest training examples in the feature space. k-NN is a type of instance-based learning, or lazy learning where the function is only approximated locally and all computation is deferred until classification. The k-nearest neighbor algorithm is amongst the simplest of all machine learning algorithms: an object is classified by a majority vote of its neighbors, with the object being assigned to the class most common amongst its k nearest neighbors (k is a positive integer, typically small). If k = 1, then the object is simply assigned to the class of its nearest neighbor.

The same method can be used for regression, by simply assigning the property value for the object to be the average of the values of its k nearest neighbors. It can be useful to weight the contributions of the neighbors, so that the nearer neighbors contribute more to the average than the more distant ones. (A common weighting scheme is to give each neighbor a weight of 1/d, where d is the distance to the neighbor. This scheme is a generalization of linear interpolation.)

The neighbors are taken from a set of objects for which the correct classification (or, in the case of regression, the value of the property) is known. This can be thought of as the training set for the algorithm, though no explicit training step is required. The k-nearest neighbor algorithm is sensitive to the local structure of the data.

Nearest neighbor rules in effect compute the decision boundary in an implicit manner. It is also possible to compute the decision boundary itself explicitly, and to do so in an efficient manner so that the computational complexity is a function of the boundary complexity.

Algorithm

The training examples are vectors in a multidimensional feature space, each with a class label. The training phase of the algorithm consists only of storing the feature vectors and class labels of the training samples.

In the classification phase, k is a user-defined constant, and an unlabeled vector (a query or test point) is classified by assigning the label which is most frequent among the k training samples nearest to that query point.

Usually Euclidean distance is used as the distance metric; however this is only applicable to continuous variables. In cases such as text classification, another metric such as the overlap metric (or Hamming distance) can be used. Often, the classification accuracy of "k"-NN can be improved significantly if the distance metric is learned with specialized algorithms such as Large Margin Nearest Neighbor or Neighbourhood components analysis.

A drawback to the basic "majority voting" classification is that the classes with the more frequent examples tend to dominate the prediction of the new vector, as they tend to come up in the k nearest neighbors when the neighbors are computed due to their large number. One way to overcome this problem is to weigh the classification taking into account the distance from the test point to each of its k nearest neighbors.

KNN is a special case of a variable-bandwidth, kernel density "balloon" estimator with a uniform kernel.

Parameter selection

The best choice of k depends upon the data; generally, larger values of k reduce the effect of noise on the classification, but make boundaries between classes less distinct. A good k can be selected by various heuristic techniques, for example, cross-validation. The special case where the class is predicted to be the class of the closest training sample (i. e. when k = 1) is called the nearest neighbor algorithm.

The accuracy of the k-NN algorithm can be severely degraded by the presence of noisy or irrelevant features, or if the feature scales are not consistent with their importance. Much research effort has been put into selecting or scaling features to improve classification. A particularly popular approach is the use of evolutionary algorithms to optimize feature scaling. Another popular approach is to scale features by the mutual information of the training data with the training classes.

In binary (two class) classification problems, it is helpful to choose k to be an odd number as this avoids tied votes. One popular way of choosing the empirically optimal k in this setting is via bootstrap method.

Properties

The naive version of the algorithm is easy to implement by computing the distances from the test sample to all stored vectors, but it is computationally intensive, especially when the size of the training set grows. Many nearest neighbor search algorithms have been proposed over the years; these generally seek to reduce the number of distance evaluations actually performed. Using an appropriate nearest neighbor search algorithm makes k-NN computationally tractable even for large data sets.

The nearest neighbor algorithm has some strong consistency results. As the amount of data approaches infinity, the algorithm is guaranteed to yield an error rate no worse than twice the Bayes error rate (the minimum achievable error rate given the distribution of the data). k-nearest neighbor is guaranteed to approach the Bayes error rate, for some value of k (where k increases as a function of the number of data points). Various improvements to k-nearest neighbor methods are possible by using proximity graphs.

For estimating continuous variables

The k-NN algorithm can also be adapted for use in estimating continuous variables. One such implementation uses an inverse distance weighted average of the k-nearest multivariate neighbors. This algorithm functions as follows:

Compute Euclidean or Mahalanobis distance from target plot to those that were sampled.
Order samples taking for account calculated distances.
Choose heuristically optimal k nearest neighbor based on RMSE done by cross validation technique.
Calculate an inverse distance weighted average with the k-nearest multivariate neighbors.
Using a weighted k-NN also significantly improves the results: the class (or value, in regression problems) of each of the k nearest points is multiplied by a weight proportional to the inverse of the distance between that point and the point for which the class is to be predicted.

Learning analytics

Learning analytics

Learning analytics is the measurement, collection, analysis and reporting of data about learners and their contexts, for purposes of understanding and optimising learning and the environments in which it occurs . A related field is educational data mining.

Contents
1 History
2 Criticism
3 Methods
4 Software
5 See also
6 References
7 External links

History

Work in progress: sociologists like Wellman and Watts. . . and mathematicians like Barabasi and Strogatz. The work of these individuals has provided us with a good sense of the patterns that networks exhibit (small world, power laws), the attributes of connections (in early 70's, Granovetter explored connections from a perspective of tie strength and impact on new information), and the social dimensions of networks (for example, geography still matters in a digital networked world).

Criticism

An earlier definition discussed by the community:
Learning analytics is the use of intelligent data, learner-produced data, and analysis models to discover information and social connections for predicting and advising people's learning.
and its criticism:
"I somewhat disagree with this definition - it serves well as an introductory concept if we use analytics as a support structure for existing education models. I think learning analytics - at an advanced and integrated implementation - can do away with pre-fab curriculum models". George Siemens, 2010.
"In the descriptions of learning analytics we talk about using data to "predict success". I've struggled with that as I pore over our databases. I've come to realize there are different views/levels of success. " Mike Sharkey 2010.

Methods

Methods for learning analytics include:
Social network analysis (SNA) - "the mapping and measuring of relationships and flows between people, groups, organizations, computers, URLs, and other connected information/knowledge entities. The nodes in the network are the people and groups while the links show relationships or flows between the nodes. SNA provides both a visual and a mathematical analysis of human relationships. Management consultants use this methodology with their business clients and call it Organizational Network Analysis [ONA]. "
Behavioral trust analysis - using instances of conversation and propagation (people communicating and using information to generate new information) as an indicator of trust.
Influence and passivity measure - assessing the influence of people and information by measuring the number of times it is passed on, cited, or retweeted.
Content analysis
Impact of interaction
Prediction

Personalization & Adaptation
Intervention
Information visualization, typically in the form of so-called learning dashboards

Software

Much of the software that is currently used for learning analytics duplicates functionality of web analytics software, but applies it to learner interactions with content. Social network analysis tools are commonly used to map social connections and discussions (see Social network analysis software). Some examples of learning analytics software tools:
SNAPP - a learning analytics tool that visualizes the network of interactions resulting from discussion forum posts and replies.
LOCO-Analyst - a context-aware learning tool for analytics of learning processes taking place in a web-based learning environment
SAM - a Student Activity Monitor intended for Personal Learning Environments

Linear regression

Linear regression

In statistics, linear regression is an approach to modelling the relationship between a scalar dependent variable y and one or more explanatory variables denoted X. The case of one explanatory variable is called simple regression. More than one explanatory variable is multiple regression. (This in turn should be distinguished from multivariate linear regression, where multiple correlated dependent variables are predicted, rather than a single scalar variable.)

In linear regression, data is modelled using linear predictor functions, and unknown model parameters are estimated from the data. Such models are called linear models. Most commonly, linear regression refers to a model in which the conditional mean of y given the value of X is an affine function of X. Less commonly, linear regression could refer to a model in which the median, or some other quantile of the conditional distribution of y given X is expressed as a linear function of X. Like all forms of regression analysis, linear regression focuses on the conditional probability distribution of y given X, rather than on the joint probability distribution of y and X, which is the domain of multivariate analysis.

Linear regression was the first type of regression analysis to be studied rigorously, and to be used extensively in practical applications. This is because models which depend linearly on their unknown parameters are easier to fit than models which are non-linearly related to their parameters and because the statistical properties of the resulting estimators are easier to determine.

Linear regression has many practical uses. Most applications of linear regression fall into one of the following two broad categories:

If the goal is prediction, or forecasting, linear regression can be used to fit a predictive model to an observed data set of y and X values. After developing such a model, if an additional value of X is then given without its accompanying value of y, the fitted model can be used to make a prediction of the value of y.
Given a variable y and a number of variables $X_1, \ldots, X_p$ that may be related to y, linear regression analysis can be applied to quantify the strength of the relationship between y and the X_j, to assess which X_j may have no relationship with y at all, and to identify which subsets of the X_j contain redundant information about y.
Linear regression models are often fitted using the least squares approach, but they may also be fitted in other ways, such as by minimizing the "lack of fit" in some other norm (as with least absolute deviations regression), or by minimizing a penalized version of the least squares loss function as in ridge regression. Conversely, the least squares approach can be used to fit models that are not linear models. Thus, while the terms "least squares" and "linear model" are closely linked, they are not synonymous.

Introduction to linear regression

Given a data set of n statistical units, a linear regression model assumes that the relationship between the dependent variable y_i and the p-vector of regressors x_i is linear. This relationship is modelled through a disturbance term or error variable ε_i — an unobserved random variable that adds noise to the linear relationship between the dependent variable and regressors. Thus the model takes the form

where T denotes the transpose, so that x_i^T is the inner product between vectors x_i and .

Often these n equations are stacked together and written in vector form as

where

Some remarks on terminology and general use:

is called the regressand, exogenous variable, response variable, measured variable, or dependent variable (see dependent and independent variables.) The decision as to which variable in a data set is modeled as the dependent variable and which are modeled as the independent variables may be based on a presumption that the value of one of the variables is caused by, or directly influenced by the other variables. Alternatively, there may be an operational reason to model one of the variables in terms of the others, in which case there need be no presumption of causality.

are called regressors, endogenous variables, explanatory variables, covariates, input variables, predictor variables, or independent variables (see dependent and independent variables, but not to be confused with independent random variables). The matrix is sometimes called the design matrix. Usually a constant is included as one of the regressors. For example we can take $x_{i1} = 1$ for $i = 1, \ldots, n$. The corresponding element of is called the intercept. Many statistical inference procedures for linear models require an intercept to be present, so it is often included even if theoretical considerations suggest that its value should be zero.

Sometimes one of the regressors can be a non-linear function of another regressor or of the data, as in polynomial regression and segmented regression. The model remains linear as long as it is linear in the parameter vector .

The regressors x_{ij} may be viewed either as random variables, which we simply observe, or they can be considered as predetermined fixed values which we can choose. Both interpretations may be appropriate in different cases, and they generally lead to the same estimation procedures; however different approaches to asymptotic analysis are used in these two situations.

is a p-dimensional parameter vector. Its elements are also called effects, or regression coefficients. Statistical estimation and inference in linear regression focuses on β.

is called the error term, disturbance term, or noise. This variable captures all other factors which influence the dependent variable yi other than the regressors xi. The relationship between the error term and the regressors, for example whether they are correlated, is a crucial step in formulating a linear regression model, as it will determine the method to use for estimation.

Example. Consider a situation where a small ball is being tossed up in the air and then we measure its heights of ascent hi at various moments in time ti. Physics tells us that, ignoring the drag, the relationship can be modelled as

where β_1 determines the initial velocity of the ball, β_2 is proportional to the standard gravity, and ϵ_i is due to measurement errors. Linear regression can be used to estimate the values of β_1 and β_2 from the measured data. This model is non-linear in the time variable, but it is linear in the parameters β_1 and β_2; if we take regressors xi = (xi1, xi2) = (ti, ti2), the model takes on the standard form

Assumptions

Standard linear regression models with standard estimation techniques make a number of assumptions about the predictor variables, the response variables and their relationship. Numerous extensions have been developed that allow each of these assumptions to be relaxed (i. e. reduced to a weaker form), and in some cases eliminated entirely. Some methods are general enough that they can relax multiple assumptions at once, and in other cases this can be achieved by combining different extensions. Generally these extensions make the estimation procedure more complex and time-consuming, and may also require more data in order to get an accurate model.

The following are the major assumptions made by standard linear regression models with standard estimation techniques (e. g. ordinary least squares):

Weak exogeneity. This essentially means that the predictor variables x can be treated as fixed values, rather than random variables. This means, for example, that the predictor variables are assumed to be error-free, that is they are not contaminated with measurement errors. Although not realistic in many settings, dropping this assumption leads to significantly more difficult errors-in-variables models.

Linearity. This means that the mean of the response variable is a linear combination of the parameters (regression coefficients) and the predictor variables. Note that this assumption is much less restrictive than it may at first seem. Because the predictor variables are treated as fixed values (see above), linearity is really only a restriction on the parameters. The predictor variables themselves can be arbitrarily transformed, and in fact multiple copies of the same underlying predictor variable can be added, each one transformed differently. This trick is used, for example, in polynomial regression, which uses linear regression to fit the response variable as an arbitrary polynomial function (up to a given rank) of a predictor variable. This makes linear regression an extremely powerful inference method. In fact, models such as polynomial regression are often "too powerful", in that they tend to overfit the data. As a result, some kind of regularization must typically be used to prevent unreasonable solutions coming out of the estimation process. Common examples are ridge regression and lasso regression. Bayesian linear regression can also be used, which by its nature is more or less immune to the problem of overfitting. (In fact, ridge regression and lasso regression can both be viewed as special cases of Bayesian linear regression, with particular types of prior distributions placed on the regression coefficients.)

Constant variance (aka homoscedasticity). This means that different response variables have the same variance in their errors, regardless of the values of the predictor variables. In practice this assumption is invalid (i. e. the errors are heteroscedastic) if the response variables can vary over a wide scale. In order to determine for heterogeneous error variance, or when a pattern of residuals violates model assumptions of homoscedasticity (error is equally variable around the 'best-fitting line' for all points of x), it is prudent to look for a "fanning effect" between residual error and predicted values. This is to say there will be a systematic change in the absolute or squared residuals when plotted against the predicting outcome. Error will not be evenly distributed across the regression line. Heteroscedasticity will result in the averaging over of distinguishable variances around the points to get a single variance that is inaccurately representing all the variances of the line. In effect, residuals appear clustered and spread apart on their predicted plots for larger and smaller values for points along the linear regression line, and the mean squared error for the model will be wrong. Typically, for example, a response variable whose mean is large will have a greater variance than one whose mean is small. For example, a given person whose income is predicted to be $100,000 may easily have an actual income of $80,000 or $120,000 (a standard deviation of around $20,000), while another person with a predicted income of $10,000 is unlikely to have the same $20,000 standard deviation, which would imply their actual income would vary anywhere between -$10,000 and $30,000. (In fact, as this shows, in many cases – often the same cases where the assumption of normally distributed errors fails – the variance or standard deviation should be predicted to be proportional to the mean, rather than constant.) Simple linear regression estimation methods give less precise parameter estimates and misleading inferential quantities such as standard errors when substantial heteroscedasticity is present. However, various estimation techniques (e. g. weighted least squares and heteroscedasticity-consistent standard errors) can handle heteroscedasticity in a quite general way. Bayesian linear regression techniques can also be used when the variance is assumed to be a function of the mean. It is also possible in some cases to fix the problem by applying a transformation to the response variable (e. g. fit the logarithm of the response variable using a linear regression model, which implies – as noted above – that the response variable has a log-normal distribution rather than a normal distribution).

Independence of errors. This assumes that the errors of the response variables are uncorrelated with each other. (Actual statistical independence is a stronger condition than mere lack of correlation and is often not needed, although it can be exploited if it is known to hold.) Some methods (e. g. generalized least squares) are capable of handling correlated errors, although they typically require significantly more data unless some sort of regularization is used to bias the model towards assuming uncorrelated errors. Bayesian linear regression is a general way of handling this issue.

Lack of multicollinearity in the predictors. For standard least squares estimation methods, the design matrix X must have full column rank p, i. e. be invertible; otherwise, we have a condition known as multicollinearity in the predictor variables. This can be triggered by having two or more perfectly correlated predictor variables (e.

g. if the same predictor variable is mistakenly given twice, either without transforming one of the copies or by transforming one of the copies linearly). It can also happen if there is too little data available compared to the number of parameters to be estimated (e. g. fewer data points than regression coefficients). In the case of multicollinearity, the parameter vector will be non-identifiable — it has no unique solution. At most we will be able to identify some of the parameters, i. e. narrow down its value to some linear subspace of Rp. See partial least squares regression. Methods for fitting linear models with multicollinearity have been developed; some require additional assumptions such as "effect sparsity" — that a large fraction of the effects are exactly zero. Note that the more computationally expensive iterated algorithms for parameter estimation, such as those used in generalized linear models, do not suffer from this problem — and in fact it's quite normal to when handling categorically-valued predictors to introduce a separate indicator variable predictor for each possible category, which inevitably introduces multicollinearity.

Beyond these assumptions, several other statistical properties of the data strongly influence the performance of different estimation methods:

The statistical relationship between the error terms and the regressors plays an important role in determining whether an estimation procedure has desirable sampling properties such as being unbiased and consistent.

The arrangement, or probability distribution of the predictor variables x has a major influence on the precision of estimates of . Sampling and design of experiments are highly-developed subfields of statistics that provide guidance for collecting data in such a way to achieve a precise estimate of .

Interpretation

A fitted linear regression model can be used to identify the relationship between a single predictor variable x_j and the response variable y when all the other predictor variables in the model are "held fixed". Specifically, the interpretation of j is the expected change in y for a one-unit change in x_j when the other covariates are held fixed—that is, the expected value of the partial derivative of y with respect to x_j. This is sometimes called the unique effect of x_j on y. In contrast, the marginal effect of x_j on y can be assessed using a correlation coefficient or simple linear regression model relating x_j to y; this effect is the total derivative of y with respect to x_j.

Care must be taken when interpreting regression results, as some of the regressors may not allow for marginal changes (such as dummy variables, or the intercept term), while others cannot be held fixed (recall the example from the introduction: it would be impossible to "hold t_i fixed" and at the same time change the value of t_{i2}).

It is possible that the unique effect can be nearly zero even when the marginal effect is large. This may imply that some other covariate captures all the information in x_j, so that once that variable is in the model, there is no contribution of x_j to the variation in y. Conversely, the unique effect of x_j can be large while its marginal effect is nearly zero. This would happen if the other covariates explained a great deal of the variation of y, but they mainly explain variation in a way that is complementary to what is captured by x_j. In this case, including the other variables in the model reduces the part of the variability of y that is unrelated to x_j, thereby strengthening the apparent relationship with x_j.

The meaning of the expression "held fixed" may depend on how the values of the predictor variables arise. If the experimenter directly sets the values of the predictor variables according to a study design, the comparisons of interest may literally correspond to comparisons among units whose predictor variables have been "held fixed" by the experimenter. Alternatively, the expression "held fixed" can refer to a selection that takes place in the context of data analysis. In this case, we "hold a variable fixed" by restricting our attention to the subsets of the data that happen to have a common value for the given predictor variable. This is the only interpretation of "held fixed" that can be used in an observational study.

The notion of a "unique effect" is appealing when studying a complex system where multiple interrelated components influence the response variable. In some cases, it can literally be interpreted as the causal effect of an intervention that is linked to the value of a predictor variable. However, it has been argued that in many cases multiple regression analysis fails to clarify the relationships between the predictor variables and the response variable when the predictors are correlated with each other and are not assigned following a study design.

Extensions

Numerous extensions of linear regression have been developed, which allow some or all of the assumptions underlying the basic model to be relaxed.

Simple and multiple regression

The very simplest case of a single scalar predictor variable x and a single scalar response variable y is known as simple linear regression. The extension to multiple and/or vector-valued predictor variables (denoted with a capital X) is known as multiple linear regression. Nearly all real-world regression models involve multiple predictors, and basic descriptions of linear regression are often phrased in terms of the multiple regression model. Note, however, that in these cases the response variable y is still a scalar.

General linear models

The general linear model considers the situation when the response variable Y is not a scalar but a vector. Conditional linearity of E(y | x) = Bx is still assumed, with a matrix B replacing the vector of the classical linear regression model. Multivariate analogues of OLS and GLS have been developed.

Heteroskedastic models

Various models have been created that allow for heteroskedasticity, i. e. the errors for different response variables may have different variances. For example, weighted least squares is a method for estimating linear regression models when the response variables may have different error variances, possibly with correlated errors. (See also Linear least squares (mathematics)#Weighted linear least squares, and generalized least squares.) Heteroscedasticity-consistent standard errors is an improved method for use with uncorrelated but potentially heteroskedastic errors.

Generalized linear models

Generalized linear models (GLM's) are a framework for modeling a response variable y that is bounded or discrete. This is used, for example:

when modeling positive quantities (e. g. prices or populations) that vary over a large scale — which are better described using a skewed distribution such as the log-normal distribution or Poisson distribution (although GLM's are not used for log-normal data, instead the response variable is simply transformed using the logarithm function);
when modeling categorical data, such as the choice of a given candidate in an election (which is better described using a Bernoulli distribution/binomial distribution for binary choices, or a categorical distribution/multinomial distribution for multi-way choices), where there are a fixed number of choices that cannot be meaningfully ordered;
when modeling ordinal data, e. g. ratings on a scale from 0 to 5, where the different outcomes can be ordered but where the quantity itself may not have any absolute meaning (e. g. a rating of 4 may not be "twice as good" in any objective sense as a rating of 2, but simply indicates that it is better than 2 or 3 but not as good as 5).
Generalized linear models allow for an arbitrary link function g that relates the mean of the response variable to the predictors, i. e. $y = g(\beta x) + \epsilon$. The link function is often related to the distribution of the response, and in particular it typically has the effect of transforming between the range of the linear predictor and the range of the response variable.

Some common examples of GLM's are:

Poisson regression for count data.
Logistic regression and probit regression for binary data.
Multinomial logistic regression and multinomial probit regression for categorical data.
Ordered probit regression for ordinal data.
Single index models[clarification needed] allow some degree of nonlinearity in the relationship between x and y, while preserving the central role of the linear predictor βx as in the classical linear

regression model. Under certain conditions, simply applying OLS to data from a single-index model will consistently estimate β up to a proportionality constant.

Hierarchical linear models

Hierarchical linear models (or multilevel regression) organizes the data into a hierarchy of regressions, for example where A is regressed on B, and B is regressed on C. It is often used where the data have a natural hierarchical structure such as in educational statistics, where students are nested in classrooms, classrooms are nested in schools, and schools are nested in some administrative grouping such as a school district. The response variable might be a measure of student achievement such as a test score, and different covariates would be collected at the classroom, school, and school district levels.

Errors-in-variables

Errors-in-variables models (or "measurement error models") extend the traditional linear regression model to allow the predictor variables X to be observed with error. This error causes standard estimators of β to become biased. Generally, the form of bias is an attenuation, meaning that the effects are biased toward zero.

Others

In Dempster–Shafer theory, or a linear belief function in particular, a linear regression model may be represented as a partially swept matrix, which can be combined with similar matrices representing observations and other assumed normal distributions and state equations. The combination of swept or unswept matrices provides an alternative method for estimating linear regression models.

Estimation methods

A large number of procedures have been developed for parameter estimation and inference in linear regression. These methods differ in computational simplicity of algorithms, presence of a closed-form solution, robustness with respect to heavy-tailed distributions, and theoretical assumptions needed to validate desirable statistical properties such as consistency and asymptotic efficiency.

Some of the more common estimation techniques for linear regression are summarized below.

Least-squares estimation and related techniques

Ordinary least squares (OLS) is the simplest and thus most common estimator. It is conceptually simple and computationally straightforward. OLS estimates are commonly used to analyze both experimental and observational data.
The OLS method minimizes the sum of squared residuals, and leads to a closed-form expression for the estimated value of the unknown parameter :

The estimator is unbiased and consistent if the errors have finite variance and are uncorrelated with the regressors

It is also efficient under the assumption that the errors have finite variance and are homoscedastic, meaning that $E[\varepsilon_i^2 | x_i]$ does not depend on i. The condition that the errors are uncorrelated with the regressors will generally be satisfied in an experiment, but in the case of observational data, it is difficult to exclude the possibility of an omitted covariate z that is related to both the observed covariates and the response variable. The existence of such a covariate will generally lead to a correlation between the regressors and the response variable, and hence to an inconsistent estimator of . The condition of homoscedasticity can fail with either experimental or observational data. If the goal is either inference or predictive modeling, the performance of OLS estimates can be poor if multicollinearity is present, unless the sample size is large.
In simple linear regression, where there is only one regressor (with a constant), the OLS coefficient estimates have a simple form that is closely related to the correlation coefficient between the covariate and the response.
Generalized least squares (GLS) is an extension of the OLS method, that allows efficient estimation of when either heteroscedasticity,

or correlations, or both are present among the error terms of the model, as long as the form of heteroscedasticity and correlation is known independently of the data. To handle heteroscedasticity when the error terms are uncorrelated with each other, GLS minimizes a weighted analogue to the sum of squared residuals from OLS regression, where the weight for the ith case is inversely proportional to var(ε_i). This special case of GLS is called "weighted least squares". The GLS solution to estimation problem is

where Ω is the covariance matrix of the errors. GLS can be viewed as applying a linear transformation to the data so that the assumptions of OLS are met for the transformed data. For GLS to be applied, the covariance structure of the errors must be known up to a multiplicative constant.

Percentage least squares focuses on reducing percentage errors, which is useful in the field of forecasting or time series analysis. It is also useful in situations where the dependent variable has a wide range without constant variance, as here the larger residuals at the upper end of the range would dominate if OLS were used. When the percentage or relative error is normally distributed, least squares percentage regression provides maximum likelihood estimates. Percentage regression is linked to a multiplicative error model, whereas OLS is linked to models containing an additive error term.

Iteratively reweighted least squares (IRLS) is used when heteroscedasticity, or correlations, or both are present among the error terms of the model, but where little is known about the covariance structure of the errors independently of the data. In the first iteration, OLS, or GLS with a provisional covariance structure is carried out, and the residuals are obtained from the fit. Based on the residuals, an improved estimate of the covariance structure of the errors can usually be obtained. A subsequent GLS iteration is then performed using this estimate of the error structure to define the weights. The process can be iterated to convergence, but in many cases, only one iteration is sufficient to achieve an efficient estimate of β.

Instrumental variables regression (IV) can be performed when the regressors are correlated with the errors. In this case, we need the existence of some auxiliary instrumental variables z_i such that $E[z_i \varepsilon_i] = 0$. If Z is the matrix of instruments, then the estimator can be given in closed form as

Optimal instruments regression is an extension of classical IV regression to the situation where $E[\varepsilon_i | z_i] = 0$.

Total least squares (TLS) is an approach to least squares estimation of the linear regression model that treats the covariates and response variable in a more geometrically symmetric manner than OLS. It is one approach to handling the "errors in variables" problem, and is sometimes used when the covariates are assumed to be error-free.

Maximum-likelihood estimation and related techniques

Maximum likelihood estimation can be performed when the distribution of the error terms is known to belong to a certain parametric family $f_\square$ of probability distributions. When $f_\square$ is a normal distribution with mean zero and variance $\square$, the resulting estimate is identical to the OLS estimate. GLS estimates are maximum likelihood estimates when $\square$ follows a multivariate normal distribution with a known covariance matrix.
Ridge regression, and other forms of penalized estimation such as Lasso regression, deliberately introduce bias into the estimation of $\square$ in order to reduce the variability of the estimate. The resulting estimators generally have lower mean squared error than the OLS estimates, particularly when multicollinearity is present. They are generally used when the goal is to predict the value of the response variable y for values of the predictors x that have not yet been observed. These methods are not as commonly used when the goal is inference, since it is difficult to account for the bias.
Least absolute deviation (LAD) regression is a robust estimation technique in that it is less sensitive to the presence of outliers than OLS (but is less efficient than OLS when no outliers are present). It is equivalent to maximum likelihood estimation under a Laplace distribution model for $\square$.
Adaptive estimation. If we assume that error terms are independent from the regressors , the optimal estimator is the 2-step MLE, where the first step is used to non-parametrically estimate the distribution of the error term.

Other estimation techniques

Bayesian linear regression applies the framework of Bayesian statistics to linear regression. (See also Bayesian multivariate linear regression.) In particular, the regression coefficients $\square$ are assumed to be random variables with a specified prior distribution. The prior distribution can bias the solutions for the regression coefficients, in a way similar to (but more general than) ridge regression or lasso regression. In addition, the Bayesian estimation process produces not a single point estimate for the "best" values of the regression coefficients but an entire posterior distribution, completely describing the uncertainty surrounding the quantity. This can be used to estimate the "best" coefficients using the mean, mode, median, any quantile (see quantile regression), or any other function of the posterior distribution.

Quantile regression focuses on the conditional quantiles of y given X rather than the conditional mean of y given X. Linear quantile regression models a particular conditional quantile, often the conditional median, as a linear function $\beta^T x$ of the predictors.

Mixed models are widely used to analyze linear regression relationships involving dependent data when the dependencies have a known structure. Common applications of mixed models include analysis of data involving repeated measurements, such as longitudinal data, or data obtained from cluster sampling. They are generally fit as parametric models, using maximum likelihood or Bayesian estimation. In the case where the errors are modeled as normal random variables, there is a close connection between mixed models and generalized least squares. Fixed effects estimation is an alternative approach to analyzing this type of data.

Principal component regression (PCR) is used when the number of predictor variables is large, or when strong correlations exist among the predictor variables. This two-stage procedure first reduces the predictor variables using principal component analysis then uses the reduced variables in an OLS regression fit. While it often works well in practice, there is no general theoretical reason that the most informative linear function of the predictor variables should lie among the dominant principal components of the multivariate distribution of the predictor variables. The partial least squares regression is the extension of the PCR method which does not suffer from the mentioned deficiency.

Least-angle regression is an estimation procedure for linear regression models that was developed to handle high-dimensional covariate vectors, potentially with more covariates than observations.

The Theil–Sen estimator is a simple robust estimation technique that choose the slope of the fit line to be the median of the slopes of the lines through pairs of sample points. It has similar statistical efficiency properties to simple linear regression but is much less sensitive to outliers.

Other robust estimation techniques, including the α-trimmed mean approach, and L-, M-, S-, and R-estimators have been introduced.

Further discussion

In statistics, the problem of numerical methods for linear least squares is an important one because linear regression models are one of the most important types of model, both as formal statistical models and for exploration of data sets. The majority of statistical computer packages contain facilities for regression analysis that make use of linear least squares computations. Hence it is appropriate that considerable effort has been devoted to the task of ensuring that these computations are undertaken efficiently and with due regard to numerical precision.

Individual statistical analyses are seldom undertaken in isolation, but rather are part of a sequence of investigatory steps. Some of the topics involved in considering numerical methods for linear least squares relate to this point. Thus important topics can be

Computations where a number of similar, and often nested, models are considered for the same data set. That is, where models with the same dependent variable but different sets of independent variables are to be considered, for essentially the same set of data points.
Computations for analyses that occur in a sequence, as the number of data points increases.
Special considerations for very extensive data sets.
Fitting of linear models by least squares often, but not always, arises in the context of statistical analysis. It can therefore be important that considerations of computational efficiency for such problems extend to all of the auxiliary quantities required for such analyses, and are not restricted to the formal solution of the linear least squares problem.

Matrix calculations, like any others, are affected by rounding errors. An early summary of these effects, regarding the choice of computational methods for matrix inversion, was provided by Wilkinson.

Applications of linear regression

Linear regression is widely used in biological, behavioral and social sciences to describe possible relationships between variables. It ranks as one of the most important tools used in these disciplines.

Trend line

Trend estimation
A trend line represents a trend, the long-term movement in time series data after other components have been accounted for. It tells whether a particular data set (say GDP, oil prices or stock prices) have increased or decreased over the period of time. A trend line could simply be drawn by eye through a set of data points, but more properly their position and slope is calculated using statistical techniques like linear regression. Trend lines typically are straight lines, although some variations use higher degree polynomials depending on the degree of curvature desired in the line.

Trend lines are sometimes used in business analytics to show changes in data over time. This has the advantage of being simple. Trend lines are often used to argue that a particular action or event (such as training, or an advertising campaign) caused observed changes at a point in time. This is a simple technique, and does not require a control group, experimental design, or a sophisticated analysis technique. However, it suffers from a lack of scientific validity in cases where other potential changes can affect the data.

Epidemiology

Early evidence relating tobacco smoking to mortality and morbidity came from observational studies employing regression analysis. In order to reduce spurious correlations when analyzing observational data, researchers usually include several variables in their regression models in addition to the variable of primary interest. For example, suppose we have a regression model in which cigarette smoking is the independent variable of interest, and the dependent variable is lifespan measured in years. Researchers might include socio-economic status as an additional independent variable, to ensure that any observed effect of smoking on lifespan is not due to some effect of education or income. However, it is never possible to include all possible confounding variables in an empirical analysis. For example, a hypothetical gene might increase mortality and also cause people to smoke more. For this reason, randomized controlled trials are often able to generate more compelling evidence of causal relationships than can be obtained using regression analyses of observational data. When controlled experiments are not feasible, variants of regression analysis such as instrumental variables regression may be used to attempt to estimate causal relationships from observational data.

Finance

The capital asset pricing model uses linear regression as well as the concept of Beta for analyzing and quantifying the systematic risk of an investment. This comes directly from the Beta coefficient of the linear regression model that relates the return on the investment to the return on all risky assets.

Economics

Linear regression is the predominant empirical tool in economics. For example, it is used to predict consumption spending, fixed investment spending, inventory investment, purchases of a country's exports, spending on imports, the demand to hold liquid assets, labor demand, and labor supply.

Environmental science

Linear regression finds application in a wide range of environmental science applications. In Canada, the Environmental Effects Monitoring Program uses statistical analyses on fish and benthic surveys to measure the effects of pulp mill or metal mine effluent on the aquatic ecosystem.

Machine learning

Machine learning

Machine learning, a branch of artificial intelligence, is a scientific discipline concerned with the design and development of algorithms that take as input empirical data, such as that from sensors or databases, and yield patterns or predictions thought to be features of the underlying mechanism that generated the data. A learner can take advantage of examples (data) to capture characteristics of interest of their unknown underlying probability distribution. Data can be seen as instances of the possible relations between observed variables. A major focus of machine learning research is the design of algorithms that recognize complex patterns and make intelligent decisions based on input data. One fundamental difficulty is that the set of all possible behaviors given all possible inputs is too large to be included in the set of observed examples (training data). Hence the learner must generalize from the given examples in order to produce a useful output in new cases.

Definition

In 1959, Arthur Samuel defined machine learning as "Field of study that gives computers the ability to learn without being explicitly programmed".

Tom M. Mitchell provided a widely quoted, more formal definition: "A computer program is said to learn from experience E with respect to some class of tasks T and performance measure P, if its performance at tasks in T, as measured by P, improves with experience E".

Generalization

Generalization in this context is the ability of an algorithm to perform accurately on new, unseen examples after having trained on a learning data set. The core objective of a learner is to generalize from its experience. The training examples come from some generally unknown probability distribution and the learner has to extract from them something more general, something about that distribution, that allows it to produce useful predictions in new cases.

Machine learning, knowledge discovery in databases

(KDD) and data mining

Two terms are commonly confused, as they often employ the same methods and overlap significantly. They can be roughly defined as follows:

Machine learning focuses on prediction, based on known properties learned from the training data
Data mining (which is the analysis step of Knowledge Discovery in Databases) focuses on the discovery of (previously) unknown properties on the data
The two areas overlap in many ways: data mining uses many machine learning methods, but often with a slightly different goal in mind. On the other hand, machine learning also employs data mining methods as "unsupervised learning" or as a preprocessing step to improve learner accuracy. Much of the confusion between these two research communities (which do often have separate conferences and separate journals, ECML PKDD being a major exception) comes from the basic assumptions they work with: in machine learning, performance is usually evaluated with respect to the ability to reproduce known knowledge, while in KDD the key task is the discovery of previously unknown knowledge. Evaluated with respect to known knowledge, an uninformed (unsupervised) method will easily be outperformed by supervised methods, while in a typical KDD task, supervised methods cannot be used due to the unavailability of training data.

Human interaction

Some machine learning systems attempt to eliminate the need for human intuition in data analysis, while others adopt a collaborative approach between human and machine. Human intuition cannot, however, be entirely eliminated, since the system's designer must specify how the data is to be represented and what mechanisms will be used to search for a characterization of the data.

Algorithm types

Machine learning algorithms can be organized into a taxonomy based on the desired outcome of the algorithm.

Supervised learning generates a function that maps inputs to desired outputs (also called labels, because they are often provided by human experts labeling the training examples). For example, in a classification problem, the learner approximates a function mapping a vector into classes by looking at input-output examples of the function.

Unsupervised learning models a set of inputs, like clustering. See also data mining and knowledge discovery.

Semi-supervised learning combines both labeled and unlabeled examples to generate an appropriate function or classifier.

Reinforcement learning learns how to act given an observation of the world. Every action has some impact in the environment, and the environment provides feedback in the form of rewards that guides the learning algorithm.

Transduction, or transductive inference, tries to predict new outputs on specific and fixed (test) cases from observed, specific (training) cases.

Learning to learn learns its own inductive bias based on previous experience.

Theory

Computational learning theory

The computational analysis of machine learning algorithms and their performance is a branch of theoretical computer science known as computational learning theory. Because training sets are finite and the future is uncertain, learning theory usually does not yield guarantees of the performance of algorithms. Instead, probabilistic bounds on the performance are quite common.

In addition to performance bounds, computational learning theorists study the time complexity and feasibility of learning. In computational learning theory, a computation is considered feasible if it can be done in polynomial time. There are two kinds of time complexity results. Positive results show that a certain class of functions can be learned in polynomial time. Negative results show that certain classes cannot be learned in polynomial time.

There are many similarities between machine learning theory and statistics, although they use different terms.

Approaches

List of machine learning algorithms

Decision tree learning

Decision tree learning
Decision tree learning uses a decision tree as a predictive model which maps observations about an item to conclusions about the item's target value.

Association rule learning

Association rule learning
Association rule learning is a method for discovering interesting relations between variables in large databases.

Artificial neural networks

Learning rule
An artificial neural network (ANN) learning algorithm, usually called "neural network" (NN), is a learning algorithm that is inspired by the structure and functional aspects of biological neural networks. Computations are structured in terms of an interconnected group of artificial neurons, processing information using a connectionist approach to computation. Modern neural networks are non-linear statistical data modeling tools. They are usually used to model complex relationships between inputs and outputs, to find patterns in data, or to capture the statistical structure in an unknown joint probability distribution between observed variables.

Genetic programming

Genetic programming (GP) is an evolutionary algorithm-based methodology inspired by biological evolution to find computer programs that perform a user-defined task. It is a specialization of genetic algorithms (GA) where each individual is a computer program. It is a machine learning technique used to optimize a population of computer programs according to a fitness landscape determined by a program's ability to perform a given computational task.

Inductive logic programming

Inductive logic programming
Inductive logic programming (ILP) is an approach to rule learning using logic programming as a uniform representation for examples, background knowledge, and hypotheses. Given an encoding of the known background knowledge and a set of examples represented as a logical database of facts, an ILP system will derive a hypothesized logic program which entails all the positive and none of the negative examples.

Support vector machines

Support vector machines
Support vector machines (SVMs) are a set of related supervised learning methods used for classification and regression. Given a set of training examples, each marked as belonging to one of two categories, an SVM training algorithm builds a model that predicts whether a new example falls into one category or the other.

Clustering

Cluster analysis
Cluster analysis is the assignment of a set of observations into subsets (called clusters) so that observations within the same cluster are similar according to some predesignated criterion or criteria, while observations drawn from different clusters are dissimilar. Different clustering techniques make different assumptions on the structure of the data, often defined by some similarity metric and evaluated for example by internal compactness (similarity between members of the same cluster) and separation between different clusters. Other methods are based on estimated density and graph connectivity. Clustering is a method of unsupervised learning, and a common technique for statistical data analysis.

Bayesian networks

Bayesian network
A Bayesian network, belief network or directed acyclic graphical model is a probabilistic graphical model that represents a set of random variables and their conditional independencies via a directed acyclic graph (DAG). For example, a Bayesian network could represent the probabilistic relationships between diseases and symptoms. Given symptoms, the network can be used to compute the probabilities of the presence of various diseases. Efficient algorithms exist that perform inference and learning.

Reinforcement learning

Reinforcement learning
Reinforcement learning is concerned with how an agent ought to take actions in an environment so as to maximize some notion of long-term reward. Reinforcement learning algorithms attempt to find a policy that maps states of the world to the actions the agent ought to take in those states. Reinforcement learning differs from the supervised learning problem in that correct input/output pairs are never presented, nor sub-optimal actions explicitly corrected.

Representation learning

Several learning algorithms, mostly unsupervised learning algorithms, aim at discovering better representations of the inputs provided during training. Classical examples include principal components analysis and cluster analysis. Representation learning algorithms often attempt to preserve the information in their input but transform it in a way that makes it useful, often as a preprocessing step before performing classification or predictions, allowing to reconstruct the inputs coming from the unknown data generating distribution, while not being necessarily faithful for configurations that are implausible under that distribution. Manifold learning algorithms attempt to do so under the constraint that the learned representation is low-dimensional. Sparse coding algorithms attempt to do so under the constraint that the learned representation is sparse (has many zeros). Deep learning algorithms discover multiple levels of representation, or a hierarchy of features, with higher-level, more abstract features defined in terms of (or generating) lower-level features. It has been argued that an intelligent machine is one that learns a representation that disentangles the underlying factors of variation that explain the observed data.

Sparse Dictionary Learning

In this method, a datum is represented as a linear combination of basis functions, and the coefficients are assumed to be sparse. Let x be a d-dimensional datum, D be a n by d matrix, where each column of D represents a basis function. r is the coefficient to represent x using D. Mathematically, sparse dictionary learning means the following

where r is sparse. Generally speaking, n is assumed to be larger than d to allow the freedom for a sparse representation.

Sparse dictionary learning has been applied in several contexts. In classification, the problem is to determine which classes a previously unseen datum belongs to. Suppose a dictionary for each class has already been built. Then a new datum is associated with the class such that it's best sparsely represented by the corresponding dictionary. Sparse dictionary learning has also been applied in image de-noising. The key idea is that a clean image path can be sparsely represented by an image dictionary, but the noise cannot. if interested.

Applications

Applications for machine learning include:

Machine perception
Computer vision
Natural language processing
Syntactic pattern recognition
Search engines
Medical diagnosis
Bioinformatics
Brain-machine interfaces
Cheminformatics
Detecting credit card fraud
Stock market analysis

Classifying DNA sequences
Sequence mining
Speech and handwriting recognition
Object recognition in Computer vision
Game playing
Software engineering
Adaptive websites
Robot locomotion
Computational finance
Structural health monitoring.
Sentiment Analysis (or Opinion Mining).
Affective computing
Information Retrieval
Recommender systems

In 2006, the on-line movie company Netflix held the first "Netflix Prize" competition to find a program to better predict user preferences and beat its existing Netflix movie recommendation system by at least 10%. The AT&T Research Team BellKor beat out several other teams with their machine learning program "Pragmatic Chaos". After winning several minor prizes, it won the grand prize competition in 2009 for $1 million.

Software

RapidMiner, LIONsolver, KNIME, Weka, ODM, Shogun toolbox, Orange, Apache Mahout, scikit-learn, mlpy, MCMLL are software suites containing a variety of machine learning algorithms.

Journals and conferences

Machine Learning (journal)
Journal of Machine Learning Research
Neural Computation (journal)
Journal of Intelligent Systems(journal)
International Conference on Machine Learning (ICML) (conference)
Neural Information Processing Systems (NIPS) (conference)

Marketing

Marketing

Marketing is "the activity, set of institutions, and processes for creating, communicating, delivering, and exchanging offerings that have value for customers, clients, partners, and society at large. "

For business to consumer marketing, it is "the process by which companies create value for customers and build strong customer relationships, in order to capture value from customers in return". For business to business marketing it is creating value, solutions, and relationships either short term or long term with a company or brand. It generates the strategy that underlies sales techniques, business communication, and business developments. It is an integrated process through which companies build strong customer relationships and create value for their customers and for themselves.

Marketing is used to identify the customer, satisfy the customer, and keep the customer. With the customer as the focus of its activities, marketing management is one of the major components of business management. Marketing evolved to meet the stasis in developing new markets caused by mature markets and overcapacities in the last 2-3 centuries. The adoption of marketing strategies requires businesses to shift their focus from production to the perceived needs and wants of their customers as the means of staying profitable.

The term marketing concept holds that achieving organizational goals depends on knowing the needs and wants of target markets and delivering the desired satisfactions. It proposes that in order to satisfy its organizational objectives, an organization should anticipate the needs and wants of consumers and satisfy these more effectively than competitors.

The term developed from an original meaning which referred literally to going to a market to buy or sell goods or services. Seen from a systems point of view, sales process engineering marketing is "a set of processes that are interconnected and interdependent with other functions, whose methods can be improved using a variety of relatively new approaches. "

Further definitions

The Chartered Institute of Marketing defines marketing as "the management process responsible for identifying, anticipating and satisfying customer requirements profitably. " A different concept is the value-based marketing which states the role of marketing to contribute to increasing shareholder value. In this context, marketing is defined as "the management process that seeks to maximize returns to shareholders by developing relationships with valued customers and creating a competitive advantage. "

Marketing practice tended to be seen as a creative industry in the past, which included advertising, distribution and selling, Merchandise support. However, because the academic study of marketing makes extensive use of social sciences, psychology, sociology, mathematics, economics, anthropology and neuroscience, the profession is now widely recognized as a science, allowing numerous universities to offer Master-of-Science (MSc) programmes. The overall process starts with marketing research and goes through market segmentation, business planning and execution, ending with pre- and post-sales promotional activities. It is also related to many of the creative arts. The marketing literature is also adept at re-inventing itself and its vocabulary according to the times and the culture.

Browne (2010) reveals that supermarkets spend millions of dollars intensively researching and studying consumer behaviour. Their aim is to make sure that shoppers leave their stores spending much more than they originally planned. 'Choice' examined the theory of trolleyology finding that many shoppers instinctively look to the right when they're in the supermarket.

Supermarkets move products around to confuse shoppers, the entry point is another marketing tactic. Consumer psychologist Dr. Paul Harrison (cited in Browne, 2010) states that supermarkets are constantly using different methodologies of selling. One method is performing regular overhauls changing the locations of products all around to break habitual shopping, and break your budget. Harrison also contends that people who are shopping in a counter clockwise direction are likely to spend more money than people shopping in a clockwise direction. Consumer psychologists (cited in Browne, 2010) reported that most people write with their right hand, thus it is a biological trait that people have the tendency of veering to the right when shopping, it is understood that supermarkets capitalize on this fact. Found on the capturing right-hand side are usually appealing products that a shopper might impulsively buy e.g. an umbrella when the weather is dull.

Evolution of marketing

History of marketing
An orientation, in the marketing context, related to a perception or attitude a firm holds towards its product or service, essentially concerning consumers and end-users. Throughout history, marketing has changed considerably in conjunction with consumer tastes. Constant throughout, however, is that marketing is some form of communication aimed broadly at improving eventual sales.

Earlier approaches

The marketing orientation evolved from earlier orientations, namely, the production orientation, the product orientation and the selling orientation.

Orientation   Profit driver   Western European timeframe   Description
Production   Production methods   until the 1950s   A firm focusing on a production orientation specializes in producing as much as possible of a given product or service. Thus, this signifies a firm exploiting economies of scale until the minimum efficient scale is reached. A production orientation may be deployed when a high demand for a product or service exists, coupled with a good certainty that consumer tastes will not rapidly alter (similar to the sales orientation).
Product   Quality of the product   until the 1960s   A firm employing a product orientation is chiefly concerned with the quality of its own product. A firm would also assume that as long as its product was of a high standard, people would buy and consume the product.
Selling Selling methods   1950s and 1960s   A firm using a sales orientation focuses primarily on the selling/promotion of a particular product, and not determining new consumer desires as such. Consequently, this entails simply selling an already existing product, and using promotion techniques to attain the highest sales possible.

Such an orientation may suit scenarios in which a firm holds dead stock, or otherwise sells a product that is in high demand, with little likelihood of changes in consumer tastes that would diminish demand.

Marketing   Needs and wants of customers   1970 to present day   The 'marketing orientation' is perhaps the most common orientation used in contemporary marketing. It involves a firm essentially basing its marketing plans around the marketing concept, and thus supplying products to suit new consumer tastes. As an example, a firm would employ market research to gauge consumer desires, use R&D to develop a product attuned to the revealed information, and then utilize promotion techniques to ensure persons know the product exists.

Contemporary approaches

Recent approaches in marketing include relationship marketing with focus on the customer, business marketing or industrial marketing with focus on an organization or institution and social marketing with focus on benefits to society. New forms of marketing also use the internet and are therefore called internet marketing or more generally e-marketing, online marketing, search engine marketing, desktop advertising or affiliate marketing. It attempts to perfect the segmentation strategy used in traditional marketing. It targets its audience more precisely, and is sometimes called personalized marketing or one-to-one marketing. Internet marketing is sometimes considered to be broad in scope, because it not only refers to marketing on the Internet, but also includes marketing done via e-mail and wireless media.

Orientation   Profit driver   Western European timeframe   Description
Relationship marketing / Relationship management   Building and keeping good customer relations   1960s to present day   Emphasis is placed on the whole relationship between suppliers and customers. The aim is to provide the best possible customer service and build customer loyalty.
Business marketing / Industrial marketing Building and keeping relationships between organizations   1980s to present day   In this context, marketing takes place between businesses or organizations. The product focus lies on industrial goods or capital goods rather than consumer products or end products. Different

forms of marketing activities, such as promotion, advertising and communication to the customer are used.
Social marketing   Benefit to society   1990s to present day
Similar characteristics to marketing orientation but with the added proviso that there will be a curtailment of any harmful activities to society, in either product, production, or selling methods.
Branding   Brand value 1980s to present day   In this context, "branding" is the main company philosophy and marketing is considered an instrument of branding philosophy.

Customer orientation

A firm in the market economy survives by producing goods that persons are willing and able to buy. Consequently, ascertaining consumer demand is vital for a firm's future viability and even existence as a going concern. Many companies today have a customer focus (or market orientation). This implies that the company focuses its activities and products on consumer demands. Generally, there are three ways of doing this: the customer-driven approach, the market change identification approach and the product innovation approach.

In the consumer-driven approach, consumer wants are the drivers of all strategic marketing decisions. No strategy is pursued until it passes the test of consumer research. Every aspect of a market offering, including the nature of the product itself, is driven by the needs of potential consumers. The starting point is always the consumer. The rationale for this approach is that there is no reason to spend R&D funds developing products that people will not buy. History attests to many products that were commercial failures in spite of being technological breakthroughs.

A formal approach to this customer-focused marketing is known as SIVA (Solution, Information, Value, Access). This system is basically the four Ps renamed and reworded to provide a customer focus. The SIVA Model provides a demand/customer-centric alternative to the well-known 4Ps supply side model (product, price, placement, promotion) of marketing management.

Product ⇨ Solution
Promotion ⇨ Information
Price ⇨ Value
Place ⇨ Access

If any of the 4Ps were problematic or were not in the marketing factor of the business, the business could be in trouble and so other companies may appear in the surroundings of the company, so the consumer demand on its products will decrease. However, in recent years service marketing has widened the domains to be considered, contributing to the 7P's of marketing in total. The other 3P's of service marketing are: process, physical environment and people.

Some qualifications or caveats for customer focus exist. They do not invalidate or contradict the principle of customer focus; rather, they simply add extra dimensions of awareness and caution to it.

The work of Christensen and colleagues on disruptive technology has produced a theoretical framework that explains the failure of firms not because they were technologically inept (often quite the opposite), but because the value networks in which they profitably operated included customers who could not value a disruptive innovation at the time and capability state of its emergence and thus actively dissuaded the firms from developing it. The lessons drawn from this work include:

Taking customer focus with a grain of salt, treating it as only a subset of one's corporate strategy rather than the sole driving factor. This means looking beyond current-state customer focus to predict what customers will be demanding some years in the future, even if they themselves discount the prediction.
Pursuing new markets (thus new value networks) when they are still in a commercially inferior or unattractive state, simply because their potential to grow and intersect with established markets and value networks looks like a likely bet. This may involve buying stakes in the stock of smaller firms, acquiring them outright, or incubating small, financially distinct units within one's organization to compete against them.
Other caveats of customer focus are:

The extent to which what customers say they want does not match their purchasing decisions. Thus surveys of customers might claim that 70% of a restaurant's customers want healthier choices on the menu, but only 10% of them actually buy the new items once they are offered. This might be acceptable except for the extent to which those items are money-losing propositions for the business, bleeding red ink. A lesson from this type of situation is to be smarter about the true test validity of instruments like surveys. A corollary argument is that "truly understanding customers sometimes means understanding them better than they understand themselves. " Thus one could argue that the principle of customer focus, or being close to the customers, is not violated here—just expanded upon. The extent to which customers are currently ignorant of what one might argue they should want—which is dicey because whether it can be acted upon affordably depends on whether or how soon the customers will learn, or be convinced, otherwise. IT hardware and software capabilities and automobile features are examples. Customers who in 1997 said that they would not place any value on internet browsing capability on a mobile phone, or 6% better fuel efficiency in their vehicle, might say something different today, because the value proposition of those opportunities has changed.

Organizational orientation

In this sense, a firm's marketing department is often seen as of prime importance within the functional level of an organization. Information from an organization's marketing department would be used to guide the actions of other departments within the firm. As an example, a marketing department could ascertain (via marketing research) that consumers desired a new type of product, or a new usage for an existing product. With this in mind, the marketing department would inform the R&D department to create a prototype of a product/service based on consumers' new desires.

The production department would then start to manufacture the product, while the marketing department would focus on the promotion, distribution, pricing, etc. of the product. Additionally, a firm's finance department would be consulted, with respect to securing appropriate funding for the development, production and promotion of the product. Inter-departmental conflicts may occur, should a firm adhere to the marketing orientation. Production may oppose the installation, support and servicing of new capital stock, which may be needed to manufacture a new product. Finance may oppose the required capital expenditure, since it could undermine a healthy cash flow for the organization.

Herd behavior

Herd behavior in marketing is used to explain the dependencies of customers' mutual behavior. The Economist reported a recent conference in Rome on the subject of the simulation of adaptive human behavior. It shared mechanisms to increase impulse buying and get people "to buy more by playing on the herd instinct. " The basic idea is that people will buy more of products that are seen to be popular, and several feedback mechanisms to get product popularity information to consumers are mentioned, including smart card technology and the use of Radio Frequency Identification Tag technology. A "swarm-moves" model was introduced by a Florida Institute of Technology researcher, which is appealing to supermarkets because it can "increase sales without the need to give people discounts. " Other recent studies on the "power of social influence" include an "artificial music market in which some 19,000 people downloaded previously unknown songs" (Columbia University, New York); a Japanese chain of convenience stores which orders its products based on "sales data from department stores and research companies;" a Massachusetts company exploiting knowledge of social networking to improve sales; and online retailers who are increasingly informing consumers about "which products are popular with like-minded consumers" (e. g. , Amazon, eBay).

Further orientations

An emerging area of study and practice concerns internal marketing, or how employees are trained and managed to deliver the brand in a way that positively impacts the acquisition and retention of customers, see also employer branding.
Diffusion of innovations research explores how and why people adopt new products, services, and ideas.
With consumers' eroding attention span and willingness to give time to advertising messages, marketers are turning to forms of permission marketing such as branded content, custom media and reality marketing.

Marketing research

Marketing research
Marketing research involves conducting research to support marketing activities, and the statistical interpretation of data into information. This information is then used by managers to plan marketing activities, gauge the nature of a firm's marketing

environment and attain information from suppliers. Marketing researchers use statistical methods such as quantitative research, qualitative research, hypothesis tests, Chi-squared tests, linear regression, correlations, frequency distributions, poisson distributions, binomial distributions, etc. to interpret their findings and convert data into information. The marketing research process spans a number of stages, including the definition of a problem, development of a research plan, collection and interpretation of data and disseminating information formally in the form of a report. The task of marketing research is to provide management with relevant, accurate, reliable, valid, and current information.

A distinction should be made between marketing research and market research. Market research pertains to research in a given market. As an example, a firm may conduct research in a target market, after selecting a suitable market segment. In contrast, marketing research relates to all research conducted within marketing. Thus, market research is a subset of marketing research.

Marketing environment

Marketing environment
The market environment is a marketing term and refers to factors and forces that affect a firm's ability to build and maintain successful relationships with customers. Three levels of the environment are: Micro (internal) environment - forces within the company that affect its ability to serve its customers. Meso environment – the industry in which a company operates and the industry's market(s). Macro (national) environment - larger societal forces that affect the microenvironment.

Market segmentation

Market segmentation
Market segmentation pertains to the division of a market of consumers into persons with similar needs and wants. For instance, Kellogg's cereals, Frosties are marketed to children. Crunchy Nut Cornflakes are marketed to adults. Both goods denote two products which are marketed to two distinct groups of persons, both with similar needs, traits, and wants.

Market segmentation allows for a better allocation of a firm's finite resources. A firm only possesses a certain amount of resources. Accordingly, it must make choices (and incur the related costs) in servicing specific groups of consumers. In this way, the diversified tastes of contemporary Western consumers can be served better. With growing diversity in the tastes of modern consumers, firms are taking note of the benefit of servicing a multiplicity of new markets.

Market segmentation can be defined in terms of the STP acronym, meaning Segment, Target and Position.

Types of Market Research

Market research, as a sub-set aspect of marketing activities, can be divided into the following parts:

Primary research (also known as field research), which involves the conduction and compilation of research for a specific purpose. Secondary research (also referred to as desk research), initially conducted for one purpose, but often used to support another purpose or end goal.
By these definitions, an example of primary research would be market research conducted into health foods, which is used solely to ascertain the needs/wants of the target market for health foods. Secondary research in this case would be research pertaining to health foods, but used by a firm wishing to develop an unrelated product.

Primary research is often expensive to prepare, collect and interpret from data to information. Nevertheless, while secondary research is relatively inexpensive, it often can become outdated and outmoded, given that it is used for a purpose other than the one for which it was intended. Primary research can also be broken down into quantitative research and qualitative research, which, as the terms suggest, pertain to numerical and non-numerical research methods and techniques, respectively. The appropriateness of each mode of research depends on whether data can be quantified (quantitative research), or whether subjective, non-numeric or abstract concepts are required to be studied (qualitative research).

There also exist additional modes of marketing research, which are:

Exploratory research, pertaining to research that investigates an assumption.
Descriptive research, which, as the term suggests, describes "what is".
Predictive research, meaning research conducted to predict a future occurrence.
Conclusive research, for the purpose of deriving a conclusion via a research process.

Marketing planning

Marketing plan
The marketing planning process involves forging a plan for a firm's marketing activities. A marketing plan can also pertain to a specific product, as well as to an organization's overall marketing strategy. Generally speaking, an organization's marketing planning process is derived from its overall business strategy. Thus, when top management are devising the firm's strategic direction or mission, the intended marketing activities are incorporated into this plan. There are several levels of marketing objectives within an organization. The senior management of a firm would formulate a general business strategy for a firm. However, this general business strategy would be interpreted and implemented in different contexts throughout the firm.

Marketing strategy

The field of marketing strategy encompasses the strategy involved in the management of a given product.

A given firm may hold numerous products in the marketplace, spanning numerous and sometimes wholly unrelated industries. Accordingly, a plan is required in order to effectively manage such products. Evidently, a company needs to weigh up and ascertain how to utilize its finite resources. For example, a start-up car manufacturing firm would face little success should it attempt to rival Toyota, Ford, Nissan, Chevrolet, or any other large global car maker. Moreover, a product may be reaching the end of its life-cycle. Thus, the issue of divest, or a ceasing of production, may be made. Each scenario requires a unique marketing strategy. Listed below are some prominent marketing strategy models.

A marketing strategy differs from a marketing tactic in that a strategy looks at the longer term view of the products, goods, or services being marketed. A tactic refers to a shorter term view. Therefore, the mailing of a postcard or sales letter would be a tactic, but a campaign of several postcards, sales letters, or telephone calls would be a strategy.

Marketing specializations

With the rapidly emerging force of globalization, the distinction between marketing within a firm's home country and marketing within external markets is disappearing very quickly. With this in mind, firms need to reorient their marketing strategies to meet the challenges of the global marketplace, in addition to sustaining their competitiveness within home markets.

Buying behaviour

A marketing firm must ascertain the nature of customers' buying behavior if it is to market its product properly. In order to entice and persuade a consumer to buy a product, marketers try to determine the behavioral process of how a given product is purchased. Buying behavior is usually split into two prime strands, whether selling to the consumer, known as business-to-consumer (B2C), or to another business, known as business-to-business (B2B).

B2C buying behaviour

This mode of behaviour concerns consumers and their purchase of a given product. For example, if one imagines a pair of sneakers, the desire for a pair of sneakers would be followed by an information search on available types/brands. This may include perusing media outlets, but most commonly consists of information gathered from family and friends. If the information search is insufficient, the consumer may search for alternative means to satisfy the need/want. In this case, this may mean buying leather shoes, sandals, etc. The purchase decision is then made, in which the consumer actually buys the product. Following this stage, a post-purchase evaluation is often conducted, comprising an appraisal of the value/utility brought by the purchase of the sneakers. If the value/utility is high, then a repeat purchase may be made. This could then develop into consumer loyalty to the firm producing the sneakers.

B2B buying behaviour

Relates to organizational/industrial buying behavior. Business buy either wholesale from other businesses or directly from the manufacturer in contracts or agreements. B2B marketing involves one business marketing a product or service to another business. B2C and B2B behavior are not precise terms, as similarities and differences exist, with some key differences listed below:

In a straight re-buy, the fourth, fifth and sixth stages are omitted. In a modified re-buy scenario, the fifth and sixth stages are precluded. In a new buy, all stages are conducted.

Use of technologies

Marketing management can also rely on various technologies within the scope of its marketing efforts. Computer-based information systems can be employed, aiding in better processing and storage of data. Marketing researchers can use such systems to devise better methods of converting data into information, and for the creation of enhanced data gathering methods. Information technology can aid in enhancing an MKIS' software and hardware components, and improve a company's marketing decision-making process.

In recent years, the notebook personal computer has gained significant market share among laptops, largely due to its more user-friendly size and portability. Information technology typically progresses at a fast rate, leading to marketing managers being cognizant of the latest technological developments. Moreover, the launch of smartphones into the cellphone market is commonly derived from a demand among consumers for more technologically advanced products. A firm can lose out to competitors should it ignore technological innovations in its industry.

Technological advancements can lessen barriers between

countries and regions. Using the World Wide Web, firms can quickly dispatch information from one country to another without much restriction. Prior to the mass usage of the Internet, such transfers of information would have taken longer to send, especially if done via snail mail, telex, etc.

Recently, there has been a large emphasis on data analytics. Data can be mined from various sources such as online forms, mobile phone applications and more recently, social media.

Services marketing

Services marketing relates to the marketing of services, as opposed to tangible products. A service (as opposed to a good) is typically defined as follows:

The use of it is inseparable from its purchase (i. e. , a service is used and consumed simultaneously)
It does not possess material form, and thus cannot be touched, seen, heard, tasted, or smelled.
The use of a service is inherently subjective, meaning that several persons experiencing a service would each experience it uniquely. For example, a train ride can be deemed a service. If one buys a train ticket, the use of the train is typically experienced concurrently with the purchase of the ticket. Although the train is a physical object, one is not paying for the permanent ownership of the tangible components of the train.

Services (compared with goods) can also be viewed as a spectrum. Not all products are either pure goods or pure services. An example would be a restaurant, where a waiter's service is intangible, but the food is tangible.

Multinomial logit

Multinomial logit

In statistics, a multinomial logit (MNL) model, also known as multinomial logistic regression, is a regression model which generalizes logistic regression by allowing more than two discrete outcomes. That is, it is a model that is used to predict the probabilities of the different possible outcomes of a categorically distributed dependent variable, given a set of independent variables (which may be real-valued, binary-valued, categorical-valued, etc.). The use of the term "multinomial" in the name arises from the common conflation between the categorical and multinomial distributions, as explained in the relevant articles. However, it should be kept in mind that the actual goal of the multinomial logit model is to predict categorical data.

In some fields of machine learning (e. g. natural language processing), when a classifier is implemented using a multinomial logit model, it is commonly known as a maximum entropy classifier, conditional maximum entropy model or MaxEnt model for short. Maximum entropy classifiers are commonly used as alternatives to Naive Bayes classifiers because they do not assume statistical independence of the independent variables (commonly known as features) that serve as predictors. However, learning in such a model is slower than for a Naive Bayes classifier, and thus may not be appropriate given a very large number of classes to learn. In particular, learning in a Naive Bayes classifier is a simple matter of counting up the number of cooccurrences of features and classes, while in a maximum entropy classifier the weights, which are typically maximized using maximum a posteriori (MAP) estimation, must be learned using an iterative procedure; see below.

Introduction

Multinomial logit regression is used when the dependent variable in question is nominal (a set of categories which cannot be ordered in any meaningful way, also known as categorical) and consists of more than two categories. Some examples would be:

Which major will a college student choose, given their grades, stated likes and dislikes, etc. ?
Which blood type does a person have, given the results of various diagnostic tests?
In a hands-free mobile phone dialing application, which person's name was spoken, given various properties of the speech signal?
These are all statistical classification problems. They all have in common a dependent variable to be predicted that comes from one of a limited set of items which cannot be meaningfully

ordered, as well as a set of independent variables (aka observations, features, etc.), which are used to predict the dependent variable. Multinomial logit regression is a particular solution to the classification problem that assumes that a linear combination of the observed features and some problem-specific parameters can be used to determine the probability of each particular outcome of the dependent variable. The best values of the parameters for a given problem are usually determined from some training data (e. g. some people for whom both the diagnostic test results and blood types are known, or some examples of known words being spoken).

Multinomial logit regression is appropriate in cases where the response is not ordinal in nature as in ordered logit. Ordered logit regression is used in cases where the dependent variable in question consists of a set number (more than two) of categories which can be ordered in a meaningful way (for example, highest degree, social class) while multinomial logit is used when there is no apparent order (e. g. the choice of muffins, bagels or doughnuts for breakfast) .

Assumptions

The multinomial logit model assumes that data are case specific; that is, each independent variable has a single value for each case. The multinomial logit model also assumes that the dependent variable cannot be perfectly predicted from the independent variables for any case. As with other types of regression, there is no need for the independent variables to be statistically independent from each other (unlike, for example, in a Naive Bayes classifier); however, collinearity is assumed to be relatively low, as it becomes difficult to differentiate between the impact of several variables if they are highly correlated.

If the multinomial logit is used to model choices, it relies on the assumption of independence of irrelevant alternatives (IIA), which is not always desirable. This assumption states that the odds of preferring one class over another do not depend on the presence or absence of other "irrelevant" alternatives. For example, the relative probabilities of taking a car or bus to work do not change if a bicycle is added as an additional possibility. This allows the choice of K alternatives to be modeled as a set of K-1 independent binary choices, in which one alternative is chosen as a "pivot" and the other K-1 compared against it, one at a time. The IIA hypothesis is a core hypothesis in rational choice theory; however numerous studies in psychology show that individuals often violate this assumption when making choices. An example of a problem case arises if choices include a car and a blue bus. Suppose the odds ratio between the two is 1 : 1. Now if the option of a red bus is introduced, a person may be indifferent between a red and a blue bus, and hence may exhibit a car : blue bus : red bus odds ratio of 1 : 0. 5 : 0. 5, thus maintaining a 1 : 1 ratio of car : any bus while adopting a changed car : blue bus ratio of 1 : 0. 5. Here the red bus option was not in fact irrelevant, because a red bus was a perfect substitute for a blue bus.

If the multinomial logit is used to model choices, it may in some situations impose too much constraint on the relative preferences between the different alternatives. This point is especially important to take into account if the analysis aims to predict how choices would change if one alternative was to disappear (for instance if one political candidate withdraws from a three candidate race). Other models like the nested logit or the multinomial probit may be used in such cases as they need not violate the IIA.

Model

Introduction

There are multiple ways to describe the mathematical model underlying multinomial logistic regression, all of which are equivalent. This can make it difficult to compare different treatments of the subject in different texts. The article on logistic regression presents a number of equivalent formulations of simple logistic regression, and many of these have equivalents in the multinomial logit model.

The idea behind all of them, as in many other statistical classification techniques, is to construct a linear predictor function that constructs a score from a set of weights that are linearly combined with the explanatory variables (features) of a given observation using a dot product:

where Xi is the vector of explanatory variables describing observation i, ▢k is a vector of weights (or regression coefficients) corresponding to outcome k, and score(Xi, k) is the score associated with assigning observation i to category k. In discrete choice theory, where observations represent people and outcomes represent choices, the score is considered the utility associated with person i choosing outcome k. The predicted outcome is the one with the highest score.

The difference between the multinomial logit model and numerous other methods, models, algorithms, etc. with the same basic setup (the perceptron algorithm, support vector machines, linear discriminant analysis, etc.) is the procedure for determining (training) the optimal weights/coefficients and the way that the score is interpreted. In particular, in the multinomial logit model, the score can directly be converted to a probability value, indicating the probability of observation i choosing outcome k given the measured characteristics of the observation. This provides a principled way of incorporating the prediction of a particular multinomial logit model into a larger procedure that may involve multiple such predictions, each with a possibility of error. Without such a means of combining predictions, errors tend to multiply. For example, imagine a large predictive model that is broken down into a series of submodels where the prediction of a given submodel is used as the input of another submodel, and that prediction is in turn used as the input into a third submodel, etc. If each submodel has 90% accuracy in its predictions, and there are five submodels in series, then the overall model has only . 95 = 59% accuracy. If each submodel has 80% accuracy, then overall accuracy drops to . 85 = 33% accuracy. This issue is known as error propagation and is a serious problem in real-world predictive models, which are usually composed of numerous parts. Predicting probabilities of each possible outcome, rather than simply making a single optimal prediction, is one means of alleviating this issue.

Setup

The basic setup is the same as in logistic regression, the only difference being that the dependent variables are categorical rather than binary, i. e. there are K possible outcomes rather than just two. The following description is somewhat shortened; for more details, consult the logistic regression article.

Data points
Specifically, it is assumed that we have a series of N observed data points. Each data point i (ranging from 1 to N) consists of a set of M explanatory variables $x_{1,i} \ldots x_{M,i}$ (aka independent variables, predictor variables, features, etc.), and an associated categorical outcome Y_i (aka dependent variable, response variable), which can take on one of K possible values. These possible values represent logically separate categories (e. g. different political parties, blood types, etc.), and are often described mathematically by arbitrarily assigning each a number from 1 to K. The explanatory variables and outcome represent observed properties of the data points, and are often thought of as originating in the observations of N "experiments" — although an "experiment" may consist in nothing more than gathering data. The goal of multinomial logistic regression is to construct a model that explains the relationship between the explanatory variables and the outcome, so that the outcome of a new "experiment" can be correctly predicted for a new data point for which the explanatory variables, but not the outcome, are available. In the process, the model attempts to explain the relative effect of differing explanatory variables on the outcome.

Some examples:

The observed outcomes are different variants of a disease such as hepatitis (possibly including "no disease" and/or other related diseases) in a set of patients, and the explanatory variables might be characteristics of the patients thought to be pertinent (sex, race, age, blood pressure, outcomes of various liver-function tests, etc.). The goal is then to predict which disease is causing the observed liver-related symptoms in a new patient.
The observed outcomes are the party chosen by a set of people in an election, and the explanatory variables are the demographic characteristics of each person (e. g. sex, race, age, income, etc.). The goal is then to predict the likely vote of a new voter with given characteristics.
Linear predictor
As in other forms of linear regression, multinomial logistic regression uses a linear predictor function to predict the probability that observation i has outcome k, of the following form:

where is a regression coefficient associated with the mth explanatory variable and the kth outcome. As explained in the logistic regression article, the regression coefficients and explanatory variables are normally grouped into vectors of size M+1, so that the predictor function can be written more compactly:

where is the set of regression coefficients associated with outcome k, and (a row vector) is the set explanatory variables associated with observation i.

As a set of independent binary regressions

One fairly simple way to arrive at the multinomial logit model is to imagine, for K possible outcomes, running K-1 independent binary logistic regression models, in which one outcome is chosen as a "pivot" and then the other K-1 outcomes are separately regressed against the pivot outcome. This would proceed as follows, if outcome K (the last outcome) is chosen as the pivot:

Note that we have introduced separate sets of regression coefficients, one for each possible outcome.

If we exponentiate both sides, and solve for the probabilities, we get:

Using the fact that all K of the probabilities must sum to one, we find:

We can use this to find the other probabilities:

The fact that we run multiple regressions reveals why the model relies on the assumption of independence of irrelevant alternatives described above.

Estimating the coefficients

The unknown parameters in each vector β_k are typically jointly estimated by maximum a posteriori (MAP) estimation, which is an extension of maximum likelihood using regularization of the weights to prevent pathological solutions (usually a squared regularizing function, which is equivalent to placing a zero-mean Gaussian prior distribution on the weights, but other distributions are also possible). The solution is typically found using an iterative procedure such as iteratively reweighted least squares (IRLS) or, more commonly these days, a quasi-Newton method such as the L-BFGS method.

As a log-linear model

The formulation of binary logistic regression as a log-linear model can be directly extended to multi-way regression. That is, we model the logarithm of the probability of seeing a given output using the linear predictor as well as an additional normalization factor:

As in the binary case, we need an extra term to ensure that the whole set of probabilities forms a probability distribution, i. e. so that they all sum to one:

The reason why we need to add a term to ensure normalization, rather than multiply as is usual, is because we have taken the logarithm of the probabilities. Exponentiating both sides turns the additive term into a multiplicative factor, and in the process shows why we wrote the term in the form rather than simply :

We can compute the value of Z by applying the above constraint that requires all probabilities to sum to 1:

Therefore:

Note that this factor is "constant" in the sense that it is not a function of Yi, which is the variable over which the probability distribution is defined. However, it is definitely not constant with respect to the explanatory variables, or crucially, with respect to the unknown regression coefficients β_k, which we will need to determine through some sort of optimization procedure.

The resulting equations for the probabilities are

Or generally:

The following function:

is referred to as the softmax function. The reason is that the effect of exponentiating the values is to exaggerate the differences between them. As a result, will return a value close to 0 whenever x_k is significantly less than the maximum of all the values, and will return a value close to 1 when applied to the maximum value, unless it is extremely close to the next-largest value. Thus, the softmax function can be used to construct a weighted average that behaves as a smooth function (which can be conveniently differentiated, etc.) and which approximates the non-smooth function . That is:

Thus, we can write the probability equations as

The softmax function thus serves as the equivalent of the logistic function in binary logistic regression.

Note that not all of the vectors of coefficients are uniquely identifiable. This is due to the fact that all probabilities must sum to 1, making one of them completely determined once all the rest are known. As a result there are only separately specifiable probabilities, and hence separately identifiable vectors of coefficients. One way to see this is to note that if we add a constant vector to all of the coefficient vectors, the equations are identical:

As a result, it is conventional to set (or alternatively, one of the other coefficient vectors). Essentially, we set the constant so that one of the vectors becomes 0, and all of the other vectors get transformed into the difference between those vectors and the vector we chose. This is equivalent to "pivoting" around one of the K choices, and examining how much better or worse all of the other K-1 choices are, relative to the choice are pivoting around. Mathematically, we transform the coefficients as follows:

This leads to the following equations:

Other than the prime symbols on the regression coefficients, this is exactly the same as the form of the model described above, in terms of K-1 independent two-way regressions.

As a latent-variable model

It is also possible to formulate multinomial logistic regression as a latent variable model, following the two-way latent variable model described for binary logistic regression. This formulation is common in the theory of discrete choice models, and makes it easier to compare multinomial logistic regression to the related multinomial probit model, as well as to extend it to more complex models.

Imagine that, for each data point i and possible outcome k, there is a continuous latent variable $Y_{i,k}^*$ (i. e. an unobserved random variable) that is distributed as follows:

where i. e. a standard type-1 extreme value distribution.

This latent variable can be thought of as the utility associated with data point i choosing outcome k, where there is some randomness in the actual amount of utility obtained, which accounts for other unmodeled factors that go into the choice. The value of the actual variable is then determined in a non-random fashion from these latent variables (i. e. the randomness has been moved from the observed outcomes into the latent variables), where outcome k is chosen if and only if the associated utility (the value of) is greater than the utilities of all the other choices, i. e. if the utility associated with outcome k is the maximum of all the utilities. (Since the latent variables are continuous, the probability of two having exactly the same value is 0, so we basically don't have to worry about that situation.) That is:

Or equivalently:

Let's look more closely at the first equation, which we can write as follows:

There are a few things to realize here:

In general, if and then That is, the difference of two independent identically distributed extreme-value-distributed variables follows the logistic distribution, where the first parameter is unimportant. This is understandable since the first parameter is a location parameter, i. e. it shifts the mean by a fixed amount, and if two values are both shifted by the same amount, their difference remains the same. This means that all of the relational statements underlying the probability of a given choice involve the logistic distribution, which makes the initial choice of the extreme-value distribution, which seemed rather arbitrary, somewhat more understandable.

The second parameter in an extreme-value or logistic distribution is a scale parameter, such that if then This means that the effect of using an error variable with an arbitrary scale parameter in place of scale 1 can be compensated simply by multiplying all regression vectors by the same scale. Together with the previous point, this shows that the use of a standard extreme-value distribution (location 0, scale 1) for the error variables entails no loss of generality over using an arbitrary extreme-value distribution. In fact, the model is nonidentifiable (no single set of optimal coefficients) if the more general distribution is used.

Because only differences of vectors of regression coefficients are used, adding an arbitrary constant to all coefficient vectors has no effect on the model. This means that, just as in the log-linear model, only K-1 of the coefficient vectors are identifiable, and the last one can be set to an arbitrary value (e. g. 0).

Actually finding the values of the above probabilities is somewhat difficult, and is a problem of computing a particular order statistic (the first, i. e. maximum) of a set of values. However, it can be shown that the resulting expressions are the same as in above formulations, i. e. the two are equivalent.

Estimation of intercept

When using multinomial logistic regression, one category of the dependent variable is chosen as the reference category. Separate odds ratios are determined for all independent variables for each category of the dependent variable with the exception of the reference category, which is omitted from the analysis. The exponential beta coefficient represents the change in the odds of the dependent variable being in a particular category vis-a-vis the reference category, associated with a one unit change of the corresponding independent variable.

Applications

Random multinomial logit models combine a random ensemble of multinomial logit models for use as a classifier.

Multivariate adaptive regression splines

Multivariate adaptive regression splines

Multivariate adaptive regression splines (MARS) is a form of regression analysis introduced by Jerome Friedman in 1991. It is a non-parametric regression technique and can be seen as an extension of linear models that automatically models non-linearities and interactions between variables.

The term "MARS" is trademarked and licensed to Salford Systems. In order to avoid trademark infringements, many open source implementations of MARS are called "Earth".

The basics

This section introduces MARS using a few examples. We start with a set of data: a matrix of input variables x, and a vector of the observed responses y, with a response for each row in x. For example, the data could be:

x   y
10.5   16.4
10.7   18.8
10.8   19.7
...   ...
20.6   77.0

Here there is only one independent variable, so the x matrix is just a single column. Given these measurements, we would like to build a model which predicts the expected y for a given x.

A linear model for the above data is

The hat on the indicates that is estimated from the data. The figure on the right shows a plot of this function: a line giving the predicted versus x, with the original values of y shown as red dots.

The data at the extremes of x indicates that the relationship between y and x may be non-linear (look at the red dots relative to the regression line at low and high values of x). We thus turn to MARS to automatically build a model taking into account non-linearities. MARS software constructs a model from the given x and y as follows

A simple MARS model of the same data

The figure on the right shows a plot of this function: the predicted versus x, with the original values of y once again shown as red dots. The predicted response is now a better fit to the original y values.

MARS has automatically produced a kink in the predicted y to take into account non-linearity. The kink is produced by hinge functions. The hinge functions are the expressions starting with (where is if , else). Hinge functions are described in more detail below.

In this simple example, we can easily see from the plot that y has a non-linear relationship with x (and might perhaps guess that y varies with the square of x). However, in general there will be multiple independent variables, and the relationship between y and these variables will be unclear and not easily visible by plotting. We can use MARS to discover that non-linear relationship.

An example MARS expression with multiple variables is

Variable interaction in a MARS model
This expression models air pollution (the ozone level) as a function of the temperature and a few other variables. Note that the last term in the formula (on the last line) incorporates an interaction between and .

The figure on the right plots the predicted as and vary, with the other variables fixed at their median values. The figure shows that wind does not affect the ozone level unless visibility is low. We see that MARS can build quite flexible regression surfaces by combining hinge functions.

To obtain the above expression, the MARS model building procedure automatically selects which variables to use (some variables are important, others not), the positions of the kinks in the hinge functions, and how the hinge functions are combined.

The MARS model

MARS builds models of the form

.

The model is a weighted sum of basis functions . Each is a constant coefficient. For example, each line in the formula for ozone above is one basis function multiplied by its coefficient.

Each basis function takes one of the following three forms:

1) a constant 1. There is just one such term, the intercept. In the ozone formula above, the intercept term is 5. 2.

2) a hinge function. A hinge function has the form or . MARS automatically selects variables and values of those variables for knots of the hinge functions. Examples of such basis functions can be seen in the middle three lines of the ozone formula.

3) a product of two or more hinge functions. These basis function

can model interaction between two or more variables. An example is the last line of the ozone formula.

Hinge functions

A mirrored pair of hinge functions with a knot at x=3. 1
Hinge functions are a key part of MARS models. A hinge function takes the form

or

where is a constant, called the knot. The figure on the right shows a mirrored pair of hinge functions with a knot at 3. 1.

A hinge function is zero for part of its range, so can be used to partition the data into disjoint regions, each of which can be treated independently. Thus for example a mirrored pair of hinge functions in the expression

creates the piecewise linear graph shown for the simple MARS model in the previous section.

One might assume that only piecewise linear functions can be formed from hinge functions, but hinge functions can be multiplied together to form non-linear functions.

Hinge functions are also called hockey stick functions. Instead of the notation used in this article, hinge functions are often represented by where means take the positive part.

The model building process

MARS builds a model in two phases: the forward and the backward pass. This two stage approach is the same as that used by recursive partitioning trees.

The forward pass

MARS starts with a model which consists of just the intercept term (which is the mean of the response values).

MARS then repeatedly adds basis function in pairs to the model. At each step it finds the pair of basis functions that gives the maximum reduction in sum-of-squares residual error (it is a greedy algorithm). The two basis functions in the pair are identical except that a different side of a mirrored hinge function is used for each function. Each new basis function consists of a term already in the model (which could perhaps be the intercept i. e. a constant 1) multiplied by a new hinge function. A hinge function is defined by a variable and a knot, so to add a new basis function, MARS must search over all combinations of the following:

1) existing terms (called parent terms in this context)

2) all variables (to select one for the new basis function)

3) all values of each variable (for the knot of the new hinge function).

This process of adding terms continues until the change in residual error is too small to continue or until the maximum number of terms is reached. The maximum number of terms is specified by the user before model building starts.

The search at each step is done in a brute force fashion, but a key aspect of MARS is that because of the nature of hinge functions the search can be done relatively quickly using a fast least-squares update technique. Actually, the search is not quite brute force. The search can be sped up with a heuristic that reduces the number of parent terms to consider at each step ("Fast MARS").

The backward pass

The forward pass usually builds an overfit model. (An overfit model has a good fit to the data used to build the model but will not generalize well to new data.) To build a model with better generalization ability, the backward pass prunes the model. It removes terms one by one, deleting the least effective term at each step until it finds the best submodel. Model subsets are compared using the GCV criterion described below.

The backward pass has an advantage over the forward pass: at any step it can choose any term to delete, whereas the forward pass at each step can only see the next pair of terms.

The forward pass adds terms in pairs, but the backward pass typically discards one side of the pair and so terms are often not seen in pairs in the final model. A paired hinge can be seen in the equation for in the first MARS example above; there are no complete pairs retained in the ozone example.

Generalized cross validation (GCV)

The backward pass uses GCV to compare the performance of model subsets in order to choose the best subset: lower values of GCV are better. The GCV is a form of regularization: it trades off goodness-of-fit against model complexity.

(We want to estimate how well a model performs on new data, not on the training data. Such new data is usually not available at the time of model building, so instead we use GCV to estimate what performance would be on new data. The raw residual sum-of-squares (RSS) on the training data is inadequate for comparing models, because the RSS always increases as MARS terms are dropped. In other words, if the RSS were used to compare models, the backward pass would always choose the largest model -- but the largest model typically does not have the best generalization performance.)

The formula for the GCV is

GCV = RSS / (N * (1 - / N)^2)

where is the residual sum-of-squares measured on the training data and is the number of observations (the number of rows in the x matrix).

The is defined in the MARS context as

= + * (- 1) / 2

where is about 2 or 3 (the MARS software allows the user to preset).

Note that (- 1) / 2 is the number of hinge-function knots, so the formula penalizes the addition of knots. Thus the GCV formula adjusts (i. e. increases) the training RSS to take into account the flexibility of the model. We penalize flexibility because models that are too flexible will model the specific realization of noise in the data instead of just the systematic structure of the data.

Generalized Cross Validation is so named because it uses a formula to approximate the error that would be determined by leave-one-out validation. It is just an approximation but works well in practice. GCVs were introduced by Craven and Wahba and extended by Friedman for MARS.

Constraints

One constraint has already been mentioned: the user can specify the maximum number of terms in the forward pass.

A further constraint can be placed on the forward pass by specifying a maximum allowable degree of interaction. Typically only one or two degrees of interaction are allowed, but higher degrees can be used when the data warrants it. The maximum degree of interaction in the first MARS example above is one (i. e. no interactions or an additive model); in the ozone example it is two.

Other constraints on the forward pass are possible. For example, the user can specify that interactions are allowed only for certain input variables. Such constraints could make sense because of knowledge of the process that generated the data.

Pros and cons

No regression modeling technique is best for all situations. The guidelines below are intended to give an idea of the pros and cons of MARS, but there will be exceptions to the guidelines. It is useful to compare MARS to recursive partitioning and this is done below. (Recursive partitioning is also commonly called regression trees, decision trees, or CART; see the recursive partitioning article for details).

MARS models are more flexible than linear regression models.
MARS models are simple to understand and interpret. Compare the equation for ozone concentration above to, say, the innards of a trained neural network or a random forest.
MARS can handle both continuous and categorical data. MARS tends to be better than recursive partitioning for numeric data because hinges are more appropriate for numeric variables than the piecewise constant segmentation used by recursive partitioning.
Building MARS models often requires little or no data preparation. The hinge functions automatically partition the input data, so the effect of outliers is contained. In this respect MARS is similar to recursive partitioning which also partitions the data into disjoint regions, although using a different method. (Nevertheless, as with most statistical modeling techniques, known outliers should be considered for removal before training a MARS model.)
MARS (like recursive partitioning) does automatic variable selection (meaning it includes important variables in the model and excludes unimportant ones). However, bear in mind that variable selection is not a clean problem and there is usually some arbitrariness in the selection, especially in the presence of collinearity and 'concurvity'.
MARS models tend to have a good bias-variance trade-off. The models are flexible enough to model non-linearity and variable interactions (thus MARS models have fairly low bias), yet the constrained form of MARS basis functions prevents too much flexibility (thus MARS models have fairly low variance).
MARS is suitable for handling fairly large datasets. It is a routine matter to build a MARS model from an input matrix with, say, 100 predictors and 105 observations. Such a model can be built in about a minute on a 1 GHz machine, assuming the maximum degree of interaction of MARS terms is limited to one (i. e. additive terms only). A degree two model with the same data on the same 1 GHz machine takes longer—about 12 minutes. Be aware that these times are highly data dependent. Recursive partitioning is much faster than MARS.
With MARS models, as with any non-parametric regression, parameter confidence intervals and other checks on the model cannot be calculated directly (unlike linear regression models). Cross-validation and related techniques must be used for validating the model instead.

MARS models do not give as good fits as boosted trees, but can be built much more quickly and are more interpretable. (An 'interpretable' model is in a form that makes it clear what the effect of each predictor is.)

The earth, mda, and polspline implementations do not allow missing values in predictors, but free implementations of regression trees (such as rpart and party) do allow missing values using a technique called surrogate splits.

MARS models can make predictions quickly. The prediction function simply has to evaluate the MARS model formula. Compare that to making a prediction with say a Support Vector Machine, where every variable has to be multiplied by the corresponding element of every support vector. That can be a slow process if there many variables and many support vectors.

Naive Bayes classifier

Naive Bayes classifier

A naive Bayes classifier is a simple probabilistic classifier based on applying Bayes' theorem with strong (naive) independence assumptions. A more descriptive term for the underlying probability model would be "independent feature model".

Introduction

In simple terms, a naive Bayes classifier assumes that the presence (or absence) of a particular feature of a class is unrelated to the presence (or absence) of any other feature, given the class variable. For example, a fruit may be considered to be an apple if it is red, round, and about 4" in diameter. Even if these features depend on each other or upon the existence of the other features, a naive Bayes classifier considers all of these properties to independently contribute to the probability that this fruit is an apple.

Depending on the precise nature of the probability model, naive Bayes classifiers can be trained very efficiently in a supervised learning setting. In many practical applications, parameter estimation for naive Bayes models uses the method of maximum likelihood; in other words, one can work with the naive Bayes model without believing in Bayesian probability or using any Bayesian methods.

In spite of their naive design and apparently oversimplified assumptions, naive Bayes classifiers have worked quite well in many complex real-world situations. In 2004, analysis of the Bayesian classification problem has shown that there are some theoretical reasons for the apparently unreasonable efficacy of naive Bayes classifiers. Still, a comprehensive comparison with other classification methods in 2006 showed that Bayes classification is outperformed by more current approaches, such as boosted trees or random forests.

An advantage of the naive Bayes classifier is that it only requires a small amount of training data to estimate the parameters (means and variances of the variables) necessary for classification. Because independent variables are assumed, only the variances of the variables for each class need to be determined and not the entire covariance matrix.

The naive Bayes probabilistic model

Abstractly, the probability model for a classifier is a conditional model

over a dependent class variable with a small number of outcomes or classes, conditional on several feature variables through . The problem is that if the number of features is large or when a feature can take on a large number of values, then basing such a model on probability tables is infeasible. We therefore reformulate the model to make it more tractable.

Using Bayes' theorem, we write

In plain English the above equation can be written as

In practice we are only interested in the numerator of that fraction, since the denominator does not depend on and the values of the features are given, so that the denominator is effectively constant.

The numerator is equivalent to the joint probability model

which can be rewritten as follows, using the chain rule for repeated applications of the definition of conditional probability:

Now the "naive" conditional independence assumptions come into play: assume that each feature is conditionally independent of every other feature for . This means that

for , and so the joint model can be expressed as

This means that under the above independence assumptions, the conditional distribution over the class variable can be expressed like this:

where (the evidence) is a scaling factor dependent only on , i. e. , a constant if the values of the feature variables are known.

Models of this form are much more manageable, since they factor into a so-called class prior and independent probability distributions . If there are classes and if a model for each can be expressed in terms of parameters, then the corresponding naive Bayes model has (k 1) + n r k parameters. In practice, often (binary classification) and (Bernoulli variables as features) are common, and so the total number of parameters of the naive Bayes model is , where is the number of binary features used for classification and prediction.

Parameter estimation

All model parameters (i. e. , class priors and feature probability distributions) can be approximated with relative frequencies from the training set. These are maximum likelihood estimates of the probabilities. A class' prior may be calculated by assuming equiprobable classes (i. e. , priors = 1 / (number of classes)), or by calculating an estimate for the class probability from the training set (i. e. , (prior for a given class) = (number of samples in the class) / (total number of samples)). To estimate the parameters for a feature's distribution, one must assume a distribution or generate nonparametric models for the features from the training set. If one is dealing with continuous data, a typical assumption is that the continuous values associated with each class are distributed according to a Gaussian distribution.

For example, suppose the training data contain a continuous attribute, . We first segment the data by the class, and then compute the mean and variance of in each class. Let be the mean of the values in associated with class c, and let be the variance of the values in associated with class c. Then, the probability of some value given a class, , can be computed by plugging into the equation for a Normal distribution parameterized by and . That is,

Another common technique for handling continuous values is to use binning to discretize the values. In general, the distribution method is a better choice if there is a small amount of training data, or if the precise distribution of the data is known. The discretization method tends to do better if there is a large amount of training data because it will learn to fit the distribution of the data. Since naive Bayes is typically used when a large amount of data is available (as more computationally expensive models can generally achieve better accuracy), the discretization method is generally preferred over the distribution method.

Sample correction

If a given class and feature value never occur together in the training set then the frequency-based probability estimate will be zero. This is problematic since it will wipe out all information in the other probabilities when they are multiplied. It is therefore often desirable to incorporate a small-sample correction in all probability estimates such that no probability is ever set to be exactly zero.

Constructing a classifier from the probability model

The discussion so far has derived the independent feature model, that is, the naive Bayes probability model. The naive Bayes classifier combines this model with a decision rule. One common rule is to pick the hypothesis that is most probable; this is known as the maximum a posteriori or MAP decision rule. The corresponding classifier is the function defined as follows:

Discussion

Despite the fact that the far-reaching independence assumptions are often inaccurate, the naive Bayes classifier has several properties that make it surprisingly useful in practice. In particular, the decoupling of the class conditional feature distributions means that each distribution can be independently estimated as a one dimensional distribution. This helps alleviate problems stemming from the curse of dimensionality, such as the need for data sets that scale exponentially with the number of features. While naive Bayes often fails to produce a good estimate for the correct class probabilities, this may not be a requirement for many applications. For example, the naive Bayes classifier will make the correct MAP decision rule classification so long as the correct class is more probable than any other class. This is true regardless of whether the probability estimate is slightly, or even grossly inaccurate. In this manner, the overall classifier can be robust enough to ignore serious deficiencies in its underlying naive probability model. Other reasons for the observed success of the naive Bayes classifier are discussed in the literature cited below.

Examples

Sex classification

Problem: classify whether a given person is a male or a female based on the measured features. The features include height, weight, and foot size.

Training

Example training set below.

sex	height (feet)	weight (lbs)	foot size(inches)
male	6	180	12
male	5.92 (5'11")	190	11
male	5.58 (5'7")	170	12
male	5.92 (5'11")	165	10
female	5	100	6
female	5.5 (5'6")	150	8
female	5.42 (5'5")	130	7
female	5.75 (5'9")	150	9

The classifier created from the training set using a Gaussian distribution assumption would be:

sex	mean (height)	variance (height)	mean (weight)	variance (weight)	mean (foot size)	variance (foot size)
male	5.855	3.5033e-02	176.25	1.2292e+02	11.25	9.1667e-01
female	5.4175	9.7225e-02	132.5	5.5833e+02	7.5	1.6667e+00

Let's say we have equiprobable classes so P(male)= P(female) = 0.5. This prior probability distribution might be based on our knowledge of frequencies in the larger population, or on frequency in the training set.

Testing

Below is a sample to be classified as a male or female.

sex	height (feet)	weight (lbs)	foot size(inches)
sample	6	130	8

We wish to determine which posterior is greater, male or female. For the classification as male the posterior is given by

For the classification as female the posterior is given by

The evidence (also termed normalizing constant) may be calculated since the sum of the posterior probabilities must equals one.

The evidence may be ignored since it is a positive constant. (That is, the evidence is the same for any sample.) We now determine the probability distribution for the sex of the sample.

where and are the parameters of normal distribution which have been previously determined from the training set. Note that a value greater than 1 is OK here – it is a probability density rather a probability, because height is a continuous variable.

Since posterior numerator is greater in the female case, we predict the sample is female.

Document Classification

Here is a worked example of naive Bayesian classification to the document classification problem. Consider the problem of classifying documents by their content, for example into spam and non-spam e-mails. Imagine that documents are drawn from a number of classes of documents which can be modelled as sets of words where the (independent) probability that the i-th word of a given document occurs in a document from class C can be written as

(For this treatment, we simplify things further by assuming that words are randomly distributed in the document - that is, words are not dependent on the length of the document, position within the document with relation to other words, or other document-context.)

Then the probability that a given document D contains all of the words, given a class C, is

The question that we desire to answer is: "what is the probability that a given document D belongs to a given class C?" In other words, what is ?

Now by definition

and

Bayes' theorem manipulates these into a statement of probability in terms of likelihood.

Assume for the moment that there are only two mutually exclusive classes, S and ¬S (e. g. spam and not spam), such that every element (email) is in either one or the other;

and

Using the Bayesian result above, we can write:

Dividing one by the other gives:

Which can be re-factored as:

Thus, the probability ratio p(S | D) / p(¬S | D) can be expressed in terms of a series of likelihood ratios. The actual probability p(S | D) can be easily computed from log (p(S | D) / p(¬S | D)) based on the observation that p(S | D) + p(¬S | D) = 1.

Taking the logarithm of all these ratios, we have:

(This technique of "log-likelihood ratios" is a common technique in statistics. In the case of two mutually exclusive alternatives (such as this example), the conversion of a log-likelihood ratio to a probability takes the form of a sigmoid curve: see logit for details.)

Finally, the document can be classified as follows. It is spam if (i. e. ,), otherwise it is not spam.

Neural network

Neural network

The term neural network was traditionally used to refer to a network or circuit of biological neurons. The modern usage of the term often refers to artificial neural networks, which are composed of artificial neurons or nodes. Thus the term has two distinct usages:

Biological neural networks are made up of real biological neurons that are connected or functionally related in a nervous system. In the field of neuroscience, they are often identified as groups of neurons that perform a specific physiological function in laboratory analysis.
Artificial neural networks are composed of interconnecting artificial neurons (programming constructs that mimic the properties of biological neurons). Artificial neural networks may either be used to gain an understanding of biological neural networks, or for solving artificial intelligence problems without necessarily creating a model of a real biological system. The real, biological nervous system is highly complex: artificial neural network algorithms attempt to abstract this complexity and focus on what may hypothetically matter most from an information processing point of view. Good performance (e. g. as measured by good predictive ability, low generalization error), or performance mimicking animal or human error patterns, can then be used as one source of evidence towards supporting the hypothesis that the abstraction

really captured something important from the point of view of information processing in the brain. Another incentive for these abstractions is to reduce the amount of computation required to simulate artificial neural networks, so as to allow one to experiment with larger networks and train them on larger data sets.
This article focuses on the relationship between the two concepts; for detailed coverage of the two different concepts refer to the separate articles: biological neural network and artificial neural network.

Overview

A biological neural network is composed of a group or groups of chemically connected or functionally associated neurons. A single neuron may be connected to many other neurons and the total number of neurons and connections in a network may be extensive. Connections, called synapses, are usually formed from axons to dendrites, though dendrodendritic microcircuits and other connections are possible. Apart from the electrical signaling, there are other forms of signaling that arise from neurotransmitter diffusion.

Artificial intelligence and cognitive modeling try to simulate some properties of biological neural networks. While similar in their techniques, the former has the aim of solving particular tasks, while the latter aims to build mathematical models of biological neural systems.

In the artificial intelligence field, artificial neural networks have been applied successfully to speech recognition, image analysis and adaptive control, in order to construct software agents (in computer and video games) or autonomous robots. Most of the currently employed artificial neural networks for artificial intelligence are based on statistical estimations, classification optimization and control theory.

The cognitive modelling field involves the physical or mathematical modeling of the behavior of neural systems; ranging from the individual neural level (e. g. modeling the spike response curves of neurons to a stimulus), through the neural cluster level (e. g. modelling the release and effects of dopamine in the basal ganglia) to the complete organism (e. g. behavioral modelling of the organism's response to stimuli). Artificial intelligence, cognitive modelling, and neural networks are information processing paradigms inspired by the way biological neural systems process data.

History of the neural network analogy

Connectionism
In the brain, spontaneous order appears to arise out of decentralized networks of simple units (neurons).

Neural network theory has served both to better identify how the neurons in the brain function and to provide the basis for efforts to create artificial intelligence. The preliminary theoretical base for contemporary neural networks was independently proposed by Alexander Bain (1873) and William James (1890). In their work, both thoughts and body activity resulted from interactions among neurons within the brain.

For Bain, every activity led to the firing of a certain set of neurons. When activities were repeated, the connections between those neurons strengthened. According to his theory, this repetition was what led to the formation of memory. The general scientific community at the time was skeptical of Bain's theory because it required what appeared to be an inordinate number of neural connections within the brain. It is now apparent that the brain is exceedingly complex and that the same brain "wiring" can handle multiple problems and inputs.

James's theory was similar to Bain's, however, he suggested that memories and actions resulted from electrical currents flowing among the neurons in the brain. His model, by focusing on the flow of electrical currents, did not require individual neural connections for each memory or action.

C. S. Sherrington (1898) conducted experiments to test James's theory. He ran electrical currents down the spinal cords of rats. However, instead of demonstrating an increase in electrical current as projected by James, Sherrington found that the electrical current strength decreased as the testing continued over time. Importantly, this work led to the discovery of the concept of habituation.

McCullouch and Pitts (1943) created a computational model for neural networks based on mathematics and algorithms. They called this model threshold logic. The model paved the way for neural network research to split into two distinct approaches. One approach focused on biological processes in the brain and the other focused on the application of neural networks to artificial intelligence.

In the late 1940s psychologist Donald Hebb created a hypothesis of learning based on the mechanism of neural plasticity that is now known as Hebbian learning. Hebbian learning is considered to be a 'typical' unsupervised learning rule and its later variants were early models for long term potentiation. These ideas started being applied to computational models in 1948 with Turing's B-type machines.

Farley and Clark (1954) first used computational machines, then called calculators, to simulate a Hebbian network at MIT. Other neural network computational machines were created by Rochester, Holland, Habit, and Duda (1956).

Rosenblatt (1958) created the perceptron, an algorithm for pattern recognition based on a two-layer learning computer network using simple addition and subtraction. With mathematical notation, Rosenblatt also described circuitry not in the basic perceptron, such as the exclusive-or circuit, a circuit whose mathematical computation could not be processed until after the backpropagation algorithm was created by Werbos (1975).

The perceptron is essentially a linear classifier for classifying data specified by parameters and an output function . Its parameters are adapted with an ad-hoc rule similar to stochastic steepest gradient descent. Because the inner product is a linear operator in the input space, the perceptron can only perfectly classify a set of data for which different classes are linearly separable in the input space, while it often fails completely for non-separable data. While the development of the algorithm initially generated some enthusiasm, partly because of its apparent relation to biological mechanisms, the later discovery of this inadequacy caused such models to be abandoned until the introduction of non-linear models into the field.

Neural network research stagnated after the publication of

machine learning research by Minsky and Papert (1969). They discovered two key issues with the computational machines that processed neural networks. The first issue was that single-layer neural networks were incapable of processing the exclusive-or circuit. The second significant issue was that computers were not sophisticated enough to effectively handle the long run time required by large neural networks. Neural network research slowed until computers achieved greater processing power. Also key in later advances was the backpropogation algorithm which effectively solved the exclusive-or problem (Werbos 1975).

The cognitron (1975) designed by Kunihiko Fukushima was an early multilayered neural network with a training algorithm. The actual structure of the network and the methods used to set the interconnection weights change from one neural strategy to another, each with its advantages and disadvantages. Networks can propagate information in one direction only, or they can bounce back and forth until self-activation at a node occurs and the network settles on a final state. The ability for bi-directional flow of inputs between neurons/nodes was produced with the Hopfield's network (1982), and specialization of these node layers for specific purposes was introduced through the first hybrid network.

The parallel distributed processing of the mid-1980s became popular under the name connectionism. The text by Rumelhart and McClelland (1986) provided a full exposition on the use of connectionism in computers to simulate neural processes.

The rediscovery of the backpropagation algorithm was probably the main reason behind the repopularisation of neural networks after the publication of "Learning Internal Representations by Error Propagation" in 1986 (Though backpropagation itself dates from 1969). The original network utilized multiple layers of weight-sum units of the type , where was a sigmoid function or logistic function such as used in logistic regression. Training was done by a form of stochastic gradient descent. The employment of the chain rule of differentiation in deriving the appropriate parameter updates results in an algorithm that seems to 'backpropagate errors', hence the nomenclature. However, it is essentially a form of gradient descent. Determining the optimal parameters in a model of this type is not trivial, and local numerical optimization methods such as gradient descent can be sensitive to initialization because of the presence of local minima of the training criterion. In recent times, networks with the same architecture as the backpropagation network are referred to as multilayer perceptrons. This name does not impose any limitations on the type of algorithm used for learning.

The backpropagation network generated much enthusiasm at the time and there was much controversy about whether such learning could be implemented in the brain or not, partly because a mechanism for reverse signaling was not obvious at the time, but most importantly because there was no plausible source for the 'teaching' or 'target' signal. However, since 2006, several unsupervised learning procedures have been proposed for neural networks with one or more layers, using so-called deep learning algorithms. These algorithms can be used to learn intermediate representations, with or without a target signal, that capture the salient features of the distribution of sensory signals arriving at each layer of the neural network.

The brain, neural networks and computers

Neural networks, as used in artificial intelligence, have traditionally been viewed as simplified models of neural processing in the brain, even though the relation between this model and brain biological architecture is debated, as it is not clear to what degree artificial neural networks mirror brain function.

A subject of current research in computational neuroscience is the question surrounding the degree of complexity and the properties that individual neural elements should have to reproduce something resembling animal cognition.

Historically, computers evolved from the von Neumann model, which is based on sequential processing and execution of explicit instructions. On the other hand, the origins of neural networks are based on efforts to model information processing in biological systems, which may rely largely on parallel processing as well as implicit instructions based on recognition of patterns of 'sensory' input from external sources. In other words, at its very heart a neural network is a complex statistical processor (as opposed to being tasked to sequentially process and execute).

Neural coding is concerned with how sensory and other information is represented in the brain by neurons. The main goal of studying neural coding is to characterize the relationship between the stimulus and the individual or ensemble neuronal responses and the relationship among electrical activity of the neurons in the ensemble. It is thought that neurons can encode both digital and analog information.

Neural networks and artificial intelligence

Artificial neural network
A neural network (NN), in the case of artificial neurons called artificial neural network (ANN) or simulated neural network (SNN), is an interconnected group of natural or artificial neurons that uses a mathematical or computational model for information processing based on a connectionistic approach to computation. In most cases an ANN is an adaptive system that changes its structure based on external or internal information that flows through the network.

In more practical terms neural networks are non-linear statistical data modeling or decision making tools. They can be used to model complex relationships between inputs and outputs or to find patterns in data.

However, the paradigm of neural networks - i. e. , implicit, not explicit , learning is stressed - seems more to correspond to some kind of natural intelligence than to the traditional symbol-based Artificial Intelligence, which would stress, instead, rule-based learning.

Background

An artificial neural network involves a network of simple processing elements (artificial neurons) which can exhibit complex global behavior, determined by the connections between the processing elements and element parameters. Artificial neurons were first proposed in 1943 by Warren McCulloch, a neurophysiologist, and Walter Pitts, a logician, who first collaborated at the University of Chicago.

One classical type of artificial neural network is the recurrent Hopfield net.

In a neural network model simple nodes (which can be called by a number of names, including "neurons", "neurodes", "Processing Elements" (PE) and "units"), are connected together to form a network of nodes — hence the term "neural network". While a neural network does not have to be adaptive per se, its practical use comes with algorithms designed to alter the strength (weights) of the connections in the network to produce a desired signal flow.

In modern software implementations of artificial neural networks the approach inspired by biology has more or less been abandoned for a more practical approach based on statistics and signal processing. In some of these systems, neural networks, or parts of neural networks (such as artificial neurons), are used as components in larger systems that combine both adaptive and non-adaptive elements.

The concept of a neural network appears to have first been proposed by Alan Turing in his 1948 paper "Intelligent Machinery".

Applications of natural and of artificial neural networks

The utility of artificial neural network models lies in the fact that they can be used to infer a function from observations and also to use it. Unsupervised neural networks can also be used to learn representations of the input that capture the salient characteristics of the input distribution, e. g. , see the Boltzmann machine (1983), and more recently, deep learning algorithms, which can implicitly learn the distribution function of the observed data. Learning in neural networks is particularly useful in applications where the complexity of the data or task makes the design of such functions by hand impractical.

The tasks to which artificial neural networks are applied tend to fall within the following broad categories:

Function approximation, or regression analysis, including time series prediction and modeling.
Classification, including pattern and sequence recognition, novelty

detection and sequential decision making.
Data processing, including filtering, clustering, blind signal separation and compression.
Application areas of ANNs include system identification and control (vehicle control, process control), game-playing and decision making (backgammon, chess, racing), pattern recognition (radar systems, face identification, object recognition), sequence recognition (gesture, speech, handwritten text recognition), medical diagnosis, financial applications, data mining (or knowledge discovery in databases, "KDD"), visualization and e-mail spam filtering.

Neural networks and neuroscience

Theoretical and computational neuroscience is the field concerned with the theoretical analysis and computational modeling of biological neural systems. Since neural systems are intimately related to cognitive processes and behaviour, the field is closely related to cognitive and behavioural modeling.

The aim of the field is to create models of biological neural systems in order to understand how biological systems work. To gain this understanding, neuroscientists strive to make a link between observed biological processes (data), biologically plausible mechanisms for neural processing and learning (biological neural network models) and theory (statistical learning theory and information theory).

Types of models

Many models are used; defined at a different levels of abstraction, and modeling different aspects of neural systems. They range from models of the short-term behaviour of individual neurons, through models of the dynamics of neural circuitry arising from interactions between individual neurons, to models of behaviour arising from abstract neural modules that represent complete subsystems. These include models of the long-term and short-term plasticity of neural systems and its relation to learning and memory, from the individual neuron to the system level.

Current research

While initially research had been concerned mostly with the electrical characteristics of neurons, a particularly important part of the investigation in recent years has been the exploration of the role of neuromodulators such as dopamine, acetylcholine, and serotonin on behaviour and learning.

Biophysical models, such as BCM theory, have been important in understanding mechanisms for synaptic plasticity, and have had applications in both computer science and neuroscience. Research is ongoing in understanding the computational algorithms used in the brain, with some recent biological evidence for radial basis networks and neural backpropagation as mechanisms for processing data.

Computational devices have been created in CMOS for both biophysical simulation and neuromorphic computing. More recent efforts show promise for creating nanodevices for very large scale principal components analyses and convolution. If successful, these efforts could usher in a new era of neural computing that is a step beyond digital computing, because it depends on learning rather than programming and because it is fundamentally analog rather than digital even though the first instantiations may in fact be with CMOS digital devices.

Architecture

The basic architecture consists of three types of neuron layers: input, hidden, and output. In feed-forward networks, the signal flow is from input to output units, strictly in a feed-forward direction. The data processing can extend over multiple layers of units, but no feedback connections are present. Recurrent networks contain feedback connections. Contrary to feed-forward networks, the dynamical properties of the network are important. In some cases, the activation values of the units undergo a relaxation process such that the network will evolve to a stable state in which these activations do not change anymore.

In other applications, the changes of the activation values of the output neurons are significant, such that the dynamical behavior constitutes the output of the network. Other neural network architectures include adaptive resonance theory maps and competitive networks.

Criticism

A common criticism of neural networks, particularly in robotics, is that they require a large diversity of training for real-world operation. This is not surprising, since any learning machine needs sufficient representative examples in order to capture the underlying structure that allows it to generalize to new cases. Dean Pomerleau, in his research presented in the paper "Knowledge-based Training of Artificial Neural Networks for Autonomous Robot Driving," uses a neural network to train a robotic vehicle to drive on multiple types of roads (single lane, multi-lane, dirt, etc.). A large amount of his research is devoted to (1) extrapolating multiple training scenarios from a single training experience, and (2) preserving past training diversity so that the system does not become overtrained (if, for example, it is presented with a series of right turns – it should not learn to always turn right). These issues are common in neural networks that must decide from amongst a wide variety of responses, but can be dealt with in several ways, for example by randomly shuffling the training examples, by using a numerical optimization algorithm that does not take too large steps when changing the network connections following an example, or by grouping examples in so-called mini-batches.

A. K. Dewdney, a former Scientific American columnist, wrote in 1997, "Although neural nets do solve a few toy problems, their powers of computation are so limited that I am surprised anyone takes them seriously as a general problem-solving tool. " (Dewdney, p. 82)

Arguments for Dewdney's position are that to implement large and effective software neural networks, much processing and storage resources need to be committed. While the brain has hardware tailored to the task of processing signals through a graph of neurons, simulating even a most simplified form on Von Neumann technology may compel a NN designer to fill many millions of database rows for its connections - which can consume vast amounts of computer memory and hard disk space. Furthermore, the designer of NN systems will often need to simulate the transmission of signals through many of these connections and their associated neurons - which must often be matched with incredible amounts of CPU processing power and time. While neural networks often yield effective programs, they too often do so at the cost of efficiency (they tend to consume considerable amounts of time and money).

Arguments against Dewdney's position are that neural nets have been successfully used to solve many complex and diverse tasks, ranging from autonomously flying aircraft to detecting credit card fraud.

Technology writer Roger Bridgman commented on Dewdney's statements about neural nets:

Neural networks, for instance, are in the dock not only because they have been hyped to high heaven, (what hasn't?) but also because you could create a successful net without understanding how it worked: the bunch of numbers that captures its behaviour would in all probability be "an opaque, unreadable table. . . valueless as a scientific resource". In spite of his emphatic declaration that science is not technology, Dewdney seems here to pillory neural nets as bad science when most of those devising them are just trying to be good engineers. An unreadable table that a useful machine could read would still be well worth having.

In response to this kind of criticism, one should note that although it is true that analyzing what has been learned by an artificial neural network is difficult, it is much easier to do so than to analyze what has been learned by a biological neural network. Furthermore, researchers involved in exploring learning algorithms for neural networks are gradually uncovering generic principles which allow a learning machine to be successful. For example, Bengio and LeCun (2007) wrote an article regarding local vs non-local learning, as well as shallow vs deep architecture .

Some other criticisms came from believers of hybrid models (combining neural networks and symbolic approaches). They advocate the intermix of these two approaches and believe that hybrid models can better capture the mechanisms of the human mind (Sun and Bookman, 1990).

Pattern recognition

Pattern recognition

In machine learning, pattern recognition is the assignment of a label to a given input value. An example of pattern recognition is classification, which attempts to assign each input value to one of a given set of classes (for example, determine whether a given email is "spam" or "non-spam"). However, pattern recognition is a more general problem that encompasses other types of output as well. Other examples are regression, which assigns a real-valued output to each input; sequence labeling, which assigns a class to each member of a sequence of values (for example, part of speech tagging, which assigns a part of speech to each word in an input sentence); and parsing, which assigns a parse tree to an input sentence, describing the syntactic structure of the sentence.

Pattern recognition algorithms generally aim to provide a reasonable answer for all possible inputs and to do "fuzzy" matching of inputs. This is opposed to pattern matching algorithms, which look for exact matches in the input with pre-existing patterns. A common example of a pattern-matching algorithm is regular expression matching, which looks for patterns of a given sort in textual data and is included in the search capabilities of many text editors and word processors. In contrast to pattern recognition, pattern matching is generally not considered a type of machine learning, although pattern-matching algorithms (especially with fairly general, carefully tailored patterns) can sometimes succeed in providing similar-quality output to the sort provided by pattern-recognition algorithms.

Pattern recognition is studied in many fields, including psychology, psychiatry, ethology, cognitive science, traffic flow and computer science.

Overview

Pattern recognition is generally categorized according to the type of learning procedure used to generate the output value. Supervised learning assumes that a set of training data (the training set) has been provided, consisting of a set of instances that have been properly labeled by hand with the correct output. A learning procedure then generates a model that attempts to meet two sometimes conflicting objectives: Perform as well as possible on the training data, and generalize as well as possible to new data (usually, this means being as simple as possible, for some technical definition of "simple", in accordance with Occam's Razor). Unsupervised learning, on the other hand, assumes training data that has not been hand-labeled, and attempts to find inherent patterns in the data that can then be used to determine the correct output value for new data instances. A combination of the two that has recently been explored is semi-supervised learning, which uses a combination of labeled and unlabeled data (typically a small set of labeled data combined with a large amount of unlabeled data). Note that in cases of unsupervised learning, there may be no training data at all to speak of; in other words, the data to be labeled is the training data.

Note that sometimes different terms are used to describe the corresponding supervised and unsupervised learning procedures for the same type of output. For example, the unsupervised equivalent of classification is normally known as clustering, based on the common perception of the task as involving no training data to speak of, and of grouping the input data into clusters based on some inherent similarity measure (e. g. the distance between instances, considered as vectors in a multi-dimensional vector space), rather than assigning each input instance into one of a set of pre-defined classes. Note also that in some fields, the terminology is different: For example, in community ecology, the term "classification" is used to refer to what is commonly known as "clustering".

The piece of input data for which an output value is generated is formally termed an instance. The instance is formally described by a vector of features, which together constitute a description of all known characteristics of the instance. (These feature vectors can be seen as defining points in an appropriate multidimensional space, and methods for manipulating vectors in vector spaces can be correspondingly applied to them, such as computing the dot product or the angle between two vectors.) Typically, features are either categorical (also known as nominal, i. e. consisting of one of a set of unordered items, such as a gender of "male" or "female", or a blood type of "A", "B", "AB" or "O"), ordinal (consisting of one of a set of ordered items, e. g. "large", "medium" or "small"), integer-valued (e. g. a count of the number of occurrences of a particular word in an email) or real-valued (e. g. a measurement of blood pressure). Often, categorical and ordinal data are grouped together; likewise for integer-valued and real-valued data. Furthermore, many algorithms work only in terms of categorical data and require that real-valued or integer-valued data be discretized into groups (e. g. less than 5, between 5 and 10, or greater than 10).

Many common pattern recognition algorithms are probabilistic in nature, in that they use statistical inference to find the best label for a given instance. Unlike other algorithms, which simply output a "best" label, oftentimes probabilistic algorithms also output a probability of the instance being described by the given label. In addition, many probabilistic algorithms output a list of the N-best labels with associated probabilities, for some value of N, instead of simply a single best label. When the number of possible labels is fairly small (e. g. in the case of classification), N may be set so that the probability of all possible labels is output. Probabilistic algorithms have many advantages over non-probabilistic algorithms:

They output a confidence value associated with their choice. (Note that some other algorithms may also output confidence values, but in general, only for probabilistic algorithms is this value mathematically grounded in probability theory. Non-probabilistic confidence values can in general not be given any specific meaning, and only used to compare against other confidence values output by the same algorithm.)
Correspondingly, they can abstain when the confidence of choosing any particular output is too low.
Because of the probabilities output, probabilistic pattern-recognition algorithms can be more effectively incorporated into larger machine-learning tasks, in a way that partially or completely avoids the problem of error propagation.
Techniques to transform the raw feature vectors are sometimes used prior to application of the pattern-matching algorithm. For example, feature extraction algorithms attempt to reduce a large-dimensionality feature vector into a smaller-dimensionality vector that is easier to work with and encodes less redundancy, using mathematical techniques such as principal components analysis (PCA). Feature selection algorithms, attempt to directly prune out redundant or irrelevant features. The distinction between the two is that the resulting features after feature extraction has taken place are of a different sort than the original features and may not easily be interpretable, while the features left after feature selection are

simply a subset of the original features.

Problem statement (supervised version)

Formally, the problem of supervised pattern recognition can be stated as follows: Given an unknown function (the ground truth) that maps input instances to output labels , along with training data assumed to represent accurate examples of the mapping, produce a function that approximates as closely as possible the correct mapping . (For example, if the problem is filtering spam, then is some representation of an email and is either "spam" or "non-spam"). In order for this to be a well-defined problem, "approximates as closely as possible" needs to be defined rigorously. In decision theory, this is defined by specifying a loss function that assigns a specific value to "loss" resulting from producing an incorrect label. The goal then is to minimize the expected loss, with the expectation taken over the probability distribution of . In practice, neither the distribution of nor the ground truth function are known exactly, but can be computed only empirically by collecting a large number of samples of and hand-labeling them using the correct value of (a time-consuming process, which is typically the limiting factor in the amount of data of this sort that can be collected). The particular loss function depends on the type of label being predicted. For example, in the case of classification, the simple zero-one loss function is often sufficient. This corresponds simply to assigning a loss of 1 to any incorrect labeling and is equivalent to computing the accuracy of the classification procedure over the set of test data (i. e. counting up the fraction of instances that the learned function labels correctly. The goal of the learning procedure is to maximize this test accuracy on a "typical" test set.

For a probabilistic pattern recognizer, the problem is instead to estimate the probability of each possible output label given a particular input instance, i. e. to estimate a function of the form

where the feature vector input is , and the function f is typically parameterized by some parameters . In a discriminative approach to the problem, f is estimated directly. In a generative approach, however, the inverse probability is instead estimated and combined with the prior probability using Bayes' rule, as follows:

When the labels are continuously distributed (e. g. in regression analysis), the denominator involves integration rather than summation:

The value of is typically learned using maximum a posteriori (MAP) estimation. This finds the best value that simultaneously meets two conflicting objects: To perform as well as possible on the training data and to find the simplest possible model. Essentially, this combines maximum likelihood estimation with a regularization procedure that favors simpler models over more complex models. In a Bayesian context, the regularization procedure can be viewed as placing a prior probability on different values of . Mathematically:

where is the value used for in the subsequent evaluation procedure, and , the posterior probability of , is given by

In the Bayesian approach to this problem, instead of choosing a single parameter vector , the probability of a given label for a new instance is computed by integrating over all possible values of , weighted according to the posterior probability:

Uses

Within medical science, pattern recognition is the basis for computer-aided diagnosis (CAD) systems. CAD describes a procedure that supports the doctor's interpretations and findings.

Other typical applications of pattern recognition techniques are automatic speech recognition, classification of text into several categories (e. g. spam/non-spam email messages), the automatic recognition of handwritten postal codes on postal envelopes, automatic recognition of images of human faces, or handwriting image extraction from medical forms. The last two examples form the subtopic image analysis of pattern recognition that deals with digital images as input to pattern recognition systems.

The method of signing one's name was captured with stylus and overlay starting in 1990. The strokes, speed, relative min, relative max, acceleration and pressure is used to uniquely identify and confirm identity. Banks were first offered this technology, but were content to collect from the FDIC for any bank fraud and did not want to inconvenience customers. .

Neural networks (neural net classifiers) have many real-world applications in image processing, a few examples:

identification and authentication: e. g. , license plate recognition, fingerprint analysis and face detection/verification;
medical diagnosis: e. g. , screening for cervical cancer (Papnet) or breast tumors;
defence: various navigation and guidance systems, target recognition systems, etc.
For a discussion of the aforementioned applications of neural networks in image processing, see e. g. .

Algorithms

Algorithms for pattern recognition depend on the type of label output, on whether learning is supervised or unsupervised, and on whether the algorithm is statistical or non-statistical in nature. Statistical algorithms can further be categorized as generative or discriminative.

Classification algorithms (supervised algorithms predicting categorical labels)

Maximum entropy classifier (aka logistic regression, multinomial logistic regression): Note that logistic regression is an algorithm for classification, despite its name. (The name comes from the fact that logistic regression uses an extension of a linear regression model to model the probability of an input being in a particular class.)
Naive Bayes classifier
Decision trees, decision lists
Support vector machines
Kernel estimation and K-nearest-neighbor algorithms

Perceptrons
Neural networks (multi-level perceptrons)

Clustering algorithms (unsupervised algorithms predicting categorical labels)

Categorical mixture models
K-means clustering
Hierarchical clustering (agglomerative or divisive)
Kernel principal component analysis (Kernel PCA)
Deep learning methods

Regression algorithms (predicting real-valued labels)

Supervised:

Linear regression and extensions
Neural networks
Gaussian process regression (kriging)
Unsupervised:

Principal components analysis (PCA)
Independent component analysis (ICA)

Categorical sequence labeling algorithms (predicting sequences of categorical labels)

Supervised:

Hidden Markov models (HMMs)
Maximum entropy Markov models (MEMMs)
Conditional random fields (CRFs)
Unsupervised:

Hidden Markov models (HMMs)

Real-valued sequence labeling algorithms (predicting sequences of real-valued labels)

Supervised (?):

Kalman filters

Particle filters
Unsupervised:

??

Parsing algorithms (predicting tree structured labels)

Supervised and unsupervised:

Probabilistic context free grammars (PCFGs)

General algorithms for predicting arbitrarily-structured labels

Bayesian networks
Markov random fields

Ensemble learning algorithms (supervised meta-algorithms for combining multiple learning algorithms together)

Bootstrap aggregating ("bagging")
Boosting (meta-algorithm)
Ensemble averaging
Mixture of experts, hierarchical mixture of experts

Physics

Physics - ,

Physics (from Ancient Greek: □□□□□ physis "nature") is a natural science that involves the study of matter and its motion through space and time, along with related concepts such as energy and force. More broadly, it is the general analysis of nature, conducted in order to understand how the universe behaves.

Physics is one of the oldest academic disciplines, perhaps the oldest through its inclusion of astronomy. Over the last two millennia, physics was a part of natural philosophy along with chemistry, certain branches of mathematics, and biology, but during the Scientific Revolution in the 17th century, the natural sciences emerged as unique research programs in their own right. Physics intersects with many interdisciplinary areas of research, such as biophysics and quantum chemistry, and the boundaries of physics are not rigidly defined. New ideas in physics often explain the fundamental mechanisms of other sciences, while opening new avenues of research in areas such as mathematics and philosophy.

Physics also makes significant contributions through advances in new technologies that arise from theoretical breakthroughs. For example, advances in the understanding of electromagnetism or nuclear physics led directly to the development of new products which have dramatically transformed modern-day society, such as television, computers, domestic appliances, and nuclear weapons; advances in thermodynamics led to the development of industrialization; and advances in mechanics inspired the development of calculus.

History

History of physics
As noted below, the means used to understand the behavior of natural phenomena and their effects evolved from philosophy, progressively replaced by natural philosophy then natural science, to eventually arrive at the modern conception of physics.

Natural philosophy has its origins in Greece during the Archaic period, (650 BCE – 480 BCE), when Pre-Socratic philosophers like Thales refused supernatural, religious or mythological explanations for natural phenomena and proclaimed that every event had a natural cause. They proposed ideas verified by reason and observation and many of their hypotheses proved successful in experiment, for example atomism.

Classical physics became a separate science when early modern Europeans used these experimental and quantitative methods to discover what are now considered to be the laws of physics. Kepler, Galileo and more specifically Newton discovered and unified the different laws of motion. Experimental physics had its debuts with experimentation concerning statics by medieval Muslim physicists like al-Biruni and Alhazen. During the industrial revolution, as energy needs increased, so did research, which led to the discovery of new laws in thermodynamics, chemistry and electromagnetics.

Modern physics started with the works of Max Planck in quantum theory and Einstein in relativity, and continued in quantum mechanics pioneered by Heisenberg, Schrödinger and Paul Dirac.

Philosophy

Philosophy of physics
In many ways, physics stems from ancient Greek philosophy. From Thales' first attempt to characterize matter, to Democritus' deduction that matter ought to reduce to an invariant state, the Ptolemaic astronomy of a crystalline firmament, and Aristotle's book Physics (an early book on physics, which attempted to analyze and define motion from a philosophical point of view), various Greek philosophers advanced their own theories of nature. Physics was known as natural philosophy until the late 18th century.

By the 19th century physics was realized as a discipline distinct from philosophy and the other sciences. Physics, as with the rest of science, relies on philosophy of science to give an adequate description of the scientific method. The scientific method employs a priori reasoning as well as a posteriori reasoning and the use of Bayesian inference to measure the validity of a given theory.

The development of physics has answered many questions of early philosophers, but has also raised new questions. Study of the philosophical issues surrounding physics, the philosophy of physics, involves issues such as the nature of space and time, determinism, and metaphysical outlooks such as empiricism, naturalism and realism.

Many physicists have written about the philosophical implications of their work, for instance Laplace, who championed causal determinism, and Erwin Schrödinger, who wrote on quantum mechanics. The mathematical physicist Roger Penrose has been called a Platonist by Stephen Hawking, a view Penrose discusses in his book, The Road to Reality. Hawking refers to himself as an "unashamed reductionist" and takes issue with Penrose's views.

Core theories

Though physics deals with a wide variety of systems, certain theories are used by all physicists. Each of these theories were experimentally tested numerous times and found correct as an approximation of nature (within a certain domain of validity). For instance, the theory of classical mechanics accurately describes the motion of objects, provided they are much larger than atoms and moving at much less than the speed of light. These theories continue to be areas of active research, and a remarkable aspect of classical mechanics known as chaos was discovered in the 20th century, three centuries after the original formulation of classical mechanics by Isaac Newton (1642–1727).

These central theories are important tools for research into more specialized topics, and any physicist, regardless of his or her specialization, is expected to be literate in them. These include classical mechanics, quantum mechanics, thermodynamics and statistical mechanics, electromagnetism, and special relativity.

Classical physics

Classical physics
Classical physics includes the traditional branches and topics that were recognized and well-developed before the beginning of the 20th century—classical mechanics, acoustics, optics, thermodynamics, and electromagnetism. Classical mechanics) is concerned with bodies acted on by forces and bodies in motion and may be divided into statics (study of the forces on a body or bodies at rest), kinematics (study of motion without regard to its causes), and dynamics (study of motion and the forces that affect it); mechanics may also be divided into solid mechanics and fluid mechanics (known together as continuum mechanics), the latter including such branches as hydrostatics, hydrodynamics, aerodynamics, and pneumatics. Acoustics, the study of sound, is often considered a branch of mechanics because sound is due to the motions of the particles of air or other medium through which sound waves can travel and thus can be explained in terms of the laws of mechanics. Among the important modern branches of acoustics is ultrasonics, the study of sound waves of very high frequency beyond the range of human hearing. Optics, the study of light, is concerned not only with visible light but also with infrared and ultraviolet radiation, which exhibit all of the phenomena of visible light except visibility, e. g. , reflection, refraction, interference, diffraction, dispersion, and polarization of light. Heat is a form of energy, the internal energy possessed by the particles

of which a substance is composed; thermodynamics deals with the relationships between heat and other forms of energy. Electricity and magnetism have been studied as a single branch of physics since the intimate connection between them was discovered in the early 19th century; an electric current gives rise to a magnetic field and a changing magnetic field induces an electric current. Electrostatics deals with electric charges at rest, electrodynamics with moving charges, and magnetostatics with magnetic poles at rest.

Modern physics

Modern physics
Classical physics is generally concerned with matter and energy on the normal scale of observation, while much of modern physics is concerned with the behavior of matter and energy under extreme conditions or on the very large or very small scale. For example, atomic and nuclear physics studies matter on the smallest scale at which chemical elements can be identified. The physics of elementary particles is on an even smaller scale, as it is concerned with the most basic units of matter; this branch of physics is also known as high-energy physics because of the extremely high energies necessary to produce many types of particles in large particle accelerators. On this scale, ordinary, commonsense notions of space, time, matter, and energy are no longer valid.

The two chief theories of modern physics present a different picture of the concepts of space, time, and matter from that presented by classical physics. Quantum theory is concerned with the discrete, rather than continuous, nature of many phenomena at the atomic and subatomic level, and with the complementary aspects of particles and waves in the description of such phenomena. The theory of relativity is concerned with the description of phenomena that take place in a frame of reference that is in motion with respect to an observer; the special theory of relativity is concerned with relative uniform motion in a straight line and the general theory of relativity with accelerated motion and its connection with gravitation. Both quantum theory and the theory of relativity find applications in all areas of modern physics.

Difference between classical and modern physics

While physics aims to discover universal laws, its theories lie in explicit domains of applicability. Loosely speaking, the laws of classical physics accurately describe systems whose important length scales are greater than the atomic scale and whose motions are much slower than the speed of light. Outside of this domain, observations do not match their predictions. Albert Einstein contributed the framework of special relativity, which replaced notions of absolute time and space with spacetime and allowed an accurate description of systems whose components have speeds approaching the speed of light. Max Planck, Erwin Schrödinger, and others introduced quantum mechanics, a probabilistic notion of particles and interactions that allowed an accurate description of atomic and subatomic scales. Later, quantum field theory unified quantum mechanics and special relativity. General relativity allowed for a dynamical, curved spacetime, with which highly massive systems and the large-scale structure of the universe can be well-described. General relativity has not yet been unified with the other fundamental descriptions; several candidate theories of quantum gravity are being developed.

Relation to other fields

Prerequisites

Mathematics is the language used for compact description of the order in nature, especially the laws of physics. This was noted and advocated by Pythagoras, Plato, Galileo, and Newton.

Physics theories use mathematics to obtain order and provide precise formulas, precise or estimated solutions, quantitative results and predictions. Experiment results in physics are numerical measurements. Technologies based on mathematics, like computation have made computational physics an active area of research.

Ontology is a prerequisite for physics, but not for mathematics. It means physics is ultimately concerned with descriptions of the real world, while mathematics is concerned with abstract patterns, even beyond the real world. Thus physics statements are synthetic, while math statements are analytic. Mathematics contains hypotheses, while physics contains theories. Mathematics statements have to be only logically true, while predictions of physics statements must match observed and experimental data.

The distinction is clear-cut, but not always obvious. For example, mathematical physics is the application of mathematics in physics. Its methods are mathematical, but its subject is physical. The problems in this field start with a "math model of a physical situation" and a "math description of a physical law". Every math statement used for solution has a hard-to-find physical meaning. The final mathematical solution has an easier-to-find meaning, because it is what the solver is looking for.

Physics is a branch of fundamental science, not practical science. Physics is also called "the fundamental science" because the subject of study of all branches of natural science like chemistry, astronomy, geology and biology are constrained by laws of physics. For example, chemistry studies properties, structures, and reactions of matter (chemistry's focus on the atomic scale distinguishes it from physics). Structures are formed because particles exert electrical forces on each other, properties include physical characteristics of given substances, and reactions are bound by laws of physics, like conservation of energy, mass and charge.

Physics is applied in industries like engineering and medicine.

Application and influence

Applied physics
Applied physics is a general term for physics research which is intended for a particular use. An applied physics curriculum usually contains a few classes in an applied discipline, like geology or electrical engineering. It usually differs from engineering in that an applied physicist may not be designing something in particular, but rather is using physics or conducting physics research with the aim of developing new technologies or solving a problem.

The approach is similar to that of applied mathematics. Applied physicists can also be interested in the use of physics for scientific research. For instance, people working on accelerator physics might seek to build better particle detectors for research in theoretical physics.

Physics is used heavily in engineering. For example, statics, a subfield of mechanics, is used in the building of bridges and other structures. The understanding and use of acoustics results in better concert halls; similarly, the use of optics creates better optical devices. An understanding of physics makes for more realistic flight simulators, video games, and movies, and is often critical in forensic investigations.

With the standard consensus that the laws of physics are universal and do not change with time, physics can be used to study things that would ordinarily be mired in uncertainty. For example, in the study of the origin of the earth, one can reasonably model earth's mass, temperature, and rate of rotation, over time. It also allows for simulations in engineering which drastically speed up the development of a new technology.

But there is also considerable interdisciplinarity in the physicist's methods and so many other important fields are influenced by physics, e. g. the fields of econophysics and sociophysics.

Research

Scientific method

Physicists use a scientific method to test the validity of a physical theory, using a methodical approach to compare the implications of the theory in question with the associated conclusions drawn from experiments and observations conducted to test it. Experiments and observations are collected and compared with the predictions and hypotheses made by a theory, thus aiding in the determination or the validity/invalidity of the theory.

A scientific law is a concise verbal or mathematical statement of a relation that expresses a fundamental principle of a theory, like Newton's law of universal gravitation.

Theory and experiment

Theorists seek to develop mathematical models that both agree with existing experiments and successfully predict future results, while experimentalists devise and perform experiments to test theoretical predictions and explore new phenomena. Although theory and experiment are developed separately, they are strongly dependent upon each other. Progress in physics frequently comes about when experimentalists make a discovery that existing theories cannot explain, or when new theories generate experimentally testable predictions, which inspire new experiments.

Physicists who work at the interplay of theory and experiment are called phenomenologists. Phenomenologists look at the complex phenomena observed in experiment and work to relate them to fundamental theory.

Theoretical physics has historically taken inspiration from philosophy; electromagnetism was unified this way. Beyond the known universe, the field of theoretical physics also deals with hypothetical issues, such as parallel universes, a multiverse, and higher dimensions. Theorists invoke these ideas in hopes of solving particular problems with existing theories. They then explore the consequences of these ideas and work toward making testable predictions.

Experimental physics informs, and is informed by, engineering and technology. Experimental physicists involved in basic research design and perform experiments with equipment such as particle accelerators and lasers, whereas those involved in applied research often work in industry, developing technologies such as magnetic resonance imaging (MRI) and transistors. Feynman has noted that experimentalists may seek areas which are not well-explored by theorists.

Scope and aims

Physics covers a wide range of phenomena, from elementary particles (such as quarks, neutrinos and electrons) to the largest superclusters of galaxies. Included in these phenomena are the most basic objects composing all other things. Therefore physics is sometimes called the "fundamental science". Physics aims to describe the various phenomena that occur in nature in terms of simpler phenomena. Thus, physics aims to both connect the things observable to humans to root causes, and then connect these causes together.

For example, the ancient Chinese observed that certain rocks (lodestone) were attracted to one another by some invisible force. This effect was later called magnetism, and was first rigorously studied in the 17th century. A little earlier than the Chinese, the ancient Greeks knew of other objects such as amber, that when rubbed with fur would cause a similar invisible attraction between the two. This was also first studied rigorously in the 17th century, and came to be called electricity. Thus, physics had come to understand two observations of nature in terms of some root cause (electricity and magnetism). However, further work in the 19th century revealed that these two forces were just two different aspects of one force—electromagnetism. This process of "unifying" forces continues today, and electromagnetism and the weak nuclear force are now considered to be two aspects of the electroweak interaction. Physics hopes to find an ultimate reason (Theory of Everything) for why nature is as it is (see section below for more information).

Research fields

Contemporary research in physics can be broadly divided into condensed matter physics; atomic, molecular, and optical physics; particle physics; astrophysics; geophysics and biophysics. Some physics departments also support research in Physics education.

Since the 20th century, the individual fields of physics have become increasingly specialized, and today most physicists work in a single field for their entire careers. "Universalists" such as Albert Einstein (1879–1955) and Lev Landau (1908–1968), who worked in multiple fields of physics, are now very rare.

Table of the major fields of physics, along with their subfields and the theories they employ[show]
Condensed matter

Condensed matter physics

Condensed matter physics is the field of physics that deals with the macroscopic physical properties of matter. In particular, it is concerned with the "condensed" phases that appear whenever the number of constituents in a system is extremely large and the interactions between the constituents are strong.

The most familiar examples of condensed phases are solids and liquids, which arise from the bonding and electromagnetic force between atoms. More exotic condensed phases include the superfluid and the Bose–Einstein condensate found in certain atomic systems at very low temperature, the superconducting phase exhibited by conduction electrons in certain materials, and the ferromagnetic and antiferromagnetic phases of spins on atomic lattices.

Condensed matter physics is by far the largest field of contemporary physics. Historically, condensed matter physics grew out of solid-state physics, which is now considered one of its main subfields. The term condensed matter physics was apparently coined by Philip Anderson when he renamed his research group—previously solid-state theory—in 1967.

In 1978, the Division of Solid State Physics at the American Physical Society was renamed as the Division of Condensed Matter Physics. Condensed matter physics has a large overlap with chemistry, materials science, nanotechnology and engineering.

Atomic, molecular, and optical physics

Atomic, molecular, and optical physics
Atomic, molecular, and optical physics (AMO) is the study of matter–matter and light–matter interactions on the scale of single atoms and molecules. The three areas are grouped together because of their interrelationships, the similarity of methods used, and the commonality of the energy scales that are relevant. All three areas include both classical, semi-classical and quantum treatments; they can treat their subject from a microscopic view (in contrast to a macroscopic view).

Atomic physics studies the electron shells of atoms. Current research focuses on activities in quantum control, cooling and trapping of atoms and ions, low-temperature collision dynamics and the effects of electron correlation on structure and dynamics. Atomic physics is influenced by the nucleus (see, e. g. , hyperfine splitting), but intra-nuclear phenomena such as fission and fusion are considered part of high-energy physics.

Molecular physics focuses on multi-atomic structures and their internal and external interactions with matter and light. Optical physics is distinct from optics in that it tends to focus not on the control of classical light fields by macroscopic objects, but on the fundamental properties of optical fields and their interactions with matter in the microscopic realm.

High-energy physics (particle physics)

Particle physics

Particle physics is the study of the elementary constituents of matter and energy, and the interactions between them. It may also be called "high-energy physics", because many elementary particles do not occur naturally, but are created only during high-energy collisions of other particles, as can be detected in particle accelerators.

Currently, the interactions of elementary particles are described by the Standard Model. The model accounts for the 12 known particles of matter (quarks and leptons) that interact via the strong, weak, and electromagnetic fundamental forces. Dynamics are described in terms of matter particles exchanging gauge bosons (gluons, W and Z bosons, and photons, respectively). The Standard Model also predicts a particle known as the Higgs boson, the existence of which has not yet been verified; as of 2010, searches for it are underway in the Tevatron at Fermilab and in the Large Hadron Collider at CERN.

Astrophysics

Astrophysics and astronomy are the application of the theories and methods of physics to the study of stellar structure, stellar evolution, the origin of the solar system, and related problems of cosmology. Because astrophysics is a broad subject, astrophysicists typically apply many disciplines of physics, including mechanics, electromagnetism, statistical mechanics, thermodynamics, quantum mechanics, relativity, nuclear and particle physics, and atomic and molecular physics.

The discovery by Karl Jansky in 1931 that radio signals were emitted by celestial bodies initiated the science of radio astronomy. Most recently, the frontiers of astronomy have been expanded by space exploration. Perturbations and interference from the earth's atmosphere make space-based observations necessary for infrared, ultraviolet, gamma-ray, and X-ray astronomy.

Physical cosmology is the study of the formation and evolution of the universe on its largest scales. Albert Einstein's theory of relativity plays a central role in all modern cosmological theories. In the early 20th century, Hubble's discovery that the universe was expanding, as shown by the Hubble diagram, prompted rival explanations known as the steady state universe and the Big Bang.

The Big Bang was confirmed by the success of Big Bang nucleosynthesis and the discovery of the cosmic microwave background in 1964. The Big Bang model rests on two theoretical pillars: Albert Einstein's general relativity and the cosmological principle. Cosmologists have recently established the ΛCDM model of the evolution of the universe, which includes cosmic inflation, dark energy and dark matter.

Numerous possibilities and discoveries are anticipated to emerge from new data from the Fermi Gamma-ray Space Telescope over the upcoming decade and vastly revise or clarify existing models of the universe. In particular, the potential for a tremendous discovery surrounding dark matter is possible over the next several years. Fermi will search for evidence that dark matter is composed of weakly interacting massive particles, complementing similar experiments with the Large Hadron Collider and other underground detectors.

IBEX is already yielding new astrophysical discoveries: "No one knows what is creating the ENA (energetic neutral atoms) ribbon" along the termination shock of the solar wind, "but everyone agrees that it means the textbook picture of the heliosphere — in which the solar system's enveloping pocket filled with the solar wind's charged particles is plowing through the onrushing 'galactic wind' of the interstellar medium in the shape of a comet — is wrong."

Current research

Research in physics is continually progressing on a large number of fronts.

In condensed matter physics, an important unsolved theoretical problem is that of high-temperature superconductivity. Many condensed matter experiments are aiming to fabricate workable spintronics and quantum computers.

In particle physics, the first pieces of experimental evidence for physics beyond the Standard Model have begun to appear. Foremost among these are indications that neutrinos have non-zero mass. These experimental results appear to have solved the long-standing solar neutrino problem, and the physics of massive neutrinos remains an area of active theoretical and experimental research. Particle accelerators have begun probing energy scales in the TeV range, in which experimentalists are hoping to find evidence for the Higgs boson and supersymmetric particles.

Theoretical attempts to unify quantum mechanics and general relativity into a single theory of quantum gravity, a program ongoing for over half a century, have not yet been decisively resolved. The current leading candidates are M-theory, superstring theory and loop quantum gravity.

Many astronomical and cosmological phenomena have yet to be satisfactorily explained, including the existence of ultra-high energy cosmic rays, the baryon asymmetry, the acceleration of the universe and the anomalous rotation rates of galaxies.

Although much progress has been made in high-energy, quantum, and astronomical physics, many everyday phenomena involving complexity, chaos, or turbulence are still poorly understood. Complex problems that seem like they could be solved by a clever application of dynamics and mechanics remain unsolved; examples include the formation of sandpiles, nodes in trickling water, the shape of water droplets, mechanisms of surface tension catastrophes, and self-sorting in shaken heterogeneous collections.

These complex phenomena have received growing attention since the 1970s for several reasons, including the availability of modern mathematical methods and computers, which enabled complex systems to be modeled in new ways. Complex physics has become part of increasingly interdisciplinary research, as exemplified by the study of turbulence in aerodynamics and the observation of pattern formation in biological systems. In 1932, Horace Lamb said:

I am an old man now, and when I die and go to heaven there are two matters on which I hope for enlightenment. One is quantum electrodynamics, and the other is the turbulent motion of fluids. And about the former I am rather optimistic.

Prediction

Prediction

A prediction or forecast is a statement about the way things will happen in the future, often but not always based on experience or knowledge. While there is much overlap between prediction and forecast, a prediction may be a statement that some outcome is expected, while a forecast is more specific, and may cover a range of possible outcomes.

Although guaranteed information about the information is in many cases impossible, prediction is necessary to allow plans to be made about possible developments; Howard H. Stevenson writes that prediction in business ". . . is at least two things: Important and hard."

Prediction is closely related to uncertainty. Reference class forecasting was developed to eliminate or reduce uncertainty in prediction.

The etymology of prediction is Latin (præ-, "before," and dicere, "to say").

Informal prediction from hypothesis

Outside the rigorous context of science, prediction is often confused with informed guess or opinion.

A prediction of this kind might be (inductively) valid if the predictor is a knowledgeable person in the field and is employing sound reasoning and accurate data. Large corporations invest heavily in this kind of activity to help focus attention on possible events, risks and business opportunities, using futurists. Such work brings together all available past and current data, as a basis to develop reasonable expectations about the future.

Opinion polls

In politics it is common to attempt to predict the outcome of elections via political forecasting techniques (or assess the popularity of politicians) through the use of opinion polls. Prediction games have been used by many corporations and governments to learn about the most likely outcome of future events.

Statistics

In statistics, prediction is a part of statistical inference. One particular approach to such inference is known as predictive inference, but the prediction can be undertaken within any of the several approaches to statistical inference. Indeed, one description of statistics is that it provides a means of transferring knowledge about a sample of a population to the whole population, and to other related populations, which is not the same as prediction over time. When information is transferred across time, often to specific points in time, the process is known as forecasting.

In many applications it is possible to estimate the models that generate the observations. If models can be expressed as transfer functions or in terms of state-space parameters then smoothed, filtered and predicted data estimates can be calculated. . If the underlying generating models are linear then a minimum-variance Kalman filter and a minimum-variance smoother may be used to recover data of interest from noisy measurements. The aforementioned techniques rely on one-step-ahead predictors (which minimise the variance of the prediction error). When the generating models are nonlinear then step-wise linearizations may be applied within Extended Kalman Filter and smoother recursions. However, in nonlinear cases, optimum minimum-variance performance guarantees no longer apply.

Supernatural (prophecy)

Prophecy
Predictions have often been made, from antiquity until the present, by using paranormal or supernatural means such as prophecy or by observing omens. Methods including water divining, astrology, numerology, fortune telling, interpretation of dreams, and many other forms of divination, have been used for millennia to attempt to predict the future. These means of prediction have not been proven by scientific experiments.

Prediction in science

In science, a prediction is a rigorous, often quantitative, statement, forecasting what will happen under specific conditions; for example, if an apple falls from a tree it will be attracted towards the center of the earth by gravity with a specified and constant acceleration. The scientific method is built on testing assertions that are logical consequences of scientific theories. This is done through repeatable experiments or observational studies.

A scientific theory whose assertions are contradicted by observations and evidence will be rejected. Notions that make no testable predictions are usually considered not to be part of science (protoscience or nescience) until testable predictions can be made.

New theories that generate many new predictions can more easily be supported or falsified (see predictive power).

In some cases the probability of an outcome, rather than a specific outcome, can be predicted, for example in much of quantum physics.

Mathematical equations and models, and computer models, are frequently used to describe the past and future behaviour of a process within the boundaries of that model.

In microprocessors, branch prediction permits avoidance of pipeline emptying at branch instructions. In engineering, possible failure modes are predicted and avoided by correcting the mechanism causing the failure.

Accurate prediction and forecasting are very difficult in some areas, such as software reliability, natural disasters, pandemics, demography, population dynamics and meteorology.

Scientific hypothesis and prediction

Established science makes useful predictions which are considered to be extremely reliable and accurate; for example, eclipses are routinely predicted.

New theories make predictions which allow them to be falsified if the predictions are not borne out in reality. For example, in the early twentieth century the scientific consensus was that there existed an absolute frame of reference, given the name luminiferous ether.

The existence of this absolute frame was deemed necessary for consistency with the established idea that the speed of light is constant. The famous Michelson-Morley experiment demonstrated that predictions deduced from this concept were not borne out in reality, falsifying the idea of an absolute frame of reference. The special theory of relativity was proposed by Einstein as an explanation for the seeming inconsistency between the constancy of the speed of light and the non-existence of a special, preferred or absolute frame of reference.

Albert Einstein's theory of general relativity could not easily be tested as it did not produce any effects observable on a terrestrial scale. However, the theory predicted that large masses such as stars would bend light, in contradiction to accepted theory; this was observed in a 1919 eclipse.

Finance

Mathematical models of stock market behaviour are also unreliable in predicting future behaviour. Consequently, stock investors may anticipate or predict a stock market boom, or fail to anticipate or predict a stock market crash.

Some correlation has been seen between actual stock market movements and prediction data from large groups in surveys and prediction games.

An actuary uses actuarial science to assess and predict future business risk, such that the risk(s) can be mitigated.

For example, in insurance an actuary would use a life table to predict (truly, estimate or compute) life expectancy.

Vision and prophecy

In literature, vision and prophecy are literary devices used to present a possible timeline of future events. They can be distinguished by vision referring to what an individual sees happen. The New Testament book of Revelation (Bible) thus uses vision as a literary device in this regard. It is also prophecy or prophetic literature when it is related by an individual in a sermon or other public forum.

Divination is the attempt to gain insight into a question or situation by way of an occultic standardized process or ritual. It is an integral part of witchcraft and has been used in various forms for thousands of years. Diviners ascertain their interpretations of how a querent should proceed by reading signs, events, or omens, or through alleged contact with a supernatural agency, most often describe as an angel or a god though viewed by Christians and Jews as a fallen angel or demon.

Prediction in fiction

Fiction (especially fantasy, forecasting and science fiction) often features instances of prediction achieved by unconventional means.

In fantasy literature, predictions are often obtained through magic or prophecy, sometimes referring back to old traditions. For example, in J. R. R. Tolkien's The Lord of the Rings, many of the characters possess an awareness of events extending into the future, sometimes as prophecies, sometimes as more-or-less vague 'feelings'. The character Galadriel, in addition, employs a water "mirror" to show images, sometimes of possible future events.
In some of Philip K. Dick's stories, mutant humans called precogs can foresee the future (ranging from days to years). In the story called The Golden Man, an exceptional mutant can predict the future to an indefinite range (presumably up to his death), and thus becomes completely non-human, an animal that follows the predicted paths automatically. Precogs also play an essential role in another of Dick's stories, The Minority Report, which was turned into a film by Steven Spielberg in 2002.
In the Foundation series by Isaac Asimov, a mathematician finds out that historical events (up to some detail) can be theoretically modelled using equations, and then spends years trying to put the theory in practice. The new science of psychohistory founded upon his success can simulate history and extrapolate the present into the future.
In Frank Herbert's sequels to Dune, his characters are dealing with the repercussions of being able to see the possible futures and select amongst them. Herbert sees this as a trap of stagnation, and his characters follow a Golden Path out of the trap.

In Ursula K. Le Guin's The Left Hand of Darkness, the humanoid inhabitants of planet Gethen have mastered the art of prophecy and routinely produce data on past, present or future events on request. In this story, this was a minor plot device.

Predictive Model Markup Language

Predictive Model Markup Language

The Predictive Model Markup Language (PMML) is an XML-based markup language developed by the Data Mining Group (DMG) to provide a way for applications to define models related to predictive analytics and data mining and to share those models between PMML-compliant applications.

PMML provides applications a vendor-independent method of defining models so that proprietary issues and incompatibilities are no longer a barrier to the exchange of models between applications. It allows users to develop models within one vendor's application and use other vendors' applications to visualize, analyze, evaluate or otherwise use the models. Previously, this was very difficult, but with PMML, the exchange of models between compliant applications is straightforward.

Since PMML is an XML-based standard, the specification comes in the form of an XML schema.

PMML Components

PMML follows an intuitive structure to describe a data mining model, be it an artificial neural network or a logistic regression model.

Sequentially, it can be described by the following components:

Header: contains general information about the PMML document, such as copyright information for the model, its description, and information about the application used to generate the model such as name and version. It also contains an attribute for a timestamp which can be used to specify the date of model creation.

Data Dictionary: contains definitions for all the possible fields used by the model. It is here that a field is defined as continuous, categorical, or ordinal (attribute optype). Depending on this definition, the appropriate value ranges are then defined as well as the data type (such as, string or double).

Data Transformations: transformations allow for the mapping of user data into a more desirable form to be used by the mining model. PMML defines several kinds of simple data transformations.

Normalization: map values to numbers, the input can be continuous or discrete.

Discretization: map continuous values to discrete values.

Value mapping: map discrete values to discrete values.

Functions (custom and built-in): derive a value by applying a function to one or more parameters.

Aggregation: used to summarize or collect groups of values.

Model: contains the definition of the data mining model. A multi-layered feedforward neural network is the most common neural network representation in contemporary applications, given the popularity and efficacy associated with its training algorithm known as backpropagation. Such a network is represented in PMML by a "NeuralNetwork" element which contains attributes such as:

Model Name (attribute modelName)
Function Name (attribute functionName)
Algorithm Name (attribute algorithmName)
Activation Function (attribute activationFunction)
Number of Layers (attribute numberOfLayers)

This information is then followed by three kinds of neural layers which specify the architecture of the neural network model being represented in the PMML document. These attributes are NeuralInputs, NeuralLayer, and NeuralOutputs. Besides neural networks, PMML allows for the representation of many other data mining models including support vector machines, association rules, Naive Bayes classifier, clustering models, text models, decision trees, and different regression models.

Mining Schema: the mining schema lists all fields used in the model. This can be a subset of the fields as defined in the data dictionary. It contains specific information about each field, such as:

Name (attribute name): must refer to a field in the data dictionary
Usage type (attribute usageType): defines the way a field is to be used in the model. Typical values are: active, predicted, and supplementary. Predicted fields are those whose values are

predicted by the model.
Outlier Treatment (attribute outliers): defines the outlier treatment to be use. In PMML, outliers can be treated as missing values, as extreme values (based on the definition of high and low values for a particular field), or as is.
Missing Value Replacement Policy (attribute missingValueReplacement): if this attribute is specified then a missing value is automatically replaced by the given values.
Missing Value Treatment (attribute missingValueTreatment): indicates how the missing value replacement was derived (e. g. as value, mean or median).
Targets: allow for post-processing of the predicted value in the format of scaling if the output of the model is continuous. Targets can also be used for classification tasks. In this case, the attribute priorProbability specifies a default probability for the corresponding target category. It is used if the prediction logic itself did not produce a result. This can happen, e. g. , if an input value is missing and there is no other method for treating missing values.
Output: this element can be used to name all the desired output fields expected from the model. These are features of the predicted field and so are typically the predicted value itself, the probability, cluster affinity (for clustering models), standard error, etc. PMML 4. 1, the latest release of PMML, extended output to allow for generic post-processing of model outputs. In PMML 4. 1, all the built-in and custom functions that were originally available for pre-processing only are now also available for post-processing.

PMML 4. 0 and 4. 1

The previous version of PMML, 4. 0, was released on June 16, 2009.

Examples of new features included:

Improved Pre-Processing Capabilities: Additions to built-in functions include a range of Boolean operations and an If-Then-Else function.
Time Series Models: New exponential Smoothing models; also place holders for ARIMA, Seasonal Trend Decomposition, and Spectral density estimation, which are to be supported in the near future.
Model Explanation: Saving of evaluation and model performance measures to the PMML file itself.
Multiple Models: Capabilities for model composition, ensembles, and segmentation (e. g. , combining of regression and decision trees).

Extensions of Existing Elements: Addition of multi-class classification for Support Vector Machines, improved representation for Association Rules, and the addition of Cox Regression Models.
The latest version of PMML, 4. 1, was released on December 31, 2011.

New features include:

New model elements for representing Scorecards, k-Nearest Neighbors (KNN) and Baseline Models.
Simplification of multiple models. In PMML 4. 1, the same element is used to represent model segmentation, ensemble, and chaining.
Overall definition of field scope and field names.
A new attribute that identifies for each model element if the model is ready or not for production deployment.
Enhanced post-processing capabilities (via the Output element).

Release history

Version 0. 7   July 1997
Version 0. 9   July 1998
Version 1. 0   August 1999
Version 1. 1   August 2000
Version 2. 0   August 2001
Version 2. 1   March 2003
Version 3. 0   October 2004
Version 3. 1   December 2005
Version 3. 2   May 2007
Version 4. 0   June 2009
Version 4. 1   December 2011

PMML Products

A range of products are being offered to produce and consume PMML:

Angoss KnowledgeSTUDIO: produces PMML 3. 2 for regression models (logistic and linear), decision trees, clustering, neural networks and ruleset models (used to represent scorecards).
Angoss KnowledgeSEEKER: produces PMML 3. 2 for decision trees.
Angoss StrategyBuilder : (a standard module in KnowledgeSEEKER and KnowledgeSTUDIO)]: produces PMML 3. 2 for decision trees (used to represent strategy trees).

Google Prediction API: consumes PMML 4.0 for data transformations.
IBM InfoSphere Warehouse: produces PMML 3.0 and 3.1 for sequences only models. Consumes (scores and visualizes) PMML 3.1 and earlier.
IBM SPSS Modeler: produces and scores PMML 3.2 and 4.0 for a variety of models.
IBM SPSS Statistics: produces PMML 3.2 and 4.0 for a variety of models.
KNIME: produces and consumes PMML 4.0 for neural networks, decision trees, clustering models, regression models, and support vector machines. As of release 2.4.0, KNIME also offers extensive pre-processing support in PMML, including the ability to edit existing PMML code.
KXEN: produces PMML 3.2 for regression models (including mining models) and clustering.
Microsoft SQL Server 2008 Analysis Services: produces and consumes PMML 2.1 for decision trees and clustering.
MicroStrategy: supports PMML 2.0, 2.1, 3.0, 3.1, 3.2 and 4.0 for linear regression, logistic regression, decision trees, clustering, association rules, time series, neural networks and support vector machines.
Open Data Group's Augustus: Produces PMML 4.0 for tree, naive-bayes and ruleset models. It consumes PMML 4.0 tree, naive-bayes, ruleset and regression models. Older versions produce and consume PMML 3.0 regression, tree and naive-bayes.
Oracle Data Mining: supports the core features of PMML 3.1 for regression models. The imported models become native Oracle Data Mining (ODM) models capable of Exadata offload.
Pervasive DataRush: produces and consumes PMML 4.0 for regression models, decision trees, and naive bayes. Produces PMML 4.0 for association rules and clustering (K-means Center-Based).
Predixion PMML Connexion: consumes PMML 2.0, 2.1, 3.0, 3.1, 3.2, and 4.0 for several mining models, including decision trees, ruleset models, support vector machines, neural networks, naive bayes, linear and logistic regression models as well as clustering models.
RapidMiner: Using the free PMML extension, several types of models can be exported to PMML.
Rattle/R: Uses the R programming language to build several predictive models. It offers a PMML package to export models built in R to PMML 3.2. This package includes export support for support vector machines, linear regression, logistic regression, decision trees, random forests, random survival forests, neural networks,

K-means and hierarchical clustering, and association rules.
Salford-Systems CART: a decision tree system that produces PMML 3.1.
SAND CDBMS 6.1 PMML Extension: consumes PMML versions 3.1 and 3.2 for several mining models, including association rules, clustering, regression, neural networks, naive bayes, support vector machines, rulesets, and decision trees. It also consumes pre-processing elements and built-in functions.
SAS Enterprise Miner: produces PMML 2.1 and 3.1 for several mining models, including linear regression, logistic regression, decision trees, neural networks, K-means clustering, and association rules. Since version 7.1, Enterprise Miner is also PMML 4.0 compliant.
STATISTICA: generates PMML 2.0 and 3.0 for analyses such as linear regression, logistic regression, decision trees, support vector machines, and neural networks
TIBCO Spotfire Miner 8.1: produces and consumes PMML 2.0 for regression models, decision trees, neural networks, clustering, and naive bayes models.
TERADATA Warehouse Miner 5.3.1: consumes PMML 2.1 through 3.2 for regression models, decision trees, neural networks, clustering, and mining models (regression type).
Weka (Pentaho): consumes PMML 3.2 for regression models, decision trees, neural networks, rule sets, and support vector machines.
Zementis ADAPA: batch and real-time scoring of PMML 2.0, 2.1, 3.0, 3.1, 3.2, and 4.0 for several mining models, including decision trees, association rules, support vector machines, neural networks, naive bayes, ruleset models, linear and logistic regression models as well as Cox regression models, clustering models and model ensembles. ADAPA also consumes all pre- and post-processing PMML elements, including transformations, built-in functions, outputs, and targets.
Zementis PMML Converter: validates, corrects, and converts PMML files expressed in versions 2.0, 2.1, 3.0, 3.1, 3.2, and 4.0.
Zementis Universal PMML Plug-in for In-Database Scoring: Scoring of PMML 2.0, 2.1, 3.0, 3.1, 3.2, and 4.0 for several mining models. Available now for the EMC Greenplum Database, Sybase IQ and IBM Netezza.
Zementis Universal PMML Plug-in for Hadoop: Scoring of PMML 2.0, 2.1, 3.0, 3.1, 3.2, and 4.0 for the Datameer Analytics Solution (DAS), an end-to-end BI solution that includes data source integration, an analytics engine, visualization and dashboarding. DAS uses Apache Hadoop, a Java-based framework that supports the parallel storage and processing of large data sets in

a distributed environment, as its back-end storage and processing engine to scale to 4000 servers and petabytes of data.

Transformations Generator

PMML provides a variety of data transformations, including value mapping, normalization, and discretization. It also offers several built-in functions as well as arithmetic and logical operators which can be combined to represent complex pre-processing steps. With the Transformations Generator tool, one can graphically design a transformation and obtain the respective PMML code.

Pruning (decision trees)

Pruning (decision trees)

Pruning is a technique in machine learning that reduces the size of decision trees by removing sections of the tree that provide little power to classify instances. The dual goal of pruning is reduced complexity of the final classifier as well as better predictive accuracy by the reduction of overfitting and removal of sections of a classifier that may be based on noisy or erroneous data.

Introduction

One of the questions that arises in a decision tree algorithm is the optimal size of the final tree. A tree that is too large risks overfitting the training data and poorly generalizing to new samples. A small tree might not capture important structural information about the sample space. However, it is hard to tell when a tree algorithm should stop because it is impossible to tell if the addition of a single extra node will dramatically decrease error. This problem is known as the horizon effect. A common strategy is to grow the tree until each node contains a small number of instances then use pruning to remove nodes that do not provide additional information.

Pruning should reduce the size of a learning tree without reducing predictive accuracy as measured by a test set or using cross-validation. There are many techniques for tree pruning that differ in the measurement that is used to optimize performance.

Techniques

Pruning can occur in a top down or bottom up fashion. A top down pruning will traverse nodes and trim subtrees starting at the root, while a bottom up pruning will start at the leaf nodes. Below are several popular pruning algorithms.

Reduced error pruning

One of the simplest forms of pruning is reduced error pruning. Starting at the leaves, each node is replaced with its most popular class. If the prediction accuracy is not affected then the change is kept. While somewhat naive, reduced error pruning has the advantage of simplicity and speed.

Cost complexity pruning

Cost complexity pruning generates a series of trees where is the initial tree and is the root alone. At step the tree is created by removing a subtree from tree and replacing it with a leaf node with value chosen as in the tree building algorithm. The subtree that is removed is chosen as follows. Define the error rate of tree over data set as . The subtree that minimizes is chosen for removal. The function defines the tree gotten by pruning the subtrees from the tree . Once the series of trees has been created, the best tree is chosen by generalized accuracy as measured by a training set or cross-validation.

RiskAoA

RiskAoA - ,

RiskAoA is a United States Department of Defense (USDoD) project Risk Management tool, allowing the instantaneous review of portfolio (see Project Portfolio Management), proposal or alternatives Risk. It was designed by Air Force Research Laboratory (AFRL) Headquarters to perform proactive risk analysis for the Analysis of Alternatives (AoA) process. The prototype, "RiskHammer" was approved by the US Air Force Electronic Systems Center-Acquisition Center of Excellence (ESC/ACE) in 2002 (see Hanscom Air Force Base). RiskAoA is proprietary to the United States Government, but is available from Air Force Materiel Command (AFMC) Headquarters, the office of AFMC/A5, in accordance with Distribution B.

RiskAoA is a simple to use Excel and Visual Basic -based program that allows the predictive and quantitative assessment of Risk. The results are statistically based values of the relative risk associated with the evaluated alternatives. The capability and algorithms for the program are unprecedented; making RiskAoA the most advanced alternatives management technology employed institutionally and the first demonstrating the predictive character of the risk discipline .

RiskAoA fulfills a unique role among risk management tools- transforming qualitative statements of an alternative or option risk into a single quantitative value as useful as the cost and schedule. An aim of the USDoD acquisition process is to maximize "value" or return on investment, using the fundamental properties of Cost, Schedule, Performance (CSP) and Risk (or CSPR) as metrics. Just as the cost of one proposal can be higher than another, or one schedule take longer, so risk can be prioritized with RiskAoA. It is further unique in being the only technology ever produced by AFRL Headquarters.

RiskAoA is also well suited for the Evaluation of Alternatives (EoA) process.

RiskAoA Objectives are:

1. Support US Government program managers and decision makers in the assessment of risks and events for any selection of alternatives for Capability-Based Planning or Joint Capabilities Integration Development System (JCIDS), the military equivalent of Enterprise Resource Planning (ERP). This application provides a predictive 'at-a-glance' assessment of the number and magnitude of difficulties expected from different alternatives, necessary for Enterprise Risk Management, supported by RiskAoA.

2. Provide easily reviewable documentation for support or defense of acquisition decisions. RiskAoA helps justify risk vs. return propositions from alternatives and proposals.

3. Provide the Risk Adjusted Life Cycle Costs (LCC) estimates required by the General Services Administration (GSA) for the Analysis of Alternatives.

The USDoD uses a "Probability-Consequence Model" (also known as "Probability-Impact" as one of its key risk metrics. A difficulty with this metric is the constructive "adding" of risk. Probabilities add as:

P1 + P2(1- P1) + P1(1- P1) (1- P2) +...; P1 is probability of event 1, P2 event 2, etc. .

Multiplying these by a consequence that can be cost, time or action, makes the addition and summary of these risks challenging. Further complicating matters is the Probability Consequence Models inability to adjust for compound effects from the same risk. An example from network security: If a network of 10 computers comes under network attack, the risk depends on the defense mechanism. If only one of the computers succumbs to the attack and infects the entire network, the risk scenario is different than if each computer must be attacked and infected individually.

RiskAoA solves these issues by developing a function which uniquely identifies each probability series as a value relative to one another, utilizing the property from probability theory that the order of occurrences does not affect the result.

The program is easy to use requiring only a few entries:

1. Name and save the analysis.

2. Determine the number of interacting systems, enter this number.

For each row:

3. Identify each risk.

3a. Name the risk

3b. Describe the risk

3c. Mitigation plan (if any)

3d. Determine the number of compounding effects from each risk-for the network attack example above, enter 10 for one attack being successful, 1/10 if all need to succumb.

3e. Assess the risk, High (H), Medium (M), Low (L), Negligible (N) or use a quantitative numbered assessment (1-99%) under the impact columns-Catastrophic, Critical, Moderate and Negligible. The text in the impact column may be changed; "Negligible" may be changed to "Schedule" or "Low" for example.

3f. Determine if this risk impacts the entire program (critical path, key performance characteristic, etc. .) and rate H,M,L.

4. Repeat step 3 for each risk for each alternative.

RiskAoA includes a forecasting tool, allowing users to determine the level of confidence in the results. The forecasting tool is based on two elements; the worst-case confidence in each of the alternative's risks, and the number of these risks. This is the equivalent of a shot-gun approach to risk management-the more germane data, the more likely the result is to be correct. If well understood data is input this function is unnecessary.

Because of the nature of the RiskAoA approach, errors tend to cancel and be moderated. This makes the forecasting tool itself a worst-case model. If the confidence in the individual risks is greater than 50%, this approach remains accurate.

RiskAoA algorithms were invented and developed by Gregory M. Tyler, and its user interface developed by the MITRE Corporation. Since it first release in 2002, it has been validated by other DoD organizations: Air Force Material Command (AFMC) Reporting Units; Validated, Verified and Accredited (VV&A) by AFRL and reviewed by AFMC/EN. It was endorsed DoD wide by the Office of the Under Secretary of Defense for Acquisition, Technology and Logistics in 2007 and by the Defense Acquisition University .

RiskAoA is available to all members of the US DoD, and Federal Government employees, in accordance with Distribution B, by contacting AFMC/A5.

Roger Jones (physicist and entrepreneur)

Roger Jones (physicist and entrepreneur)

Roger D. Jones
For Roger Jones the mathematician see Roger Jones (mathematician)
Roger D. Jones
Born   1953
Nationality   United States
Fields   Physics
Adaptive Computation and Machine Learning
Healthcare analytics
Banking and Finance
Institutions   Qforma (formerly CommodiCast) (Chairman, Chief Operating Officer, Chief Scientific Officer)

Complexica (CEO)

Los Alamos National Laboratory (Staff Physicist)

Assistant Professor, Department of Physics, Dartmouth College
Alma mater   University of Florida (BS)
Dartmouth College (PhD)
Roger D. Jones, PhD (born 1953) is an American physicist and entrepreneur.
Roger D. Jones is currently Chairman, Chief Operating Officer, and Chief Scientific Officer of Qforma, Inc. located in Santa Fe, New Mexico, USA. Trained in physics at Dartmouth College, Jones worked as a staff physicist at Los Alamos National Laboratory from 1979 to 1995. His primary research interests were in laser fusion and machine learning. In the early nineties he headed projects that applied his machine learning inventions to technical problems in the private sector. At that time he became embroiled in controversy over corporate welfare and the role of technology transfer from the national laboratories to the private sector. In 1995 in collaboration with Citibank, Jones co-founded the Center for Adaptive Systems Applications (CASA), a company that applied neural network and adaptive technology to consumer banking. CASA was acquired by HNC Software in March 2000, at the peak

of the dotcom boom. HNC Software was subsequently acquired by Fair Isaac Corporation. Much of the technology developed at CASA became part of the credit scoring offerings of Fair Isaac. Jones along with other Santa Fe scientists and entrepreneurs such as Doyne Farmer, Norman Packard, Stuart Kauffman, and David Weininger founded several other high-technology startup companies in the emerging Santa Fe technology community, dubbed by Wired Magazine as the "Info Mesa. " Jones introduced the first entirely virtual company. Much of the effort of these startups focused on finance and the catastrophic reinsurance industry. By 2004 the companies Jones co-founded merged into a single company, Qforma, Inc. , that focused on adaptive and predictive technologies for the pharmaceutical and financial industries.

Roger Jones has an Erd☐s number of 4.

SPSS

Statistics program

SPSS is a computer program used for survey authoring and deployment (IBM SPSS Data Collection), data mining (IBM SPSS Modeler), text analytics, statistical analysis, and collaboration and deployment (batch and automated scoring services).

SPSS (originally, Statistical Package for the Social Sciences) was released in its first version in 1968 after being developed by Norman H. Nie and C. Hadlai Hull. SPSS is among the most widely used programs for statistical analysis in social science. It is used by market researchers, health researchers, survey companies, government, education researchers, marketing organizations and others. The original SPSS manual (Nie, Bent & Hull, 1970) has been described as one of "sociology's most influential books". In addition to statistical analysis, data management (case selection, file reshaping, creating derived data) and data documentation (a metadata dictionary is stored in the datafile) are features of the base software.

Statistics included in the base software:

Descriptive statistics: Cross tabulation, Frequencies, Descriptives, Explore, Descriptive Ratio Statistics

Bivariate statistics: Means, t-test, ANOVA, Correlation (bivariate, partial, distances), Nonparametric tests
Prediction for numerical outcomes: Linear regression
Prediction for identifying groups: Factor analysis, cluster analysis (two-step, K-means, hierarchical), Discriminant

The many features of SPSS are accessible via pull-down menus or can be programmed with a proprietary 4GL command syntax language. Command syntax programming has the benefits of reproducibility, simplifying repetitive tasks, and handling complex data manipulations and analyses. Additionally, some complex applications can only be programmed in syntax and are not accessible through the menu structure. The pull-down menu interface also generates command syntax; this can be displayed in the output, although the default settings have to be changed to make the syntax visible to the user. They can also be pasted into a syntax file using the "paste" button present in each menu. Programs can be run interactively or unattended, using the supplied Production Job Facility. Additionally a "macro" language can be used to write command language subroutines and a Python programmability extension can access the information in the data dictionary and data and dynamically build command syntax programs. The Python programmability extension, introduced in SPSS 14, replaced the less functional SAX Basic "scripts" for most purposes, although SaxBasic remains available. In addition, the Python extension allows SPSS to run any of the statistics in the free software package R. From version 14 onwards SPSS can be driven externally by a Python or a VB. NET program using supplied "plug-ins".

SPSS places constraints on internal file structure, data types, data processing and matching files, which together considerably simplify programming. SPSS datasets have a 2-dimensional table structure where the rows typically represent cases (such as individuals or households) and the columns represent measurements (such as age, sex or household income). Only 2 data types are defined: numeric and text (or "string"). All data processing occurs sequentially case-by-case through the file. Files can be matched one-to-one and one-to-many, but not many-to-many.

The graphical user interface has two views which can be toggled by clicking on one of the two tabs in the bottom left of the SPSS window. The 'Data View' shows a spreadsheet view of the cases (rows) and variables (columns). Unlike spreadsheets, the data cells can only contain numbers or text and formulas cannot be stored in these cells. The 'Variable View' displays the metadata dictionary where each row represents a variable and shows the variable name, variable label, value label(s), print width, measurement type and a variety of other characteristics. Cells in both views can be manually edited, defining the file structure and allowing data entry without using command syntax. This may be sufficient for small datasets. Larger datasets such as statistical surveys are more often created in data entry software, or entered during computer-assisted personal interviewing, by scanning and using optical character recognition and optical mark recognition software, or by direct capture from online questionnaires. These datasets are then read into SPSS.

SPSS can read and write data from ASCII text files (including hierarchical files), other statistics packages, spreadsheets and databases. SPSS can read and write to external relational database tables via ODBC and SQL.

Statistical output is to a proprietary file format (*. spv file, supporting pivot tables) for which, in addition to the in-package viewer, a stand-alone reader can be downloaded. The proprietary output can be exported to text or Microsoft Word, PDF, Excel, and other formats. Alternatively, output can be captured as data (using the OMS command), as text, tab-delimited text, PDF, XLS, HTML, XML, SPSS dataset or a variety of graphic image formats (JPEG, PNG, BMP and EMF).

SPSS Server is a version of SPSS with a client/server architecture. It had some features not available in the desktop version, such as scoring functions (Scoring functions are included in the desktop version from version 19).

Versions

Early versions of SPSS were designed for batch processing on mainframes, including for example IBM and ICL versions, originally using punched cards for input. A processing run read a command file of SPSS commands and either a raw input file of fixed format data with a single record type, or a 'getfile' of data saved by a previous run. To save precious computer time an 'edit' run could be done to check command syntax without analysing the data.

From version 10 (SPSS-X) in 1983, data files could contain multiple record types.

SPSS versions 16.0 and later run under Windows, Mac, and Linux. The graphical user interface is written in Java. The Mac OS version is provided as a Universal binary, making it fully compatible with both PowerPC and Intel-based Mac hardware.

Prior to SPSS 16.0, different versions of SPSS were available for Windows, Mac OS X and Unix. The Windows version was updated more frequently, and had more features, than the versions for other operating systems.

SPSS version 13.0 for Mac OS X was not compatible with Intel-based Macintosh computers, due to the Rosetta emulation software causing errors in calculations. SPSS 15.0 for Windows needed a downloadable hotfix to be installed in order to be compatible with Windows Vista.

Ownership history

Between 2009 and 2010, the premier vendor for SPSS was called PASW (Predictive Analytics SoftWare) Statistics. The company announced on July 28, 2009 that it was being acquired by IBM for US$1.2 billion. As of January 2010, it became "SPSS: An IBM Company". Complete transfer of business to IBM was done by October 1, 2010. By that date, SPSS: An IBM Company ceased to exist. IBM SPSS is now fully integrated into the IBM Corporation, and is one of the brands under IBM Software Group's Business Analytics Portfolio, together with IBM Cognos.

Add-ons

Add-on modules provide additional capabilities. The available modules are:

SPSS Programmability Extension (added in version 14). Allows Python, R, and .NET programming control of SPSS.
SPSS Data Preparation (added in version 14). Allows programming of logical checks and reporting of suspicious values.
SPSS Regression - Logistic regression, ordinal regression, multinomial

logistic regression, and mixed models.
SPSS Advanced Models - Multivariate GLM and repeated measures ANOVA (removed from base system in version 14).
SPSS Decision Trees. Creates classification and decision trees for identifying groups and predicting behaviour.
SPSS Custom Tables. Allows user-defined control of output for reports.
SPSS Exact Tests. Allows statistical testing on small samples.
SPSS Categories
SPSS Forecasting
SPSS Conjoint
SPSS Missing Values. Simple regression-based imputation.
SPSS Complex Samples (added in Version 12). Adjusts for stratification and clustering and other sample selection biases.
AMOS (Analysis of Moment Structures) - add-on which allows modeling of structural equation and covariance structures, path analysis, and has the more basic capabilities such as linear regression analysis, ANOVA and ANCOVA

Release history

SPSS 15. 0. 1 - November 2006
SPSS 16. 0. 2 - April 2008
SPSS Statistics 17. 0. 1 - December 2008
PASW Statistics 17. 0. 3 - September 2009
PASW Statistics 18. 0 - August 2009
PASW Statistics 18. 0. 1 - December 2009
PASW Statistics 18. 0. 2 - April 2010
PASW Statistics 18. 0. 3 - September 2010
IBM SPSS Statistics 19. 0 - August 2010
IBM SPSS Statistics 20. 0 - August 2011
IBM SPSS Statistics 21. 0 - August 2012

Tibco Software

Tibco Software

TIBCO Software Inc. (NASDAQ: TIBX) is a provider of infrastructure software for companies to use on-premise or as part of cloud computing environments. TIBCO manages information, decisions, processes and applications in real-time for over 4,000 customers with a market cap of $5. 1 billion. Clients have included Yahoo,

NASDAQ, Charles Schwab, Oracle, Major League Baseball, and the Golden State Warriors. It has headquarters in Palo Alto, California, and offices in North America, Europe, Asia, the Middle East, Africa and South America. The company's major commercial competitors are IBM and Oracle Corporation.

History

Beginnings and Teknekron

In 1985, Teknekron Corp. , a technology incubator, provided $250,000 in seed capital to Vivek Ranadivé. In 1986 Teknekron Software Systems was born, and in 1987, it was spun off into an independent company. The company's principal innovation was the software bus (abbreviated as TIB), which transfers vital data between software programs.

In 1986, Teknekron embarked on a consulting project with Goldman Sachs to redefine the "trading floor of the future. " In 1987, the first TIB — for the integration and delivery of market data such as stock quotes, news and other financial information — went live at Fidelity, followed by First Interstate Bank[disambiguation needed] and Salomon, eventually digitizing all of Wall Street. Teknekron's software bus programming allowed data to be shared between computers using different languages and different applications. Wall Street trading firms used the software for trading systems, and eventually, large-scale manufacturers employed the technology as well. Ranadivé said, ''We digitized Wall Street. You had 20 television monitors that you had to look at. What we did was get rid of all that and replaced it with a Sun workstation. All of that information could now be treated as digitized information. ''

In December 1993, Reuters Holdings PLC bought Tenekron for $125. 1 million in cash.

TIBCO and IPO

In 1997, Ranadivé founded TIBCO (The Information Bus Company). The Bus software allowed communication within the financial markets to happen in real-time and without human intervention.

The technology was used by companies like SAP, IBM, and Oracle. Later in 1997, TIBCO became one of 13 of Microsoft's partners in "push" technology, which delivers internet content to users for free through web browsers.

Before going public, Gail Bronson, a senior analyst at IPO Monitor, said that TIBCO "is going to be huge" because of the company's underwriting, venture capital and corporate connections. TIBCO issued its IPO in July 1999 with a range value of $9 to $11 In its first day of trading, TIBCO's stock doubled, from $17. 38 to $32. 38 per share and in early 2000, the software maker's value went from $22. 75 to $244. 88 per share, the company's record high at the time. After its IPO, TIBCO raised $109. 5 million and 7. 3 million common shares sold for $15 each, above its range value.

In 2000, Yahoo introduced Corporate Yahoo, a platform developed using TIBCO Software that allowed companies to develop customized communications between computers. Corporate Yahoo contained early examples of bundled e-mail, calendars, stock prices, and news displayed on intranet homepages. Hewlett-Packard was one of the partners in the software's development.

Post-IPO

TIBCO survived the the dot-com bubble burst and was listed among USA Today's e-Consumer and e-Business index of 50 technology companies that remained relevant in 2001 following the boom. During the first and second quarters of 2001, the firm's market capitalization approached $2 billion.

In 2003, mobile operator Vodafone and Indian mobile provider Reliance Communications began using the firm's software, and Delta Air Lines used TIBCO software to organize its operation systems, including baggage handling, ticketing, and check-in. The same year, Lufthansa also used their software, and Deutsche Bahn used it to construct digitally integrated train stations.

In 2004, Wellpoint and RealMed used TIBCO technology to process HIPAA claims, and Harrah's casinos used predictive software to analyze system demands. After Hurricane Katrina, Allstate Insurance used their programming to process insurance claims. Since its release in 2007, Apple's iPhone has used their software to process user requests and facilitate sales. Xcel Energy launched its SmartGridCity program in 2009, which provided assistance to companies seeking to reduce carbon emissions, while using TIBCO software.

By 2011, the firm's annual revenues had grown to $920 million, its customer base to 4,000, and its number of employees to 2,500.

Products

TIBCO's infrastructure software focuses on real-time communication for business-to-business, business-to-consumer and business-to-employee data transfers, including facilitation of communication between otherwise incompatible software. The company provides middleware, which allows for access to real-time data between multiple systems while predicting users' needs. The software appears in Amazon.com's personalized product recommendations, and FedEx's package tracking system. Clients also use the software's feedback to deliver special offers to customers based on their browsing habits.

TIBCO ActiveMatrix is a technology-neutral platform for composite business process management (BPM) and service-oriented architecture (SOA) applications. The platform includes products for service creation and integration, distributed service and data grids, packaged applications, BPM and governance.

TIBCO BusinessEvents is complex event processing (CEP) software to identify meaningful patterns across a business by correlating massive volumes of data with discrete events and applying predefined rules to identify situations that require a response.

TIBCO Collaborative Information Manager is master data management for aligning enterprise data across multiple business units, departments and partners, synchronizing the information with downstream IT transactional systems.

TIBCO Silver is an infrastructure platform for cloud applications in enterprise IT environments. It includes BPM, composite application development and analytics products.

TIBCO Spotfire is an analytics and business intelligence platform for analysis of data by predictive and complex statistics. During the 2010 World Cup, FIFA used this software to give viewers analytics on country teams' past performances.

TIBCO tibbr, launched January 2011, is a social media system for the workplace. It manages input and output feeds to outside programs and integrates with other social media platforms. Sixty companies, or 50,000 users, have signed up. tibbr 3. 0, lanched in June 2011, added HD video conferencing, and distinguishes between public and private information sharing.

TIBCO FTL is an extreme-low-latency messaging technology for electronic trading, using high performance algorithms on massively multi-core machines.

TIBCO ActiveSpaces Datagrid is a distributed elastic peer-to-peer transactional datastore based on the tuple space concepts. It stores, retrieves and queries data stored into Spaces and distributes changes to that data in real-time in a true 'push' manner. It can function as an alternative datastore (with ACID properties and query filtering criteria expressed as SQL-compatible strings), messaging system (or a combination of the two) , processing large amounts of data in a distributed manner.

TIBCO TopLink a highly-secure version of tibbr, is a private social network for world leaders. introduced at the World Economic Forum in 2012. Its goal is to "unlock the collective wisdom of the world's best and brightest" .

Acquisitions

TIBCO has acquired several companies to extend and enhance its technology offerings. Most notably:

In 2002, TIBCO acquired Talarian, adding SmartSockets to its portfolio of high-performance messaging solutions.
In 2004, they acquired Staffware for automating, integrating and dynamically managing business processes.
In 2005, they acquired Objectstar, a mainframe integration solutions provider.
In 2007, they entered the analytics business intelligence markets by

acquiring Spotfire.
In 2009, the company entered the grid computing and cloud computing markets with its acquisition of DataSynapse.
On March 25, 2010, the company acquired Netrics, a privately-held provider of enterprise data matching software products.
On September 16, 2010, the company acquired Proginet (file transfer).
On September 23, 2010, company acquired OpenSpirit, an independent provider of data and application integration solutions for the exploration and production segment of the global oil and gas market.
On December 8, 2010, company acquired Loyalty Lab Inc. , an privately-held independent provider of loyalty management solutions.
On August 30, 2011, company acquired Nimbus a UK-headquartered provider of business process discovery and analysis applications.
On April 12, 2012, company acquired LogLogic, a log management company.

Reception and awards

Named among This Year's Intelligent Dozen by TechWeb's Intelligent Enterprise
Winner of the Stevie Business Award for Women in Business
Finalist, Business Innovation Category at 2010 American Business Awards
Named Company to Watch, TechWeb's Intelligent Enterprise 2010 Editors' Choice Awards.
Spotfire named Best-Ranked Solution by Yphise.
Editor's Choice for CMP's Intelligent Enterprise.
Multiple award winner, SYS-CON Media's 2007 SOAWorld Readers' Choice Awards.
Top Vendor across BPM, SOA and Web 2. 0 technology categories.
CEO Vivek Ranadivé won the 2005 Wharton Infosys Business Transformation technology change agent Award.
Named in Chronicle 500 list of the Bay Area's "top publicly traded companies. "

Underwriting

Underwriting

Underwriting refers to the process that a large financial service provider (bank, insurer, investment house) uses to assess the eligibility of a customer to receive their products (equity capital, insurance, mortgage, or credit). The name derives from the Lloyd's of London insurance market. Financial backers, who would accept some of the risk on a given venture (historically a sea voyage with associated risks of shipwreck) in exchange for a premium, would literally write their names under the risk information that was written on a Lloyd's slip created for this purpose.

Securities underwriting

Securities underwriting refers to the process by which investment banks raise investment capital from investors on behalf of corporations and governments that are issuing securities (both equity and debt capital). The services of an underwriter are typically used during a public offering.

This is a way of selling a newly issued security, such as stocks or bonds, to investors. A syndicate of banks (the lead managers) underwrite the transaction, which means they have taken on the risk of distributing the securities. Should they not be able to find enough investors, they will have to hold some securities themselves. Underwriters make their income from the price difference (the "underwriting spread") between the price they pay the issuer and what they collect from investors or from broker-dealers who buy portions of the offering.

Risk, exclusivity, and reward

Once the underwriting agreement is struck, the underwriter bears the risk of being unable to sell the underlying securities, and the cost of holding them on its books until such time in the future that they may be favorably sold.

If the instrument is desirable, the underwriter and the securities issuer may choose to enter into an exclusivity agreement. In exchange for a higher price paid upfront to the issuer, or other favorable terms, the issuer may agree to make the underwriter the exclusive agent for the initial sale of the securities instrument. That is, even though third-party buyers might approach the issuer directly to buy, the issuer agrees to sell exclusively through the underwriter.

In summary, the securities issuer gets cash up front, access to the contacts and sales channels of the underwriter, and is insulated from the market risk of being unable to sell the securities at a good price. The underwriter gets a nice profit from the markup, plus possibly an exclusive sales agreement.

Also, if the securities are priced significantly below market price (as is often the custom), the underwriter also curries favor with powerful end customers by granting them an immediate profit (see flipping), perhaps in a quid pro quo. This practice, which is typically justified as the reward for the underwriter for taking on the market risk, is occasionally criticized as unethical, such as the allegations that Frank Quattrone acted improperly in doling out hot IPO stock during the dot com bubble.

Bank underwriting

In banking, underwriting is the detailed credit analysis preceding the granting of a loan, based on credit information furnished by the borrower, such as employment history, salary and financial statements; publicly available information, such as the borrower's credit history, which is detailed in a credit report; and the lender's evaluation of the borrower's credit needs and ability to pay. Examples include mortgage underwriting.

Underwriting can also refer to the purchase of corporate bonds, commercial paper, government securities, municipal general-obligation bonds by a commercial bank or dealer bank for its own account or for resale to investors. Bank underwriting of corporate securities is carried out through separate holding-company affiliates, called securities affiliates or Section 20 affiliates.

Insurance underwriting

Insurance underwriters evaluate the risk and exposures of potential clients. They decide how much coverage the client should receive, how much they should pay for it, or whether even to accept the risk and insure them. Underwriting involves measuring risk exposure and determining the premium that needs to be charged to insure that risk. The function of the underwriter is to protect the company's book of business from risks that they feel will make a loss and issue insurance policies at a premium that is commensurate with the exposure presented by a risk.

Each insurance company has its own set of underwriting guidelines to help the underwriter determine whether or not the company should accept the risk. The information used to evaluate the risk of an applicant for insurance will depend on the type of coverage involved. For example, in underwriting automobile coverage, an individual's driving record is critical. As part of the underwriting process for life or health insurance, medical underwriting may be used to examine the applicant's health status (other factors may be considered as well, such as age & occupation). The factors that insurers use to classify risks should be objective, clearly related to the likely cost of providing coverage, practical to administer, consistent with applicable law, and designed to protect the long-term viability of the insurance program.

The underwriters may either decline the risk or may provide a quotation in which the premiums have been loaded or in which various exclusions have been stipulated, which restrict the circumstances under which a claim would be paid. Depending on the type of insurance product (line of business), insurance companies use automated underwriting systems to encode these rules, and reduce the amount of manual work in processing quotations and policy issuance. This is especially the case for certain simpler life or personal lines (auto, homeowners) insurance. Some insurance companies, however, rely on agents to underwrite for them. This arrangement allows an insurer to operate in a market closer to its clients without having to established a physical presence. A Lloyd's Coverholder is one such example in which a Lloyd's Syndicate (an insurer who is a member of Lloyd's of London) delegates its underwriting authority to, hence allowing that syndicate to operate in a region or country as if it is a local insurer. In Hong Kong, where the largest number of Approved Lloyd's Coverholders are domiciled in Asia Pacific, insurers and their potential clients seek a closer way for the Lloyd's market to access the emerging insurance market of Asia Pacific and vice versa.

Other forms of underwriting

Real estate underwriting

In evaluation of a real estate loan, in addition to assessing the borrower, the property itself is scrutinized. Underwriters use the debt service coverage ratio to figure out whether the property is capable of redeeming its own value or not.

Forensic underwriting

Forensic underwriting is the "after-the-fact" process used by lenders to determine what went wrong with a mortgage. Forensic underwriting refers to a borrower's ability to work out a modification scenario with their current lien holder, not to qualify them for a new loan or a refinance. This is typically done by an underwriter staffed with a team of people who are experienced in every aspect of the real estate field.

Sponsorship underwriting

Underwriting spot
Underwriting may also refer to financial sponsorship of a venture, and is also used as a term within public broadcasting (both public television and radio) to describe funding given by a company or organization for the operations of the service, in exchange for a mention of their product or service within the station's programming.

Thomson Financial League Tables

Underwriting activity reported in Thomson Financial League Tables(numbers in $ billion) (number of issues in parentheses):

Global Debt, Equity & Equity-related

Year	Underwriting Activity	Source
2008	4,715 (13,542)	Q4 2008 report
2007	7,510 (22,256)	Q4 2007 report

2006   7,643 (21,818)   Q4 2006 report
2005   6,511 (20,118)   Q4 2005 report
2004   5,693 (20,066)   Q4 2004 report
2003   5,326 (19,706)   Q4 2003 report
2002   4,257 (14,070)   Q4 2002 report
2001   4,112 (NA)   Q4 2001 report

Zementis Inc

Zementis Inc

Zementis, Inc. is a company that makes software for the operational deployment and integration of predictive analytics and data-mining solutions. Its main products are the ADAPA decision engine, a platform for statistics and data processing, and the Universal PMML plug-in for Hadoop and in-database scoring.

The "Zementis" Name

The name Zementis, symbolizing "concrete thoughts", is derived from the German word Zement (cement, concrete) and the Latin word Mentis (thought, intellect) and relates to the company's core competence in machine learning and AI.

The Road to ADAPA

Founded in 2004 with the goal of providing predictive analytics to the marketplace, Zementis is composed of two main divisions, analytics and engineering. Although it started as a company focused on building predictive models, Zementis scientists soon realized that their models needed a platform in which they could be easily deployed and managed. From this need, the ADAPA Decision Engine came to be.

ADAPA initially supported only neural networks, but it soon became a platform for the deployment of a myriad of statistical techniques as well as data processing. From its inception, ADAPA has been based on open-standards, including PMML, the Predictive Model Markup Language. As a member of the Data Mining Group (DMG), the committee defining PMML, Zementis has helped shaped the standard as it becomes the necessary vehicle for the sharing of predictive solutions between applications.

In 2008, ADAPA was launched as a service on the Amazon Elastic Compute Cloud and is currently being used worldwide by companies and individuals who want to execute their predictive models and decision logic.

In 2011, building on the heritage of its ADAPA Decision Engine, Zementis launched the Universal PMML Plug-in (UPPI), a highly optimized, in-database scoring engine for predictive models, fully supporting the PMML standard. With PMML, the Plug-in delivers a wide range of predictive analytics for high performance scoring. It shortens time to market for predictive models and empowers users through instant deployment of predictive models. UPPI is available for the EMC GreenPlum Database, Sybase IQ, and IBM Netezza. It is also available for Datameer for scoring in Hadoop.

In 2012, ADAPA cloud offering was extended to the IBM SmartCloud. In this way, IBM cloud computing provides companies around the world predictive decisions when and where they are needed.

Zementis is a privately held company with offices in the USA and in Asia.

Zementis Locations

Zementis HQ is located in San Diego in California. It also has an office in Hong Kong for servicing clients in the Asia-Pacific region.

CPSIA information can be obtained at www.ICGtesting.com
Printed in the USA
LVOW13s0337040813

346133LV00002B/492/P